Creating the College Man

STUDIES IN AMERICAN THOUGHT
AND CULTURE

Series Editor

PAUL S. BOYER

Advisory Board

Charles M. Capper
Mary Kupiec Cayton
Lizabeth Cohen
Nan Enstad
James B. Gilbert
Karen Halttunen
Michael Kammen
James T. Kloppenberg
Colleen McDannell
Joan S. Rubin
P. Sterling Stuckey
Robert B. Westbrook

Creating
the College Man

*American Mass Magazines and
Middle-Class Manhood,
1890–1915*

Daniel A. Clark

THE UNIVERSITY OF WISCONSIN PRESS

Publication of this volume has been made possible, in part, through support from the Anonymous Fund of the College of Letters and Science at the University of Wisconsin–Madison and from Indiana State University College of Arts and Sciences.

1930 Monroe Street, 3rd Floor
Madison, Wisconsin 53711-2059
uwpress.wisc.edu

3 Henrietta Street
London WC2E 8LU, England
eurospanbookstore.com

1   3   5   4   2

Printed in the United States of America

Library of Congress Cataloging-in-Publication Data
Clark, Daniel A. (Daniel Andrew), 1967–
Creating the college man: American mass magazines and
middle-class manhood, 1890–1915 / Daniel A. Clark.
p.   cm. — (Studies in American thought and culture)
Includes bibliographical references and index.
ISBN 978-0-299-23534-5 (pbk.: alk. paper)
ISBN 978-0-299-23533-8 (e-book)
1. Middle-class men—Press coverage—United States—History.
2. Male college students—Press coverage—United States—History.
3. Education, Higher—United States—Sociological aspects—History.
I. Title.   II. Series: Studies in American thought and culture
LA227.1.C56   2010
378.1′9820810973—dc22
2009040636

Contents

Acknowledgments

One accumulates a great many debts in the course of researching, writing, and publishing a book. This project began in graduate school as a dissertation, and as with any scholar, many readings and conversations helped to frame my understanding and pursuit of this topic. I want to thank Jon Teaford, John Lauritz Larson, Michael Morrison, and Jim Farr, for their guidance (and the readings they insisted upon). A special mention goes to my major professor, Susan Curtis, whose exacting expectations and belief in me sustained me at the early stages of this project. I also must acknowledge graduate student colleagues: Linda Phillips, Cherry Spruill, Chris Corley, Steve Wagner, Matt Loayza, and especially Tom Pendergast. I conducted most of the research for this book in Louisiana and must thank Bill Robeson and my colleagues at Southeastern Louisiana University, who always supplied good food and camaraderie. Indiana State University has provided a true intellectual home, and I am pleased to thank Rich Schneirov, Bob Hunter, Bill Giffin, Chris Fischer, Rob Fish, Jay Gatrell, and Tom Sauer, with a very special thanks to Chris Olsen. They and my other colleagues at ISU always believed in my abilities, and I am deeply indebted. Two undergraduate research assistants, Perry Clark and Lori Enright, provided key aid at critical times. Roger Geiger, Bruce Leslie, Christine Ogren, Chris McKenna, Matthew Schneirov, and John Pettegrew formed a set of scholarly colleagues, playing a vital role in my professional development over the years. I also want to thank the anonymous readers, who critically appraised my manuscript. Their insights made this book immeasurably better. Finally, Gwen Walker, Adam Mehring, and the staff and editors at the University of Wisconsin Press, along with series editor Paul Boyer, have been models of professionalism. I am deeply grateful that they saw the potential of the manuscript and helped shepherd me through the process.

On a personal level, I must thank my close friends (Matt, John, and Curt) and my brothers and sisters, who always believed in me and kept life fun. My only wish is that my parents, Don and Shirley, had lived to see this book published. Mom instilled a love of history, and Dad set an example of steady work and perseverance. My deepest debt of gratitude goes to my immediate family—my two girls, Betsy and Abby, and my wife Janet. The girls make it all worthwhile, and I quite frankly owe all my achievements to Janet. Without her unwavering love and support, I could not have pursued my life as a scholar, and it is to her that I dedicate this book.

Creating the College Man

Introduction

Piggy Goes to Harvard:
Mass Magazines, Masculinity, and College Education
for the Corporate Middle Class

D uring the late nineteenth and early twentieth centuries, many businessmen proudly echoed Andrew Carnegie's well-known denunciation
that "a college education unfits rather than fits men to affairs."[1]
What a difference a century makes. While Carnegie would change his tune,
such a sentiment as his could hardly be conceivable today. College and university bumper stickers have become notorious markers of presumed social status.
Access to college education is a major political, economic, and social concern,
swirling with issues of gender equity and racial and class preference. *The U.S.
News and World Report*'s annual college ratings issue has emerged as a much an-
ticipated media event. With the skyrocketing costs of higher education has come
renewed focus on improving access and evaluating quality in higher education.
And for the last several years educational and social researchers have lamented
a decline in male college enrollments and graduation rates (especially acute for
African Americans) as a part of a broader "crisis of masculinity" in modern
America.[2] All of these contemporary concerns assume the central importance
of college education in conceptions of power in America.

3

But how did a college education become so vital to our notions of advancement? We Americans tend to forget what a fundamental shift in thinking the integration of college within our popular cultural assumptions of success and authority represented. Might not our present debates about the purpose and place of college education (what value it adds) be advanced by a deeper understanding of the genesis of the American embrace of college education almost a century ago? What originally made a college education so attractive, particularly to American men, who overwhelmingly had few historic connections to formal education or credentialing and who were in fact part of the broad American public largely regarded as anti-intellectual in the nineteenth century? We have neglected to understand how current concerns encompassing American higher education (and even masculinity) may be tied intimately to cultural reconstructions of college arising at the very beginning of the modern era—vitally connected to reformulations of power and identity for white, middle-class men in America during the turn of the last century. Native-born, white American men at that time confronted a set of issues not dissimilar to today—a shifting economy, the threat of massive immigration, and the challenge of women rising in the workplace and in politics.

This book began, then, with a very simple but inadequately understood question: What informed the modern demand for college education in America? This scholarly quest led me back to find the metaphorical first of the first-generation collegians of the modern period in order to understand what forces shaped the popular acceptance of college in American life during that critical formative era. To ponder the growing importance of college education in American society during that time is, in reality, to explore how Americans reformulated dominant notions of male authority and power (interlaced with shifts in conceptions of gender, race, and business success) as they adjusted to the creation of a corporate and consumer-oriented world. One thing Carnegie's statement should remind us of is just how different concepts of success and manhood were within the dominant ideology of nineteenth-century America.

The dominant ideal of success in the nineteenth century—the autonomous, self-made man—was based around an economic world of small farmers and businessmen, as one scholar has termed it, "traditional entrepreneurial individualism."[3] Any kind of formal education beyond the three Rs had a very limited, even dubious place in manly notions of success. The vast majority of the eminent businessmen listed in a *Who's Who of Americans* in 1900 (84) noted no education beyond the high school years.[4] In 1900 American institutions of higher education enrolled only 4 percent of all college-age youth, women included.[5] Success literature of the nineteenth century rarely mentioned education, emphasizing instead the necessity of character and self-discipline instilled by simple hard work. And well into the twentieth century such literature, in fact, assigned the college graduate a place alongside the eccentric genius, figures dismissed as lazy and undisciplined—men "who sought a conspicuous place, short work, and large rewards." Colleges crippled the faculties required for business success—will, diligence, persistence, health, and discipline. College had ruined more men than it had helped.[6]

A glimpse forward into the 1920s, however, reveals that a shocking and relatively rapid transition had occurred regarding Americans' perceptions of the college man and the popular acceptance of higher education as a stepping stone to success and manhood even in business. College athletes like Red Grange became national heroes. Eminent writers, such as F. Scott Fitzgerald in *This Side of Paradise*, integrated college life and characters into their work and, thus, more deeply into the national consciousness. Several feature length movies— *The Blot* (1921), *Braveheart* (1924), *College* (1927), and Harold Lloyd as "Speedy" Lamb in *The Freshman* (1925)—focused on college characters and their campus activities.[7] Even Sinclair Lewis's George Babbitt, the decade's quintessential middle-class businessman, sported a college education and sent his son. College enrollments had risen remarkably as well—from 237,000 (or 4 percent of the college-age cohort) in 1900 to 1.1 million (or almost 13 percent of the age cohort) in 1930.[8] Even more telling, a survey of American business leaders in 1928 found that college graduates filled fully 32 percent of all executive positions.[9] In other words, college graduates were disproportionately represented among the nation's business elite, a trend that would only continue. Going to college had entered squarely into the popular consciousness of America by the 1920s and into notions of business success, establishing patterns for the massive growth of higher education during the rest of the century.

When the businessman who had long rejected the necessity of any formal education (who even had prided himself on his lack of education) accepted college as a rung on the ladder of success, something clearly had changed. Americans had crossed a cultural Rubicon. The embrace of college education by the American businessman, representing the vast majority of aspiring middle-class American men, unquestionably involved massive shifts in thinking about success that cut to the core of male identity and authority. But how did college become part of the new formula for American success and middle-class identity in the dawning corporate age? What could college offer the aspiring middle-class man that he could find nowhere else and that bolstered emerging ideals of corporate identity and middle-class masculinity? In short, how was college education invested with new meaning? How did it become cultural capital for the middle-class man, and for the businessman in particular?[10] For too long we have neglected to explore the formation of popular perceptions and expectations involving college, focusing instead on institutional change or specific professions.

It is true that the late nineteenth century witnessed a profound transformation in American higher education, with the proliferation of institutions (both state and private), the emergence of electives, and the rise of technical, scientific, and professional courses. This metamorphosis coincided with the growth of a new middle class of urban professionals and managers, many of whom pioneered novel forms of professional organization and certification, often involving education (as with law, medicine, and accounting, and including new academic professionals in the sciences and social sciences). Proceeding from these changes, many argue that the growing importance of higher education evolved as a function of the changing economy (simple modernization theory).[11] But this set of explanations only seems to explain all, while in fact illuminating very little of the actual transformation; it assumes far too much. Corporations did not begin to systematically comb the campuses for new hires until after 1920.[12] And despite the increased prominence of science and utilitarian studies in college and university curricula, corporate professionals did not flock to create university-level programs or to limit their ranks to the college educated as would occur in law and medicine in the early twentieth century.[13] Accountants, engineers, and managers first formed loose organizations to certify themselves.[14] And when corporations did begin to hire college graduates for executive positions more systematically, the vast majority entering business remained liberal arts graduates of some variety, not technical specialists. Engineering graduates, for instance, comprised only 13 percent of executives in one 1925 survey.[15] Professional organizations, high schools, proprietary business colleges, or simply self-education sufficed for quite some time.[16] With a high school education and perseverance on the job, one could train in-house (as most engineers still did in 1900).[17]

For college education to form an ingredient of a professional, middle-class business identity, it would not come via a specific curriculum or managerial model. It would come through a cultural construction of an ideal manager and businessman (really a generic ideal American man), a professional vision that would include more than practical expertise.[18] It would encompass breadth of vision, integrity, and leadership.[19] The allure of a professional identity for businessmen as it developed in America, was not simply based on the rise of science, but also an almost pre-democratic notion of power and authority that recalled the English gentleman, a vision that would involve both culture and the liberal arts.[20] How did an emerging corporate, white-collar class of (would-be "professional") businessmen construct novel identifications that went beyond mere utility?[21]

Another typical interpretation of the growth of college enrollments is to dismiss it as a growing middle-class desire for signs of status or cultural capital.[22] In the late nineteenth century an urban upper-middle class developed and established exclusive avenues of education to solidify their identity, creating boarding schools on the English model (like Groton) and patronizing Ivy League institutions. This upper-middle class and their idealization of liberal culture and muscular Christianity would prove an important model for wider emulation, but as with modernization theory, it cannot wholly account for the broader middle-class embrace of college.[23] A college education still remained only one of many legitimate avenues to acquire the proper cultural habits of the American middle class (a cultivated taste in music, art, drama, and literature, along with a knowledge of proper dress and etiquette).[24] College education would emerge as the ideal site to cultivate "Culture" and character, linked to the liberal arts and athletics, but how was this communicated? How were such conceptions integrated into visions of broader middle-class success and manhood to become normative concepts? If college education became a critical component of middle-class "cultural capital," it was not an obvious choice, especially for American men.[25] Before the average American man would invest in a college education literally, he would have to be invested in it *culturally*. We know several key pieces of the story, but not the whole.

Indeed, the key to understanding the rising prominence of college in modern American society lies in comprehending how the college experience was redefined for native-born, American men during a time of profound transformation in notions of manhood. The advent of industrialization and massive bureaucratic organizations placed a distinct strain on traditional models of Victorian manhood. The rise of a corporate and modern consumer-based economy challenged American beliefs about work, leisure, and identity. The middle-class businessman, especially, faced a psychic crisis. The typical businessman became not an owner but rather a permanently subordinate employee.[26] Most white-collar employees saw their work routinized as part of a stultifying bureaucracy. Whereas the self-made man succeeded through inner character (grit, perseverance, honesty, self-discipline) and proved his manhood in the battle of commerce, the corporate employee worked in a team, subordinate to others' authority, often performing dreary paperwork—hardly the stuff to challenge character and build manhood.[27]

Other factors exacerbated male anxieties during these years, as well, contributing to a sense of crisis, such as sons laboring in the shadows of heroic Civil War fathers, who had tested their manhood under fire, or the real (and symbolic) closing of the frontier and its promise of manly regeneration. Women agitated for a political voice (both to vote and through reform groups) and entered the workforce, upsetting the separate spheres balance. Working-class immigrant men, through their rugged labor and rough leisure pursuits, challenged middle-class notions of virile superiority, a particularly troubling issue for middle-class managers of such men.[28] And these "white" new immigrants found not only the voting rolls open to them but also traditional American notions of success and self-made manhood, a troubling prospect given that their fitness for citizenship increasingly became an issue.[29]

How did native-stock American men respond? The most basic response revolved around a rise in what scholars term *passionate masculinity*.[30] Middle-class men in particular compensated for the loss of autonomy and manly identity in the workplace by cultivating a hypermasculinity exhibited through once-suspect leisure activities rather than one's occupation. They embraced rugged, competitive sports as a place to forge character—the "cult of the strenuous life."[31] Men flocked to join fraternal associations, lodges, and clubs for a sense of rough camaraderie.[32] There arose a fascination with and indulgence in the more "authentic" and manly urban sporting culture of gambling, saloons, and "rough" sports such as boxing. This often translated into the reshaping of such activities into more respectable forms, but the indulgence in such un-Victorian leisure activities was remarkable.[33] The turn of the century also witnessed the rise of new fantasy heroes in men's popular literature, the explosion of such a market itself indicative of massive change. The cowboy, the great athlete, and white primitives like Tarzan offered vicarious regeneration to American men.[34] The characterization of business practice received a similar makeover, appropriating martial references to define activities as aggressively masculine—moving armies of men and fighting business campaigns.[35] This redefinition of masculinity, while seeming to preserve self-made notions of independence and the accompanying Victorian values, in fact facilitated their transformation and American men's adaptation to a new set of values aligned with the dictates of the corporation and a consumer-oriented culture.[36]

Still, the critical importance of college education in defining male power and authority has not been carefully factored into the whole equation of evolving masculinity in America.[37] If the college man made it into the tale of shifting manhood at all, it was through the rise of sports on campus—vitally important but still only a fraction of the story.[38] White American men around the turn of the century exhibited almost as keen a concern for proving their contributions to civilization as to reassuring their primitive vigor in the face of ethnic and racial challenges.[39] The significance of college to modern men had to be created and justified. In fact the single most potent appeal of the college experience would be the way it could seamlessly unite the various discordant facets of ideal masculinity in transition. The college man could be the vigorous athlete and the civilized scholar, the genteel leader and the modern professional. He could find fraternal bonding and "instant" tradition, while indulging in a raucous sporting culture. He could simultaneously prove his self-made worth through athletics and work (as a student or after graduation). But all this required conjuring in the realm of American culture.

This book places the formation of such popular expectations back in the center of the story. Rather than examine an institution (or a set of institutions), the rise of a profession, or the makeup of college and university boards, I explore how the concept of going to college evolved in the sphere of American culture—how the notion of going to college seeped into the commonplace assumptions surrounding middle-class male identity, success, and mobility. My research was informed in part by the work of Michel Foucault and Edward Said. Similar in approach to Said's *Orientalism*, this book is not concerned with uncovering a "real" college experience, or the difference between that real college experience and an imagined one.[40] This study examines the discourse on college to uncover how the concept of going to college became invested with new meaning, integrated into dominant notions of authority, especially with regard to the "business man," the archetypical American man of the late nineteenth and early twentieth centuries. My prime concern here is the cultural construction of the college experience (and a generic college man) as a vital component of a broader American transformation in middle-class and masculine ideals. This cultural process corresponded to the rising power of the corporate businessman (and supporting corporate professionals), so that the investing of the college experience with new meanings was intimately interconnected with an emerging new class, maturing in its notions of identity and authority, and facing challenges from women and immigrants in the realm of the workplace and politics even as they faced a very different work environment for men reared on the self-made ideal. It proved to be a complex and nuanced cultural process, one that worked to subtly exclude many Americans from this new avenue to authority by fashioning the parameters of the possible for only a few, while doing this within the language of democratic meritocracy. Ultimately (and ironically), though, this new narrative of authority involving college would prove an inclusive and open avenue for a broad middle-class identity. Examining the cultural discourse on the value of the college experience and its relevance to the identity of the middle-class corporate business man offers a window as to how culturally hegemonic ideals, visions of authority, and pathways to power (involving not only class but also race and gender), were transformed at the dawning of the new corporate and consumer-oriented age—how new cultural narratives of middle-class identity and masculine authority arose to replace the traditional self-made man of the receding era.

The emerging mass media served as the prime vehicle of this critically transforming discourse, facilitating the interconnected makeover of the college experience and the middle-class corporate businessman as part of a shifting hegemonic ideology of masculine authority in America. With their editorial attention focused chiefly on men during this period, and with the businessman as the archetype, such magazines as the *Saturday Evening Post, Munsey's, Cosmopolitan,* and *Collier's Weekly* became the nation's first truly national media, achieving unprecedented circulation (*Munsey's* 500,000 alone beating all of the old, nineteenth-century genteel monthlies combined). These magazines emerged alongside and catered to a unique group, America's "plain business men" as *Post* editor George Horace Lorimer called them, part of a new corporate middle class. These mass magazines would play an integral role in helping this class navigate through and wrestle with the new imperatives of the dawning corporate and consumer age. As the economy transformed, these magazines repeatedly fixated on the future paths to success and opportunity for their male readers. For the new middle class, the question of college education would figure prominently in their evolving process of self-awareness. Mass-media magazines would play a pivotal role in the cultural reconstruction of ideal middle-class manhood and its dynamic new connection with college, a phenomenon at the dawn of the modern consumer age that in many ways only such a consumer medium could have sustained. And no magazine articles captured the profound generational angst, the question of how to prepare young men for a changing world, better than the *Post*'s series "Letters from a Self-Made Merchant to His Son."

Piggy Goes to Harvard

"Letters from a Self-Made Merchant" and its successor "Old Gorgon Graham," ran from 1901 through 1904. Written anonymously by *Post* editor George Horace Lorimer and so enormously popular that they were later published as a collection, the articles take the form of letters written by John "Old Gorgon" Graham to his son. Graham was the fictitious head of his own Chicago pork-packing firm that in self-made fashion he built up from scratch. With the rushing tide of changes sweeping a rapidly industrializing America, Lorimer could have used such a voice as Graham's to address any number of pressing social issues (labor troubles or the "Trust" problem for instance). But significantly, the overarching issue Lorimer wished to confront—the most alarming one to him that surpassed all other concerns—was the passing of the torch from the self-made men to their more privileged sons, and through this issue, the greater problem of fashioning leadership, manhood, and success for a new industrial and commercial age.

The topic of generational transition and the opportunities for manly success amid the new business conditions deeply troubled Lorimer, and his concerns cut to the core of transforming cultural notions of class and manhood in America. Numerous editorials and articles ran in the *Post* warning of and pondering the maxim "from shirtsleeves to shirtsleeves" in three generations. The great self-made man builds up his business and fortune only to watch his son lose it through sloth, luxury, and inattention, so that the grandson must go back to scrambling for a living. Lorimer never tired of berating the idle sons of the rich, especially the nouveau riche, and he saw to it that many short stories dealt with this topic as well. How could sons be groomed for leadership when their fathers had learned the hard-knock lessons struggling up from the bottom? How then to instill the staunch Victorian manly values of hard work and diligence that would make them fit to assume the mantle of leadership the fathers wished to bestow? How could they ensure the forging of character but also the vision and skill necessary to pilot the huge companies the fathers had built? How could the values of the self-made man translate to the dawning age of corporate organization?

The very first letter indicated the radical element of this proposed new training, as John Graham addressed his son Pierrepont (affectionately known as "Piggy") preparing for his final year at Harvard.[41] Why a college education for a future meat packer? "Like most fellows who haven't any too much of it," wrote John, "I've a great deal of respect for education." For John Graham (Lorimer), this meant an education rooted in Matthew Arnold–style liberal culture, acquainting oneself with the best that has been thought and done, and thus satisfying one honored component of Victorian manhood.[42] But, significantly, culture hardly constituted the sole reason Old Gorgon Graham sent Piggy to Harvard. Times had changed, and the college man, according to Graham, could prove a valuable asset. To demonstrate, Graham recounted the tale of the first college man he ever hired—the son of a friend fallen on hard times. Putting the fellow to work on a loading gang, Graham expected the boy to break, only to find later that the college man had been promoted. And he continued to progress up through the ranks by thinking of ways to make the work easier—an overhead rail system for the loading gang, a time clock to keep track of men, and ordering typewriters rather than copying letters by hand as a personal secretary. College had trained his mind to consider the big picture, to look beyond his narrow job, and to use the newest scientific technology to solve problems. Finally, Graham's college man excelled at advertising, the new frontier of scientific commercial conquest that also required creativity and breadth.[43] Lorimer, as Graham, depicted the college man as possessing the ideal education for the future executive—liberal education endowing the proper culture of a gentleman yet also bestowing the mental precision and breadth to bring scientific order and creativity into the modern business world.

Lorimer's endorsement of the college man came with numerous caveats, however. Mindful of the common complaints lodged against the college bred in business, he also filled Gorgon Graham's letters with advice, aimed no doubt for all college boys who aspired to rise in commercial life. Many of the warnings sought to temper the assumed pretentiousness and effete snobbery associated with the college man. John Graham consistently admonished his son to work harder, not be "chesty" (prideful), to use direct and manly language, and not to socialize on business time—all common knocks against college graduates.[44] Furthermore, throughout the length of the series, Lorimer paraded an assortment of college-educated foils. These rich men's sons invariably sponged off their fathers or their fathers' friends and always expected a better job than they deserved.[45] And most importantly, from the very first letter Graham preached that his son (that representative college man) "will have to earn his way in the world and in the firm," starting at the bottom.[46]

The series did far more than simply offer folksy observations. As the iconic self-made man, Graham was the aging hero of self-made America, and his concerns were those of an entire generation. In essence, Lorimer formulated a new cultural narrative of manly authority, a blueprint for the proper training not only for fortunate sons but for all who aspired to be the lieutenants and captains, the managers and executives of the emerging corporate world. The "Letters" series represented how the magazines, in their efforts to address the concerns and aspirations of their readers, posited the American college as an experience uniquely suited to fulfill emerging notions of success and masculinity. Piggy went to Harvard to become cultured and a gentleman. This liberal breadth seemed particularly important for a future leader, but so did the problem-solving skills a liberal education simultaneously imparted, reflecting higher education's new association with modern science. Hard work in the stockyards and working up through the ranks purged the unmanly elements still associated with college, as did the advent of college athletics. One letter specifically highlighted the example of a college fullback meant to inspire Piggy to assume a more manly business demeanor.[47]

For all its sincere democratic tones, however, powerful assumptions about ethnicity, class, and gender informed this new narrative of manly success. Immigrants when noted remained decidedly subordinate workers, while naturally well-bred Piggy and his kind assumed managerial roles. And the educational background of a love interest of Piggy's (and his eventual wife) never even merited mention in these letters. The series, then, exemplified the magazine's attempt to resonate with and guide its readers, actively participating not only in a reconfiguration of the channels to success and manhood in a new age, and reconceptualizing the benefits of college to fit these new demands, but also marking out fitting parameters of who could conceive of embarking upon such a path to power.

At the same time Lorimer's "Letters" series grew in popularity, coverage of college life and curricular changes grew dramatically in the middle-class magazines right alongside (and intimately bound together with) the concern over shifting requirements for business success and male identity. The *Post* published several entire issues revolving around college topics and the magazine continually reported on the advent of science and more practical studies in the college curriculum.[48] Even earlier than the *Post*'s attention, *Cosmopolitan* ran a long series on "Modern Education" (beginning in 1897) that focused exclusively on American colleges, inviting distinguished college presidents and professors to address the issue of curricular change and the purpose of college education in America.[49] At the same time, magazines grew fascinated with fraternities and college athletics. *Munsey's* and *Cosmopolitan* ran long pieces on "College Fraternities," delighting in the rough camaraderie and manly rituals.[50] Magazines reveled in the manly competition of football, too, usually through short stories as with the *Post*'s "The Last Five Yards."[51] On a different yet related note, *Munsey's*, *Cosmopolitan*, and the *Post* pondered the pressing social question of the day, "How Business Success Will Be Won in the Twentieth Century," and the need for business leaders and attempted to offer direction to such questions, as well, as with *Cosmopolitan*'s series "Choice of a Profession."[52] And these same magazines also brought these currents of concern and interest together. The *Post* asked, "Should the Business Man Have a College Education?" and *Munsey's* examined "The College Man and the Corporate Position."[53] In addition to "Letters from a Self-Made Merchant to His Son," the *Post* ran "Talks with a Kid Brother at College," in which an older brother already in the business world advised the younger sibling on how the college experience prepared one for future business battles.[54] Juxtaposed alongside these articles came a deluge of fictional accounts of college life, many involving business in their plots, as well as a cascade of advertising (especially from ready-made apparel companies), which incorporated idealized collegiate scenes and references in their ad copy aimed at positing idealized models of masculinity for all men.[55] And, finally, what is missing in all these visions of college and the college man is just as important. The magazines formed a vision of college for an assumed homogenous native-born, white readership. No minorities and very few new (and racially suspect) immigrants enter into these media depictions of the college man. The female college student formed a conspicuous presence, but magazine coverage effectively diffused the threat of the "new woman" by endorsing her but situating her almost always in the subordinate role of worthy consort (supportive girlfriend or wife) to the male, college-educated leaders of this bold new era.

The *Post, Munsey's, Cosmopolitan,* and *Collier's Weekly* all became infatuated with college life while they pondered the shifting requirements of middle-class manhood and business success, and they all simultaneously devoted increasing attention to the college man as a possible solution to the problem of industrial leadership. This solution was predicated on a new image of college not only as a place to gain culture and refinement but also acquire mental training, scientific skills, and the gritty, manly experiences of the athletic field, along with the male bonding and adventure represented by fraternity life and other extracurricular activities. In other words, a reworked vision of the college experience (one that satisfied longings for a sense of community and tradition as well as allowed outlets for manly aggression and modern professional training) arose in combination with the college man as a feasible heir to assume the reins of business leadership—a hybrid, new and improved self-made man for a modern era. What other experience could unify and satisfy so many conflicting currents of evolving male identity and authority, combining links with genteel culture and Victorian character along with an indulgence of the masculine passions, all while preparing a young man intellectually and professionally? And in this cultural endeavor, the magazines did not reflect a changing reality; they actively crafted it, positing a new vision of college and manhood for their readers. In effect, college was remade in the pages of these periodicals to conform to transforming economic and cultural demands, reconfigured in alignment with the emerging identity of a new white-collar, managerial middle class. And magazines, then, presented the college man (in articles, fiction, and especially advertising) as a model for emulation to all American men, playing a vital role in fashioning a new national cultural narrative of masculine authority. Editors, writers, and advertisers promoted this new ideal and did so both with rational argument and by conjuring desirable images and references. This consumer medium sold their male readers on college as the ideal route to manhood and success in a new age.

This book, then, is not wholly about college education, the middle-class businessman, or evolving gender and racial definitions, but rather where they all interconnected amid the changing ideals and expectations constructed by businessmen and their cultural spokesmen (editors, writers, and advertisers) in the pages of middle-class magazines. One might ask, were not new developments in the college curriculum and extracurricular occurring independently of magazines? Were not businessmen shaping a professional ideal of the business administrator on their own? Were not many Americans coping with shifting gender expectations and the troubling influx of immigrants without the aid of the media? Certainly all these points are accurate. But to dismiss these magazines as mere passive reflectors of social trends is to ignore the power of the media in modern society to inform ideals and to guide values, to set cultural parameters, or to establish idioms for understanding change.[56] And these new mass magazines that emerged around 1900 formed the vanguard of the modern media, the nation's first national mass media.

The Magazine Revolution

Geographically vast and institutionally diverse compared to European nations, the United States contained no entrenched elite and no truly dominant national institutions, especially with regard to higher education, that could spearhead cultural transformation on a national scale.[57] Moreover, America also valued the tradition of democratic opportunity and revered the icon of the self-made man, so that again unlike European nations, top-down alterations in licensing or professionalization—whether emanating from academia or the business world—could not readily develop. All these considerations factored heavily into my decision to focus solely on the first national media, the mass magazines, as the key sites of the cultural reconstruction of college, and the positing of college attendance as vital cultural capital. Two prominent monthlies (*Munsey's* and *Cosmopolitan*) and two prominent weeklies (the *Saturday Evening Post* and *Collier's*) together constituted the industry leaders. Highly innovative, and culturally unique, nothing like them had existed before.

Mass magazines such as *Munsey's* and *Cosmopolitan* pioneered a mass-media revolution in the early 1890s by drastically lowering prices (five and ten cents compared to thirty-five cents for the old genteel monthlies) and generating profits instead from advertising attracted to their massive circulation numbers (700,000 for *Munsey's* and 300,000 for *Cosmopolitan* in 1897, the weekly *Collier's* ran above 500,000 after 1905, with the new industry leader, the *Saturday Evening Post*, topping one million by 1909; compare this to 150,000 for a genteel monthly).[58] Many factors coalesced to enable this revolution to occur—technical breakthroughs in printing, the marketing needs of mass-produced consumer goods, and the rise of advertising.[59] But the editors (Frank Munsey, George Horace Lorimer at the *Post*, John Brisbane Walker at *Cosmopolitan*, and Norman Hapgood *at Collier's*) supplied the key ingredient. Unlike the literary luminaries of the older monthlies like *Harper's* or the *Nation*, these new editors were entrepreneurs, active leaders of their magazines rather than passive voices from an easy chair.[60] They gave these magazines an expansive, confident ethos, far different from the mood and purpose of the old monthlies, which often deplored the changes sweeping late nineteenth-century America. And they charted a new editorial direction astutely in tune with (and helping to inform) the budding consciousness of their prime readership, what one may term a new corporate or urban middle class of professionals and managers.[61]

While no surveys of readers existed until much later, and the editors usually refused to define their readers as a special class, their readership unquestionably was not the highbrow set of the old genteel monthlies nor the working-class, mass readership of the daily newspapers. Edward Bok of the *Ladies Home Journal* described these readers as the "broad middle class" or the "literate middle class."[62] Readers were also assumed to be native-born, white Americans or "old-stock" immigrants, and predominantly male. Even as they all became more "general" in the 1910s, these magazines primarily targeted male readers. My characterization of the typical reader as the generic businessman stemmed entirely from my sources. I took my lead from Lorimer at the *Post*, who regarded his readers generally as businessmen, although he used this term in a broadly inclusive fashion—the average American man not a specialized type.[63] Similarly, *Cosmopolitan*'s "Making a Choice of a Profession" series involved mainly "business" fields. Contemporary fiction, which all these magazines championed, also usually involved some kind of business venture or setting. And, quite significantly, advertising aimed at male readers posited the generic businessman as their typical American. Most critically, though, when the issue of a college education arose, all the magazines debated its merits with an eye toward business fields and not the traditional professions. They were a new type of American—urban residents, middle-class professionals and businessmen, managers, and white-collar employees, and reasonably well educated, with comfortable incomes and the aspiration to acquire a modicum of culture to mark them as respectable.[64] It was this readership that editors in fact "sold" to advertisers, meaning that the magazines had to connect with this new middle class in order to be successful.[65] They had to not just appeal to but also inspire and flatter along lines that resonated with their readers.

A world ordered around corporate capitalism was in its earliest formative stages. Aware of fundamental transformations in America, magazine editors sensed and responded to the need of their middle-class readers "to fix their bearings in the fluid social space of the moment."[66] These magazines and the new middle class grew up together, born of the same process—mass production and corporate industrialization—and these magazines acted as cultural forums. On some levels, they preserved cherished vestiges of Victorian culture while helping to establish the cultural parameters of a new and very different age. These mass periodicals indeed endorsed (in fact, played a critical role in) the rising corporate and consumer-oriented world, and they would help readers "adjust" to shifting economic and cultural imperatives. The magazines functioned as a unique site of cultural negotiation regarding the major issues of the day, a place where meanings and identities were hammered out for this new group.[67]

How did the mass magazines both reflect and help to define the lives of their readers? Answers emerge from every element of the magazines—their editorial content, their advertising, and their fiction. They all constructed their readers as modern participants in a new economic order, situating readers "on the crest of progress" and their magazines as central instruments of education to help readers comprehend those exciting times.[68] In marked contrast to the quality monthlies, all of the mass periodicals celebrated the promise of new technology. Articles highlighted skyscrapers, electrical power, automobiles, and exalted in the efficiency of the new corporations. Even their muckraking stemmed more from a desire to channel the promises of modern life.[69] Each of these magazines endorsed a more energetic, vital, and healthy lifestyle, their conception of their readers seeming to reflect the energy and action of the day.[70] The magazines also championed a new social ethic centered on material abundance and consumption. Indeed, their advertising sections (integrated prominently within the content in the weeklies) grew enormously, with ads covering an entire page and beckoning with arresting images. They still preached hard work and perseverance, but also that one could now enjoy more fully the fruits of that labor through modern efficiency.[71] Advertisers and editors in promoting a new way of life—active, healthy, leisured, and full of commodities— all encouraged the middle class to identify with and revel in modern, progressive changes.[72] Nevertheless, the mass magazines continued the quality monthlies' project of traditional cultural uplift, by disseminating informational articles on singers, poets, writers, musicians, and thinkers, and by presenting "the best" contemporary poetry and fiction.[73] The magazines "acted as cultural gatekeepers and tutors," responding to the desires of readers who "wanted to be both taught and to be addressed as knowing"—a class, "feeling its way into culture."[74]

Building on the work of Martin Sklar, Matthew Schneirov's judgment of the new mass magazines captured my view that "corporate capitalism and consumer culture were not 'things' they [the magazine editors and contributors] adapted to or legitimated. They were phenomena the popular magazines helped, directly and indirectly to create."[75] In other words, as an unprecedented national media forum, the magazines formed a key part of the process of cultural evolution, of helping the one in four Americans who read these magazines to define themselves, sift through possibilities, and to make sense of their place in America. This project of middle-class cultural definition shaped the content of the magazines, and then helped to redefine America. The swirling nature of this process (part traditional, part modern) impacted visions of the college experience in profound ways that helped render it an ideal place to acquire the evolving aspects of middle-class masculine identity. To ponder such a seemingly simple question as why college became more popular, actually entails far broader and deeper issues that cut straight to shifting notions of masculinity and, thus, authority in a rapidly changing society.

A New Vision of the College Experience in Mass Magazines

Mass magazines formed the principal cultural forum where the perception of college was recrafted and worked into the cultural horizon of the plain middle-class businessman. The magazines did not reflect a changing reality in the image of college portrayed on their pages; they actively created this ideal out of a response to the sense of crisis perceived among their male readers. How could one sustain the ideal of the cultured gentleman? Where could one find the hard lessons associated with self-made manhood? How could one fulfill the notion of rugged masculinity? Where could one attain the modern training of a professional in order to more equitably guide the American economy? Where could one find rough manly, communal bonding? How could one possibly experience the manly temptations and lessons of an urban sporting culture without too much sinful risk? How could native-born, middle-class American men counter the very real challenges posed by an influx of immigrant men and by the "new woman" of the era? These were some of the longings, anxieties, and concerns of the emerging corporate middle class as they straddled the Victorian and modern ages, and they went to the core of the transforming notions of masculinity, race, and middle-class authority.

The college experience could (and would) provide all of this, but it had to be constructed in such a way. Parents did not simply wake up one morning with the idea of sending their sons to college for success in life. Employers did not suddenly begin to comb campuses for graduates. And while many college presidents, professors, and students at several institutions worked to alter the curriculum and the conceptions of the college man in America, they alone could not meaningfully affect wide public perceptions and discourse. College as a viable rung on the ladder of success and as a fit site to form an ideal middle-class manhood, one that combined Victorian and modern masculinity, had to be literally created for mass consumption. Many individuals helped to reshape the place of college in American life, but only the new middle-class magazines occupied the perfect position in American culture to fashion such a broad vision, to bring all of the elements together.

Four mass magazines (*Munsey's*, *Cosmopolitan*, the *Post*, and *Collier's*) were consistently at or near the top in circulation. *Munsey's* peaked in the 1890s and first evidenced a clear infatuation with college life (articles on athletics and secret societies) connected with success in business ("Should Your Boy Go to College?" in 1895). *Cosmopolitan* was the strongest monthly in the early 1900s. Distinct from the weeklies, monthlies could be well over one hundred pages (the *Post* would eventually approach that, but like *Collier's* began at under thirty pages). Monthlies devoted more space to fiction by far, while their short stories and articles easily tripled (usually) the standard length of those in the weeklies. All promoted "culture," but *Munsey's* pursued this most vigorously. The weeklies differed in important ways from each other as well. *Collier's* published only one or two short stories per issue and focused on news events, while the *Post* ran three or four stories and focused on domestic and business-related topics.

I read these magazines cover to cover from the years 1893–1912 for the monthlies and 1899–1915 for the weeklies.[76] Reading each issue so extensively was time consuming but necessary in order to appreciate how these magazines functioned as a whole in doing their "cultural work." Using a guide to parachute in to read a relevant article or story does not allow one to witness the interconnected nature of this media. It was amazing to see how thoroughly issues of masculinity, success, and authority (including conceptions of college and professionalism) intertwined and permeated every aspect of these magazines (editorials, articles, fiction, and advertising).

Table 1 charts the changing volume and nature of collegiate references in these periodicals. The coverage peaked during what I term a "foundational period," roughly 1898–1904, a period that began with *Cosmopolitan*'s "Modern Education" series and running through the *Post*'s major infatuation with the

Table 1. Collegiate References in Mass Magazines, 1893 to 1915

	Munsey's							Cosmopolitan							Saturday Evening Post							Collier's						
	A	Am	E	Em	F	Fm	T	A	Am	E	Em	F	Fm	T	A	Am	E	Em	F	Fm	T	A	Am	E	Em	F	Fm	T
1893	—	5	2	—	1	1	9	4	8	—	—	—	4	16	—	—	—	—	—	—	—	—	—	—	—	—	—	—
1894	5	6	1	2	2	2	18	—	9	—	—	—	1	10	—	—	—	—	—	—	—	—	—	—	—	—	—	—
1895	3	4	3	1	—	—	11	2	5	—	—	—	1	8	—	—	—	—	—	—	—	—	—	—	—	—	—	—
1896	1	1	4	3	—	—	9	2	4	1	2	—	2	11	—	—	—	—	—	—	—	—	—	—	—	—	—	—
1897	—	2	2	3	—	1	6	10	4	2	—	—	—	16	—	—	—	—	—	—	—	—	—	—	—	—	—	—
1898	1	2	3	2	—	1	11	7	8	1	—	—	2	18	3	3	—	—	5	2	13	12	—	3	1	—	1	16
1899	2	1	2	1	—	1	5	6	5	1	1	—	1	14	4	8	9	5	5	5	30	11	—	5	4	—	1	21
1900	2	1	1	—	2	1	7	7	4	3	3	—	1	18	18	14	7	1	11	7	62	13	2	4	8	—	1	28
1901	6	2	1	1	—	—	9	5	2	1	3	—	—	11	20	5	7	1	17	7	57	11	3	4	8	1	1	26
1902	5	3	2	—	—	2	12	7	4	—	—	—	1	12	11	5	5	1	7	4	33	11	3	5	2	—	1	26
1903	1	3	1	4	—	2	12	2	4	3	3	—	2	11	5	3	6	2	14	4	34	13	4	6	2	—	1	27
1904	3	3	2	4	—	2	14	—	12	3	3	—	2	20	3	3	10	3	7	6	29	9	4	4	6	2	2	27
1905	3	4	1	2	1	2	13	—	10	2	3	2	3	15	2	2	6	—	3	3	17	13	5	2	5	—	2	28
1906	3	3	2	2	—	4	11	5	5	2	2	—	2	14	4	3	12	—	3	3	21	14	6	7	7	—	2	36
1907	1	5	2	3	—	3	13	1	3	2	2	—	4	11	8	5	5	4	2	6	26	12	7	7	7	—	1	34
1908	2	3	3	3	3	3	12	3	3	2	2	2	2	10	2	—	2	1	1	2	11	15	9	3	3	—	2	30
1909	1	3	3	2	3	4	16	2	3	5	1	2	3	17	1	1	7	—	8	3	21	16	5	5	6	1	1	34
1910	2	3	2	3	2	2	14	3	1	5	—	1	—	10	2	1	6	—	7	4	20	17	2	6	6	—	1	32
1911	2	3	3	3	—	2	12	2	2	3	3	1	3	15	5	1	4	2	5	5	19	12	4	9	13	—	1	39
1912	1	3	2	4	1	3	12	3	4	4	2	2	1	15	2	9	1	—	3	4	21	15	5	11	12	—	1	44
1913	—	—	—	—	—	—	—	—	—	—	—	—	—	—	3	3	5	2	6	4	20	14	3	8	6	—	1	32
1914	—	—	—	—	—	—	—	—	—	—	—	—	—	—	3	6	5	7	3	5	29	10	2	7	5	—	3	27
1915	—	—	—	—	—	—	—	—	—	—	—	—	—	—	4	8	7	6	4	6	35	9	3	8	7	—	1	28

Note: If an article (A), editorial (E), or work of fiction (F) focused on a direct college topic (featured an institution, college characters, etc.), then it was listed as such. An article (Am), editorial (Em), or work of fiction (Fm) was counted separately if it *mentioned* a college topic. Ideally another category—significant mentions—should be added since a collegiate background for a character in a work of business fiction could be quite significant. Note the large number of mentions for articles in *Cosmopolitan* for 1904. It ran a "Making a Choice of Profession" series during that year in which many businessmen who held a college degree were mentioned—something quite significant, but again hidden from view unless one truly digs through the entire discourse of the magazines, reading articles and contemporary fiction carefully.

It is tempting to pay attention to the totals (T), and that is important. One should also note the number of focused articles, editorials, and works of fiction. Taking this into account, the *Post's* obvious fascination with college falls into stark relief, especially during the "foundational period" (1898–1904), as does *Cosmopolitan's* attention during its "Modern Education" series in the late 1890s. *Collier's* numbers in this regard are inflated due to its intense and consistent coverage of athletics.

college experience with its College Man issues and several pieces of serialized fiction focused on college life. *Munsey's* early interest coincided with a concern over future opportunities that would remain a constant undercurrent throughout the foundational period. Not surprisingly given his editorial interest in business, Lorimer's *Post* focused the most on the question of college and success, with two full College Man numbers given to the issue, and in the foundational period ran at least two other stories per year on it, plus the Gorgan Graham and another letters series ("Talks with a Kid Brother at College") revolving around this new phenomenon. But all the magazines ran featured stories on this central question as well as stories on fraternities and athletics. *Collier's* main contribution, for example, came through its intense coverage of college athletics and particularly football (Walter Camp's All-American teams), although publishing football fiction (something it regularly did after 1920) was left mainly to the *Post*.

During the foundational period the most distinctive aspect of this explosion of interest in college hinged on several interrelated themes related to the evolving identity of the middle-class male reader: the college curriculum and its utility (usually raised in reference to the business world); a fascination with football and other "rugged" elements of college life; and the appeal of college as an elite and sophisticated setting, the flip side of which were articles in a humorous tone that rendered college as appropriately democratic and accessible. Flowering a bit later came the deluge of ad copy portraying the idealized young American in now-familiar college settings. Aside from some muckraking on college topics after 1909 (*Collier's* publishing the most serious pieces, while *Cosmopolitan's* were essentially more positive), the obvious infatuation with college as a new and rich experience for American men faded as a focus in articles after the foundational period. But the usage of college references in fiction subtly increased in profound ways, and in this respect charts of statistical references prove no substitute for simply reading these magazines from cover to cover.

Fiction was vital for each of these magazines, and the rise of fiction featuring college characters or college settings proved remarkable. Accounts of pranks, hazing, and the football tale became the most popular and built on a wave of fascination with college life in book publishing in the 1890s.[77] Magazine coverage of college life took some of the themes of this subgenre to new levels, introducing college life to a broader spectrum of Americans and linking it more directly with their readers' middle-class concerns. But such college fiction coincided with and was bound up in a broader phenomenon—the rise of the male reader. Every issue in each of these magazines contained a Western tale or a martial-themed story (medieval knights, Napoleonic battles, the Civil War). Gritty literary realism proved popular as well, with business settings and plots of manly regeneration through competition quite common, all reflecting a preoccupation with reviving male potency through these literary models.[78] One can find stories by Stephen Crane, Frank Norris, and Jack London. The college tale of rough hazing and rugged football certainly fits within this rising new genre of male fiction. One must go beyond the obvious college tales, though, to appreciate the transformation taking shape. For example, in general fiction we can see "mentions," in general fiction (usually on contemporary business topics), and the way college enters into character backgrounds (see table 1). Whereas mentions of a college background for a character occurred prior to 1900, such characters usually were traditional professionals. Increasingly business-related characters in this male genre sported a college background, a phenomenon that coincided after 1905 with the massive influx of ad copy integrating college themes. This evidences how the reformulated vision of the college man, stemming from the earlier makeover in the foundational period had worked its cultural magic and rendered the college experience as an increasingly normative part of ideal middle-class manhood.

Perhaps having all gone to college, publishers, editors, and writers conspired in some fashion to shape the vision of the ideal American man in their own image. Of the publishers and editors of the magazines in this study, most either attended or graduated from college.[79] And of the forty-two writers and contributors (not counting academics) who authored articles or fiction in these magazines (and for whom I could find biographical information), twenty-two had graduated from college, and eleven had some postsecondary experience— either attending college or graduating from law or medical school. Only eight had attained no higher formal education.[80] Such evidence might suggest that these editors, at least, guided the discourse on college to reflect a bias toward attending. Nevertheless, such simplistic reductions do not succeed in illuminating the central issue—how was college invested with meaning. The two editors who inserted their voices most pointedly on this subject (Walker and Lorimer) were hardly uncritical. Perhaps their college experiences informed their perspective. Overall, however, this issue, while important, could hardly have consumed every layer of editorial decision making, let alone the content of ad copy, since the discourse on college and college education encompassed articles, stories, and ad copy with little obvious bearing on the topic of "should your boy go to college."

The larger and most relevant point remains that the animating concern of these editors, where college was concerned, was not necessarily to change the system or simply prompt more people to attend. Their vision of the place of college in American life grew out of their prime desire to connect with and guide their readers. The editors who piloted these magazines chose contributors and fiction writers who had their fingers on the pulse of changes in their readers' lives. They understood the pressures on middle-class men, and they fashioned a college experience that met all of the desired self-conceptions and assuaged the anxieties. This is why I have chosen not to focus on singular authors or editors. If one searches for the most significant editor or author or story (or institution or college president for that matter) to pinpoint the transition, then I believe one searches in vain. The evolutionary perceptions of college in this instance were part of a broader, gradual process that must be surveyed on a more collective level, which is why the consumer medium of the magazines as a whole are so essential.

Amplifying some elements of college life over others, magazine writers, editors, and advertisers integrated their revamped version of the college experience into a new vision of ideal manhood for a dawning corporate age, one that fused the best of past and present. This new vision did not emanate solely from the editors or contributors. All offered bits and pieces: some emphasized athletics, others science and utility, and still others liberal culture or the allure of a collegiate lifestyle. At times these various elements could oppose each other, but these facets of college life did indeed remain juxtaposed with each other, offering readers new and valuable ways to reconsider college education in their identities. Gradually, the elements fused into a unified whole, an attractive vision of college life and the college man for a new age. The magazines functioned as points of assembly and re-presentation, where all of the components (conceptions of college, business, racial superiority, and middle-class masculinity) met, reacted to each other, and gelled together into something new, establishing many of the key parameters of authority for middle-class American men for the rest of the century. Only in these magazines was a recrafted vision of the college experience that satisfied several parallel currents of middle-class manhood and business identity fully articulated and integrated. And only the magazines disseminated these ideals throughout the United States at a critical point in time, while also filtering conceptions of college, manhood, and success through a consumer medium, helping to weave college into the cultural fabric of middle-class masculinity and identity. In many ways only a consumer medium could have effectively constructed college in such a multilayered fashion, accommodating so many discordant and incongruous strains of evolving American masculine ideals, effectively cordoning off college as an avenue for advancement primarily for native-born white men, all while employing the language of democratic meritocracy. In the United States, it was the national media of that time, as the cultural spokesmen of the emerging corporate middle class, that invested new meanings in the college experience and through this agent re-formed the perceived matrices of male authority and power.

Magazines by nature were a consumer medium, so collegiate expectations and their connections to ideal middle-class manhood were filtered through the portal of consumption. But while the refashioning of college at first seemed to preserve many Victorian ideals (the importance of forming character and cul-ture), the magazine rendering of them also collapsed such ideals into a set of stylized and desirable images. Advertising did this most pointedly, but to some degree the magazines generally promoted this trend. By the 1920s, much of the original appeal of college (though still present in images and characterizations) had been translated and worked into something quite different that promoted more a modern masculine ideal exalting appearance over substance. Even if college did still preserve the possibility for very real and substantive personal transformation, the college man effectively had become more the model of corporate suave than the heir of the self-made man.[81]

The cultural reconstruction of college in redefining middle-class mascu-linity functioned to reformulate channels to power and authority during a time of profound transition. It facilitated new avenues for reasserting native-born, white male hegemony in an emerging corporate America. For the executives and managers of the new corporations to possess legitimacy in wielding au-thority, for themselves as much as for their workers, their positions had to be justified within a matrix of male authority that was also in flux. The cultural re-envisioning of college in the mass magazines helped to rationalize this author-ity, to recalibrate the channels for achieving masculine power for a new age. It essentially offered WASP men a new and convenient way to preserve claims to superiority on multiple fronts, both traditional (Victorian character and self-made achievement by working through college or up-through-the-ranks), and modern (passionate masculinity and scientific professionalism). Through a college education, the aspiring corporate executive could be a traditional gentleman-leader *and* the technical professional as corporate executive, while he could also lay claim (through the same college experience) to identifying himself as the impassioned footballer or the fraternity brawler—claims that buttressed his "manliness" against the threat of his virile immigrant workers even as his college education simultaneously reinforced his educated, "civil-ized" superiority. In other words, the attraction of college as an aspect of one's identity and its growing popularity in the twentieth century involved far more than rational economic calculations.[82] What this book illuminates, then, is nothing less than a discourse that facilitated a transformation of hegemonic vi-sions of power, and how this discourse helped to fashion a new multifaceted (and attractive) narrative of masculine authority in a corporate age, with a re-vamped vision of college and the college man as a central component.

Unquestionably this narrative functioned as a potent cultural barrier that privileged native-born, white American men, yet it was a complex narrative of exclusion. For all of the dominant visions of WASP college men as the new leaders of an emerging corporate America, the meritocratic ideals inherent in the construction of this new narrative of authority rendered it open to those implicitly excluded. Ultimately most Americans could conceive of using the same pathway for themselves (working through college or playing football there, and then rising through the corporation). Certainly it would prove an attractive avenue for new European immigrant men to become more fully "white" Americans, but the concept of going to college, with all its accumulated meanings for power and authority, would eventually prove adaptable for minorities and women. Pregnant within the very language of that exclusionary concept of "going to college" was the cultural ammunition to foment a push for inclusion, for others to live that vision.

The Crisis of the Clerks

Magazines, Masculine Success, and the Ideal Businessman in Transition

Keenly aware that times were changing, the new middle-class periodicals that arose around the turn of the century seemed particularly interested in addressing the question of opportunities for young men entering the business world or "the world of affairs" as it was often called. Alongside the issue of whether the modern "trusts" multiplied or hindered these opportunities recurred the question of whether your boy should go to college. On this topic most writers would have agreed with Herbert Vreeland in "the Young Man's Opportunity in the New Business Order" when he opined that "no man can get too much education . . . but the absence of an educational equipment at the start is no barrier to success."[1] In fact, a loud and substantial minority proclaimed college a clear hindrance to business success. One contributor to the *Post* lectured in reassuring terms about the handicap of the college man at twenty-two rubbing elbows with the "common school man," who started in the office at fifteen. The college man, this writer predicted, would come "face to face with the realization that he is not so gifted . . . that much of his time at college has been wasted in acquiring useless learning; that the dead languages which he has taken so much pains to acquire are not of the slightest help to him in buying, selling, or in the making of common records."[2]

Each of the industry-leading, new middle-class magazines, *Munsey's, Cosmopolitan, Collier's,* and especially the *Saturday Evening Post,* stalwartly upheld the self-made businessman as their quintessential American man. Opportunities abounded for men imbued with that ideal Victorian virtue of character. If young men worked diligently, persevered through hardships, and possessed an iron will and courage, they could educate themselves through their work as craftsmen or clerks and, thus, rise to own their shop or business. Articles and fiction in these periodicals endlessly championed such ideal figures.

But times were indeed changing. By the end of the first decade, even the *Post,* the greatest promoter of traditional self-made manhood, admitted a problem. In 1909 the *Post* ran a series covering a "crisis" for the clerk, the stereotypical aspiring businessman of the nineteenth century.[3] No longer could a man learn the business firsthand by doing the mountain of monotonous tasks required in the huge modern office surrounded by legions of clerks now using typewriters. No longer did such work experience foster and nurture the growth of Victorian values and character, nor did the clerk sit at the elbow of the business master learning the practical secrets of success. And now women had infiltrated the office, assuming the secretarial and office positions that had traditionally served as training-ground and stepping-stones for aspiring businessmen. Finally, and most alarming, hordes of new immigrant men arrived yearly, hungry for work and advancement, adding a new dimension to the competition to get ahead. In the space of a decade, story headlines in the *Post* went from advice to aspiring clerks, "The Clerk Who Saves," to lamentations, "The Clerk Who Isn't Young."[4] Ironically, by 1910 an alternative avenue for molding ideal business men had emerged—the college—with magazines as a principal vehicle celebrating this new route to business success.

Before we can understand how these magazines refashioned the image of college to meet this crisis of business masculinity, we need to grasp not only the pressures on traditional models of business success but also the alternative ideals crafted to cope with the corporate transformation prior to the full acceptance of college as an ideal place to cultivate businessmen. College as an accepted rung on the ladder of American success eventually would occur owing to the way that college, as a single formative experience, could interweave several attributes increasingly deemed essential to advancement—an acquaintance with science, the breadth of liberal culture, and a brush with the so-called manly athletics. While all of these motives served as links between college, business success, and masculinity, in fact college was not a necessary component for any of them. Modern scientific training, the polish of genteel culture, the fortitude and toughness bred by sports, all of these could be acquired outside the ivied walls and, thus, without the many negative stereotypes attached to college life. Indeed, the middle-class magazines promoted the acquisition of all of these attributes as components of ideal manhood, while often ignoring the need for any formal education and viewing college as a detriment to success.

Exploring the various currents of American masculinity and notions of business success in the early throes of evolution from the proprietary to the corporate age shows how these new conceptions of ideal business manhood were constructed, interpreted, and filtered through the first truly national media— the mass middle-class magazine. Even though the magazines collectively pushed the need for more scientific training and for cultural breadth in order for their readers to succeed in this brave new corporate world, college was not automatically a part of the new success formula. Although these magazines collectively would play the key role in refashioning the college experience as part of middle-class identity in this particular time frame, we cannot ignore the fact that most articles, editorials, and fiction dealing with the generic business-man failed to mention college. College often proved irrelevant in profiles of businessmen or accounts of industries. But conditions were changing, and all these magazines covered the rise of the corporation and the altered opportunities for advancement. The *Saturday Evening Post* focused most intensely on this issue. Every issue featured at least two articles and one short story involving a business topic. Other magazines also ran frequent profiles of business leaders and articles on corporate organization, and each increasingly featured contemporary fiction in a business setting (although *Collier's* lagged here). Out of this coverage and concern would flower the new vision of college.[5]

Many complex issues heralded the death knell of the traditional self-made man in business. Not only did this final crisis involve the new realities of the massive bureaucratic corporate office (the impossibility of "learning on the job" or rising from the legions of workers), it also swirled with interlaced anxieties of racial and masculine inferiorities occasioned by the arrival of female office secretaries and the massive influx of supposedly inferior but aggressive immigrant men. In the context of these final and interrelated crises, it was clear that a new ideal route to success had to be crafted, but in no small way the initial accommodations would set the tone and mark the route that a college education would conveniently fulfill.

Business Success and Victorian Manhood in Transition

In 1899 the *Saturday Evening Post* ran a story titled, "The New Outlook for Young Men." The advice offered in anticipation of the new century was anything but novel. "Pluck, honesty, good address and manly earnestness," would prevail for those hoping to feast on the "incredible opportunities" of the next century.[6] The *Post*, *Cosmopolitan*, *Collier's*, and *Munsey's* all predicted great opportunities ahead, but the formula for business success evidently would not change. Each magazine printed regular profiles of the "Captains of Industry" and how they rose. John D. Rockefeller proved a popular hero, a man of action who rose from poverty to wrestle a wasteful industry into shape.[7] And the maxims for success never varied—honesty, frugality, sobriety, and hard work, the same key ingredients for the Victorian self-made man. So powerful was this ideal that even J. P. Morgan's life was filtered through the model of the self-made man. Though the *Cosmopolitan* profiler admitted Morgan "to the purple born," he praised Morgan's work ethic. The young Morgan could have acceded to the life of a rich loafer. Instead he took up his father's business "as good a man as if he had begun without a dollar."[8]

Late nineteenth-century Americans built their conceptions of manhood and success around the self-made man, with the businessman as the quintessential archetype. The stereotypical hero usually hailed from humble origins such as the farm or small town and, having completed his common schooling, set out to make his fortune. From there the typical hero rose from the office boy to a clerk and eventually to the head of the firm. In each case the hero relied on nothing more than the cardinal virtues of Victorian manhood. He worked hard, persevered, lived simply, and applied his common sense to impress his superiors. His fortunes resulted from the solid foundation of his inner character. The self-made businessman in particular represented one of America's most cherished models of success.[9]

Tales of business success and the self-made hero saturated the pages of the *Post*, *Collier's*, *Munsey's*, and *Cosmopolitan*. Certainly, these new popular periodicals aimed at a broader audience than the businessman as demonstrated in their fiction, which often focused on female characters and with various "departments" or series devoted to the theater, poetry, or home décor. Their frequent advice articles on career opportunities often included insight into traditional professions.[10] But the requirements for success rarely varied, and the American businessman in his myriad forms remained the center of editorial attention. Turn-of-the-century magazines celebrated the rags-to-riches tales and the rugged, individualistic qualities of Victorian manhood. The title "From Brakeman to President," the success story of a railroad president in *Munsey's*, said it all. *Cosmopolitan's* series on the "Dreamers of the Business World" and the "Captains of Industry" were meant to instruct and inspire the next generation of self-made men. The *Post* took its edifying mission even more seriously, running articles directly geared for instruction of the young clerk. Consider some of the titles: "The Clerk Who Saves," "What Constitutes 'Self-Made' Man," "Getting and Keeping a Business Position," "Why Young Men Fail: A Clear Explanation by Shrewd Business Men." All emphasized the traditional route to business success, revolving around character and perseverance, never mentioning anything but self-education.[11]

The editors of *Munsey's*, *Cosmopolitan*, and the *Post* (Frank Munsey, John Brisben Walker and G. H. Lorimer, respectively) certainly would continue to sustain Victorian virtues as the true source of success and ideal manhood. The editors of these magazines were themselves pathbreaking entrepreneurs, raised in an American culture that venerated these Victorian ideals. Nevertheless, a careful reader of their pages would have noticed unfamiliar settings and terms creeping into the business profiles that pointed to the beginning of dramatic changes. *Cosmopolitan* in their "Captains of Industry" series in 1902, for instance, featured Charles M. Schwab. Although the article chronicled his rise from poverty to great power and wealth in a typical rags-to-riches format—he began as a grocery boy—it concluded that he "represents the highest development of the salaried employee." "Though a glorified wage-earner," the writer added that Schwab was content.[12] The narratives of business success had begun to integrate the terms of the corporate world and the characterizations of the ideal businessman now began their remarkable transformation.

Of course, anxiety caused by the rapidly changing economic structure precipitated the vigorous affirmations of the traditional success ethic one finds in the popular magazines. Despite their celebration of the self-made man and Victorian virtues, the editors were hardly reactionary in their attitudes toward modern changes or in their confrontation of what Munsey categorized as one of the vital concerns of the day, "organized capital."[13] These magazines' content blended both the traditional genteel project of disseminating culture with a hearty embrace of modern life—technology, skyscrapers, and the modern "trust."[14] Munsey thought the modern trusts crude, but he featured articles marveling at the great organizations of the day as the way of the future.[15] And while Walker and Lorimer would publish antitrust fiction and articles, they both qualified their stance on the trusts by noting that they endorsed "good" trusts as models of modern efficiency.[16] While critiques of voracious capital and longings for simpler times entered into editorial content, these editors in many ways reflected their readers—born in one era of the small entrepreneurs, but proudly creating and trying to make sense of their place in a promising new corporate age.

These editors' visions of the ideal businessman and his qualities transferred much of the cherished self-made man to the corporate setting, trying to make sense of the world their readers increasingly inhabited. Each of these magazines stalwartly denied that trusts had ruined the opportunities for young men. One series in the *Post*, "Limiting Opportunity," pointedly addressed this issue. Was the only chance for a young man in business to marry the daughter of a Captain of Industry? Was the aspiring businessman doomed to be "a minion of some corporation on a meager salary?" Emphatically the answer was no. The "trusts" desperately sought good men. All one needed to do to become a responsible, high-salaried employee was start at the bottom, be loyal, and work hard.[17] Munsey conceded that the "big combinations of capital" indeed made it more difficult for young men to become independent businessmen. But both he and Lorimer lectured that these big enterprises actually heightened the chances for young men to rise on their own merits to great salaried positions. The call issuing from great railroads and manufacturers, asserted Munsey in what would become a common refrain, "is for men of brains—clever, keen, enterprising men of executive ability . . . men who think, men who do things." In fact, this enhanced the opportunities for self-made men to rise, argued both editors, since brains trumped capital as the essential ingredient for leadership.[18]

Numerous articles trumpeted the increased opportunities—"How the Trusts Promote Men," and "The Young Man's Opportunities," but these articles tellingly emphasized something not necessarily a part of the traditional success tale, attributes that heralded the rise of the modern corporate professional—technical knowledge.[19] In the *Post* two new business heroes emerged as manly ideals to strive for—the scientific, expert manager, and the salesman. While the figure of the salesman retained the ideal of learning informally through experience in true self-made fashion, the expert manager presaged the future.[20] In one of the *Post*'s continuing series of "How Business Success Will Be Won in the Twentieth Century," one contributor spelled it out plainly: "the specialist will be the dominating force in the business world," he predicted, and "the road to success lies along that line." For this writer, the "new method," being a highly trained specialist in the modern corporation, ranked as the epitome of "scientific and civilized" progress.[21] Articles like "The Business Expert: Stories of a New Profession" in 1902 further trumpeted this new hero as a true professional among the "modern expert callings," a "methodizer" and "system expert" in the office and shop, noting how the efficiency expert fixed the auditing office of a manufacturer after diagnosing "too much faith and not enough system."[22] Before long the term *scientific management* or the

"Science of Business" entered numerous articles. Advice on "Cutting Out the Motions in Business" and how to become a "General Manager" proliferated, peppered with references of business professionals applying scientific technique to business.[23] The *Post*'s business advice gradually shifted from how to help clerks rise in the office to advice or "shop talk" for managers and executives in order to help them organize their business more efficiently.[24] A *Post* editorial of 1909 even rejoiced in the ascension of the "Professional Business Man," who managed businesses and properties he did not own, just as a surgeon or lawyer provided professional services for clients.[25]

Men in business were being asked to apply their varied skills to systematize work, regimenting the office and the shop, and to make the workplace function more effectively. The vast majority of these men had received no formal education on these subjects, but the phenomenon must be counted as part of the rationalization and ordering of a chaotic yet promising world in transition, and it necessitated further alteration in the qualities required for business success. The issue of how best to obtain such scientific or technical training, however, had yet to be fully resolved.

Attaining Science and Culture: The Lingering Ambivalence toward the College-Bred

The image of the ideal businessman presented in these magazines, then, encouraged the notion of the businessman as a budding modern professional expert. Nevertheless, this expertise still did not inevitably require any formal education, so the ideal of the self-educated man remained a powerful model for success. Most business advice articles, including those that espoused the need for scientific training, often failed to mention college or any formal education beyond the common school.

Even as these magazines' contributors would refashion college as a suitable preparation for business, for several years hearty condemnations of college-going continued, a testament to the difficulty in rapidly altering the long-held belief in self-education. For example, a railroad executive in the featured 1903 *Cosmopolitan* series, "Making a Choice of a Profession," assured readers that "real" education that formed character, whether formal or informal, was always good, but through "application and study" a young man could master the knowledge necessary, adding that between the self-trained man and the "educated numbskull," there was no comparison.[26] Consider the Carnegies, Fricks, and Schwabs, urged one *Post* writer on the subject. Charles M. Schwab was made chief engineer at the Homestead steelworks at twenty-three yet never spent a day in college. He picked up all the knowledge necessary to him during working hours. The writer believed technical education vital, but in the tradition of self-education and the shop-trained engineer, he viewed college as a hindrance, citing how few college men had reached the "upper places of great corporations" by 1901. Books were cheap, argued another railroad officer in the *Post*, and they placed the wisdom of the ages at the bright young man's disposal.[27]

Such sentiments surfaced regularly in other articles featuring the opportunities that abounded due to modern industrial change. While preaching the "Gospel of Saving" to young men starting out, Russell Sage in a *Post* article, commented that in this age of specialization, sixteen was not too young an age to adopt a specialty and to "work up to it." For such special skills, he considered college a waste of time and, in fact, a severe handicap due to the delay it caused business aspirants.[28] Writing on the "consulting engineer" and trumpeting the new "science of business," *Post* regular Forrest Crissey in 1903 never referred to formal educational credentials. And articles like "Mind Training in Business," while still touting the "cardinal virtues" of "honesty, sobriety, truthfulness and industry," urged readers to pursue self-training to become experts.[29] One writer observed that modern department stores discounted even a high school education as a substitute for practical experience.[30]

As the corporate age dawned, businessmen and their myriad champions in the magazines increasingly promoted what might be termed a "scientific idiom" that began to professionalize business occupations. They described modern business and its contributions to American life through managerial expertise, specialization, and public service. Inevitably this would pull businessmen closer to formal education, but the process was not automatic. Neither businessmen nor corporate specialists immediately looked to formal education in a knee-jerk reaction. It was not an obvious choice. Most businessmen and magazine writers themselves had not gone to college. And budding business professionals first organized themselves into associations—engineers, accountants, bankers, chemists—to certify their skills. Most men still learned on the job. Even as the magazines helped culturally to define professionals in the business world, several new paths opened to supply the requisite business education, and together they formed a huge and underappreciated set of options that merged the traditional idea of self-training with the modern notion of learning from "experts." Proprietary business colleges, business periodicals (often specializing in subfields), business training and success books, as well as the correspondence school all enjoyed enormous popularity and began catering to this new dynamic group of businessmen on the rise. And the multitude of advertisements in the popular magazines promoting such avenues of business education high-lighted that modern training could be had without the "taint" of college educa-tion. In fact, many ads for such endeavors encouraged an open contempt for higher education.

Publishers offered an array of self-help literature aimed specifically at the aspiring businessman. Their messages sustained the ideal of self-help but also offered expert advice and knowledge. Most publications like "Keys to Success" and organizations like The Success Company supplied business biographies that aspiring youth could read and therein find inspiration and models to emu-late.[31] The *Self-Educator* magazine promised to keep the "busy man of affairs" abreast of the latest innovations and discoveries in industry, commerce, and science, so that one could, "Help You Fit Yourself" to succeed in a changing world.[32] Few magazines, however, rivaled Orison Swett Marden's *Success Maga-zine*. It provided motivational business fiction ("love, heroism, adventure and world conquest"), guidance on etiquette and correct dress, along with advice on choosing a career.[33]

Still other business-oriented publications—*Beach's Magazine, Business*, and *System*—emphasized that they relayed practical experience, hands-on know-how and, most significantly, modern expert advice. According to one of their ads, business called for "more strategy than football . . . more skill than base-ball"; it was indeed a "scientific game." Through the metaphor of sport, *Sys-tem's* ads reflected how the magazines encouraged a new business ideal that seamlessly united the traditional need for fortitude and courage with the new demand in business for expert, scientific skills.[34] They and other publications promised modern, expert knowledge to complement their readers' Victorian character, and all without the vaguest mention of formal education.[35]

Nevertheless, more than any others, large advertisements (often taking up a quarter to a half page) for correspondence schools and proprietary business colleges bombarded periodical readers with information on the changing de-mands of the business world. Never has the demand for "brains and executive ability been so great," noted an International Correspondence Schools (ICS) advertisement, adding that "for the man of character and initiative . . . special training is the key to success." With lines like "Break Away from the Ranks of the Untrained" and "The Trained Man Wins" blazing across the ad pages, ICS and other correspondence schools endlessly reminded the aspiring corporate employees of the new middle class what it took to be promoted. And the refer-ences were always on promotion, not ownership, indicating the recognition of shifting business realities.[36] Correspondence schools offered courses in engi-neering, accounting, bookkeeping, stenography, and commercial law, allowing one to advance from "too much rule-of-thumb methods."[37]

A variety of proprietary schools (usually one- and two-year programs, although one could take a single course) vied to supply this training as well—The Railway Commercial Training School, Gem City Business College, The Tulloss School, Bryant and Stratton's College, Banks Business College, and the National Mercantile Training School, to name only a few.[38] Such schools focused primarily on traditional clerking skills, with some new attention to law, marketing, accounting, and sales. But they all tapped into and fueled the excitement surrounding the opportunities posed by corporate expansion. Business now carried forward the "progress of the world," a "calling higher than warriors or diplomats or politicians," declared a Peirce School advertisement.[39] And though more eloquent than similar business school ads, Peirce's notion of the business man's proper training perpetuated the common notion that such a training combined traditional business skills with "the best of modern methods."[40]

It was an age of modern specialization, and all of these ads assumed rising up in an organization rather than ownership as the ideal goal, yet the path was still open to any ambitious young man looking to the broad world of business. Often, these ads specifically disavowed the necessity of formal education. "When your boy leaves school for business, his employer won't give a rap whether he can recite Homer's *Iliad*, or in what year some Roman Emperor reigned," warned one advertisement for the Commercial Correspondence School of Rochester, adding that they made "a specialty of commercial subjects alone."[41] Similarly, an ICS ad touting the need for technical training cautioned, "this does not mean you must have an elaborate school or college education, but that you must have the good, sound, practical training that makes you an expert."[42]

Why did the strenuous denunciations of college surface so frequently? Many Americans around 1900, particularly businessmen, still attached powerful negative stereotypes to the college man, which continued to influence media treatments of the college bred and reinforced the sacred ideal of the self-made man, even as the same media sources simultaneously would work to rehabilitate the college man. College education suffered from two associations. It was traditionally the route to the ministry, and it was increasingly linked, due to its focus on classical literature, with cultural attainment. Both piety and culture remained honored components of manhood, but they also constituted two elements most often associated with the influence of women in restraining men's passions. And as the veneration of male aggressiveness rose in the latter years of the nineteenth century, college men found themselves often branded as "girlie," effeminate, and overcivilized.[43] Unless a man exercised caution in his displays of cultured learning or piety by the end of the nineteenth century, he could find himself branded a "sissy."[44]

Through such connections, the college man shared many of the same traits as the "dandy," or the overcultured genius, and such linkages came through in periodical literature. In defending higher education in 1906, for instance, George Horace Lorimer plainly discussed the stereotype. He contended that the practical American, despite his avowed reverence for education, clearly held the term *academic* in contempt. The term usually meant "unpractical, foolish, womanish, beneath the attention of real men." The professor, he noted, "should wear petticoats as the badge of his estate."[45] For the practical world of affairs, the "college man, like the genius, was thought to be [simultaneously] awkward, hypersensitive, impatient, conceited, pedantic, confused tactless, bookish and utterly impractical," the exact opposite of an ideal self-made American.[46]

Since at least the mid-nineteenth century, success books warned that colleges (wholly devoted in the popular mind to a classical education) robbed men of their natural vigor. It had directly and indirectly ruined more men than it had benefited, and this attitude still held a powerful appeal at the dawn of the new century; the colleges produced no business leaders. Some "antiquarians" might have a use for reading Ovid's *Metamorphoses*, but most young men "suffer a net loss by every moment they devote to such reading."[47] In his much read *Empire of Business*, Andrew Carnegie stated that non-college men claimed most of the positions of honor, while college men usually worked underneath onetime clerks and mechanics.[48]

The new mass magazines sustained much of these self-made prejudices and offered numerous answers as to why the self-made clerks consistently bested college men. Collegians aimlessly learned abstract facts, "mental gymnastics invested with holy authority," that bore no relation to practical life.[49] Henry Clews, a wealthy banker and renowned critic of the college man, stated the case against hiring the college man in that three-fourths of their heads were "filled with classical knowledge, dead languages, and high sounding unpractical ideals."[50] All great business leaders, according to *Ladies' Home Journal* editor Edward Bok, were the graduates of the "school of hard knocks," not college.[51] Such references became a common refrain for businessmen and champions of the self-made man.

Writing for the *Post* specifically on the topic, Bird S. Coler, then comptroller of New York, noted, "the pinch comes as soon as he [the college man] is started in business competition with the bright, clever, earnest young men . . . who have not the artificial polish of a collegiate course, but the practical, stirring, vigorous experiences of actual business life." Led to think his knowledge had high value, the college man would find a rude awakening in the business world.

Eventually, according to Andrew Carnegie (quoted in another article), the college man would realize "that he is not so gifted outside the college walls," his time at college "wasted in acquiring useless . . . dead languages." The boy who started in a business at fifteen, in contrast, content with a nominal wage, was worth a great deal to the firm after seven years of experience, about the same time the college boy came along feeling that he should be given the same pay even though he could not make common records. The young man at his side, "who doesn't know a Greek root from a tulip bulb is relied on more."[52] "The average graduate," according to Clews, "does not even know enough of arithmetic and of calligraphy to earn, upon his arrival, a salary of five dollars a week." Moreover, since he regarded himself as brilliant, the collegian often refused to humble himself "to learn the rudiments [of the] business man's vocation."[53] Advice offered to clerks even admonished them to avoid dressing and acting like the "college chap."[54] Artificial, proud, impatient, impractical, the college man could not compete with the self-made man's vigor and more alert manhood.

Compounding these traditional negative attitudes toward the college man, many thought that the relative freedom of the college years actually corrupted the virtues of young men. This seemed especially so as the phenomenon of college-going among the nation's elite received increasing attention. One *Post* writer inveighed against sending sons to college, since there they only acquired "tastes and habits" that proved burdensome later in life.[55] A commentator in *Munsey's* was more precise: "there is too much luxury" in the colleges. "Frugal habits, frugal associations" were the key to the "building of the character of the commercial, professional man," and college corrupted those ideals.[56] For example, in one article on handling men, the dissipated college youth is shown with a rakish hat, cigarette dangling from the mouth, wholly disinterested.[57]

Magazine fiction added vivid reinforcement of such stereotypes as well. "Summer Girls and Idle Fellows," for example, featured college men and professors idly whiling away summer days with the ladies, reading poetry and discussing socialism.[58] The elite college "sport"—often a drinking gambler, flaccid and weak—became a common character, the foil to the self-made businessman, in an eruption of periodical fiction that focused on the business world. Many stories of rising young businessmen, in particular, began with the boy first leaving college due to ill health, sloth, or rebelliousness.[59] In addition to the college man as effeminate and overcultured, then, increasingly they also received the stigma of being morally and physically dissipated, the opposite of the vigorous, disciplined self-made man. Great business leaders were the graduates of the "school of hard knocks," not college.[60]

Culture was not a dirty word to the middle-class businessman, however. Supposedly, the overeducated, effeminate college boy could never make it in the real world, but this did not mean that the businessman should remain uncultured.[61] Self-made manhood required the development of culture as part of the nurturing of one's character. In fact, late nineteenth-century Americans accorded the clerk or bookkeeper a special status. They identified men in such positions not as permanently subordinate employees but as future proprietors in training. Clerks themselves shared this attitude, which helps explain why they endured lower pay than many skilled labor jobs. Moreover, it was assumed that the clerk would acquire a measure of culture commensurate with his future middle-class status.[62] Just as the young clerk need not attend college (or any school) to acquire the necessary expertise even to qualify as a "scientific manager," so he need not attend any school to acquire his requisite culture. As with business specialization or scientific knowledge, culture too could readily be attained through self-education.

Editors wanted to help all of their readers and especially the aspiring businessman to fulfill the ideal of becoming more cultured. Certainly their magazines celebrated modern life, but the editors also clung to the avowed mission of the genteel literary monthlies to disseminate the benefits of culture to those Americans in need of it. *Cosmopolitan*, *Munsey's*, *Collier's*, and the *Post* each viewed their missions, in part, as bringing the best fiction and poetry, art reproductions, and (more typically) news and information of the arts, culture, and theater to inform and elevate the tastes of their readers. *Munsey's* offered regular "departments" such as "Literary Chat," "The Stage," and "Artists and their Work."[63] Along with such articles as "The Progress of Science," "Captains of Industry," and "The Methods of Banking," *Cosmopolitan* also ran "In the World of Arts and Letters," "John Milton," and "Balzac and His Work" in addition to the standard offerings of art reprints, poetry, and fiction.[64] *Collier's Weekly* also published such articles as "Opera and Drama," "New Plays and Players," and "A Glimpse at Recent Fiction."[65] These magazines invited their readers to consider themselves cultured and encouraged longings to become even more erudite.

At the *Post* Lorimer exhibited his enthusiastic admiration for the cultured businessman by often featuring those he thought set an ideal. The leading men of the business world whom Lorimer invited to give practical advice to young men often ended up recommending the importance of reading broadly. The president of Chemical National Bank in "Getting On: A Young Man's Business Reading," advised wide and thoughtful reading in order to develop wisdom and character.[66] More pointedly, Frank Vanderlip's "The Business Man's Reading" detailed a program of reading that included a liberal array of classics to develop character in the hypothetical young bank clerk. In a telling piece of advice, he warned that the young clerk would find such a broad and liberal self-education necessary if he did not plan to remain a clerk.[67] Similarly, when the *Post* started its short-lived Home College Course in 1902, the very first article, "The Home College Course: Literature and Its Uses," aimed its persuasive arguments directly at the businessman. "The mental life of a practical man of affairs is likely limited," the author noted. In order to achieve "mental flexibility" and to avoid the glut in the market for men who were "mere narrow specialists," the author advised a wider reading to develop "breadth and power."[68]

To promote such erudite men of affairs, the *Post* repeatedly ran articles to educate young men to their cultural duties. Articles like "The Clerk Who Reads" and "How Shall a Young Man Educate Himself?" advised partaking of wide cultural subjects as well as those of specialized (practical) depth for the self-educated, aspiring businessman.[69] Even articles such as "The Money Matters of the Young Businessman," commented that since issues of character were so critical to success, young men needed to attend to their personal cultivation. Church attendance, careful dress, and boarding with a family received mention right alongside attending the theater for cultural elevation.[70] *Cosmopolitan* offered similar counsel. James Canfield, the author of "The Average Young Man and His Library," noted the importance of self-preparation for a career, but thought it more critical for success to read broadly: the subjects he listed sounded much like a modern liberal education.[71] Many of the critics of college education for the businessman railed not against culture but wasted years. They quite often noted that one could gain a true liberal education from the library and not waste time learning the dead languages. As one business man intoned, "all the culture and all the breadth that lie within the four walls of a university lie also on the shelves of our public libraries."[72] The self-made businessman seeking cultural enlightenment also appeared in magazine fiction. In a typical business fiction plot in *Munsey's*, a young clerk in New York, fresh from the farm and trying to make his way in an insurance company, began attending the opera and reading to raise his level of cultural appreciation.[73] Within the evolving discourse on success in the middle-class magazines, then, a rough consensus emerged that endorsed "culture" but as something divorced from the typical classical college curriculum then obtaining.

Alongside articles and editorials touting the benefits of refinement, advertisers encouraged the very same ideas and offered myriad opportunities for self-culture. A vast array of products offered the reader access to the best literature, music, and art. For "the man of affairs with countless calls upon his time," the "Library of the World's Best Literature" was available in forty-six volumes.[74]

Every issue of every magazine contained ads for compilations of history such as Professor Ridpath's *History of the World*, often accompanied by lavish illustrations of Julius Caesar or Napoleon in some famous battle.[75] The University Society, another regular on the ad pages, presented sets of Shakespeare's works with commentaries, warning that "a knowledge of Shakespeare's plays is essential to the well-informed man or woman."[76] Readers were presented with collections of classics (Dante and Tennyson, Kant and Shakespeare), histories, cyclopedias, and modern literature in the pages of these magazines.[77]

Culture was important for the businessman, and every element of the magazines pushed the acquisition of culture as a desired component of ideal manhood. Such messages, especially in advertising, perpetuated the ideal of middle-class cultural acquisition and played upon the anxieties of readers, who were prompted to question their level of appreciation and cultivation. Long honored but often downplayed as an ideal component of manhood, the magazines collectively enhanced the acquisition of culture in their constructions of masculinity, and tied self-refinement unequivocally to business success. Thus, the magazines began to amplify the manliness of culture, but one also must note that self-culture rather than formal education remained the principal avenue for its acquisition.

From the late 1890s through the first decade of the new century, the new middle-class periodicals helped to craft a vision of the ideal businessman for a new age. Magazines urged an embrace of the modern world, the promises of the great trusts or corporations, and advised aspiring businessmen to learn a specialty, become an expert, and fit into the corporation to rise. They endorsed new corporate ideals of manhood. Yet the methods for learning such skills and the requirements for advancement continued to resonate with the myths and ideals of the self-made man. Self-education remained a highly visible option for attaining specialized knowledge and culture. From this foundation the young clerk or shop hand, even in the modern corporation, rose through character and perseverance, and learned business skills as always through a sort of apprenticeship. Scores of characters in business fiction provided vivid illustration of the new avenues leading to success. So, as Americans adapted to a changing world and magazines helped them cope, the vision of business success mixed the necessities of corporate employment with the ideals of the self-made man—scientific specialization but also traditional culture through self-education and rising through the ranks. And college was not the default option for acquiring the requisite training to succeed in the dawning age. But by championing the scientific professional businessman and by amplifying the importance of attaining cultured breadth for success, magazine visions of ideal manhood established some of the key ideals that would allow for the easy routing of the American Dream of business success through the college gates.

The Crisis of the Clerks and the "Racial" Threat to Self-Made Ideals

All of this sound and fury in the middle-class magazines over the shifting economic conditions and opportunities for young men did indeed indicate the recognition of monumental socio-economic changes. And for a time, the magazines vigorously asserted that opportunities for business success remained brighter than ever in the corporation. Nevertheless, the glowing language began to fade during the first decade of the new century. For the first time even Lorimer's *Post* acknowledged that shadows of doubt clouded some of the traditional assumptions of business success.

In 1909 *Post* business writer Will Payne, who normally presented a parade of real-life self-made business success stories, raised a new alarm with "Those Contented Clerks: The Broad Line Between Making Good and Making Money." He first reiterated that clerks traditionally accepted low pay as the price of learning the business firsthand. They would sort the mail, take letters, copy contracts with open ears, eyes, and minds in order to soak in experience. They endured the meager existence because of the implicit promise that they would rise on their own merits to eventually own their own business or step into top management. But the offices had grown monstrously large. While the manager Payne interviewed asserted that he had risen from the bottom, the clerks Payne spoke with did not hide their disillusionment. They all had expected to learn business firsthand, but as one noted sarcastically, all he had learned was where people sat. "An educated monkey could do it [the work] as well as I can," added another clerk. These clerks never came within earshot of real business activities and had to read the newspapers to see what their bosses had done in the business and social whirl of activities.[78]

Other such articles surfaced in the usually upbeat *Post* on this growing "crisis." An editorial, "Getting a Business Education," lamented the hundreds of thousands of job seekers flocking to the "citadels of business" to learn the trade only to find themselves filing letters. They would soon discover that they could learn as much operating the elevator.[79] Articles noted how the long hours of monotonous work with little prospect of promotion drove some to suicide.[80] The very title of the *Post* editorial, "The Clerk Who Isn't Young," captured the shocking realization that not all clerks became entrepreneurs. The once proud clerk, the editorial noted, was now often a pathetic figure, "gray haired . . . exploited and helpless."[81]

What had happened? Learning business by observing as an office boy and then working as a clerk had worked in an earlier age of individual proprietors and much smaller firms. But business had changed with the growth of bureaucratic offices in large firms and corporations. By 1910 the waves of mergers, consolidations, and simple growth of big business had produced staggering alterations not only on the shop floor but in the office organization and management as well. Typewriters, carbon paper, duplicating machines, vertical files, and the advent of managerial hierarchies and decision making by committees permanently altered the dynamics of success for the office clerk. Bigger offices and firms reduced interaction between clerks and bosses. The increasingly efficient technology kept the clerk busy with menial tasks while vital business decisions no longer passed by word-of-mouth but by telegram and telephone and were made in committee behind closed doors.[82] The bookkeeper, as a *Post* article acknowledged in 1913, hardly needed any of his traditional skills such as a good writing hand or quick mathematical acumen since the office was modernized with typewriters and even stamp-licking machines.[83] This same article observed that increasingly office "girls" performed many of the menial office tasks. Editors imagined that women did not mind being "clerical laborers," as they nourished no "economic ambition."[84] In a telling commentary Lorimer voiced his hearty support for such a trend in hiring since young aspiring businessmen learned nothing from the "mountain of monotonous clerical chores," and most women simply wanted to earn something before marriage. Learning business was learning about people, reasoned Lorimer, and if the clerk could no longer do this, then the old route of business apprenticeship no longer sufficed.[85]

While the ubiquitous correspondence school ads promoted the ideal of rising from the ranks, their messages also articulated the anxieties of the emasculated clerk or worker in the changing economy. The International Correspondence Schools (ICS) continually asked shop workers and clerks, "Are You a Cog?" and targeted "The Man Who is Bottled Up . . . in Shop or Office."[86] "Are you the man who knows . . . or the man who must be told?" taunted another ICS ad.[87] Such ads highlighted the widening gap between those with special skills or knowledge of "the bigger phases" of business and those without. Formal training rather than long years of patient office apprenticeship seemed to be the answer.[88] Only training "gives a man confidence—that means MONEY-POWER-INFLUENCE."[89] These ads reinforced the perception that the rules of the game had indeed changed and, thus, they played upon fears of lost potency.

Most magazine fiction continued to pulsate with stories of rising men and success, but some also picked up on the theme of declining opportunities and a changing workplace. As early as 1898 in *Cosmopolitan*, "The Mills of the Little

Tin Gods" relayed the disappointments of the little men who keep business going. The story began with the typical country boy seeking his fortune and starting out as a clerk. He found his hopes gradually crushed. "Men are dying on the vast treadmill everyday, the very souls flayed out of them . . . [from] the slow sloughing away of ambition," their faith fed to the business machine "that it might run smoothly."[90] Such an early indictment was uncommon. But by 1910, around the same time the *Post* exposed the crisis of the clerk, stories surfaced adding vivid detail to their plight. In "Getting a Start at Sixty," the narrator recounted his replacement by a younger man after forty years in a dead-end position.[91]

This crisis for the clerk was accompanied by other unsettling consequences of economic transformations. One *Collier's* writer articulated the interconnected dilemmas. As parents cried, "what shall we do with our boys," Poultney Bigelow wrote, the "Captains of industry" echoed parental worries as they searched "in vain for the men who can act as lieutenants in the great army of industrial workers." Bankers, managers, railroad officers, all looked for men, and "they look in vain."[92] Business and industrial leaders could no longer patiently wait for the boy sweeping the floor to rise through the ranks as critical as that seemed for the traditional formation of character. Even for those preparing themselves to become managers, salesmen, or other budding business specialists the question was: How could they be chosen and where would they receive their training (and character)? The issues of a young man's proper preparation and the need for more and more business "lieutenants" flowed together.

A generational angst had arisen steadily across the land. The big men who industrialized America were aging and looking apprehensively for their replacements. The media would highlight these fears, and they were real. A 1907 study commissioned by a Massachusetts Industrial Commission concluded that "all industries were in need of more competent foremen, factory directors and managers than were available." Industry wanted men with "broad perspective and interests as well as the qualifications necessary to organize and direct a department or a factory division." And those currently filling these duties had arrived there by chance; of necessity they were self-made men, at once celebrating and fretting over the achievement.[93]

Related to this crisis of generational leadership, many believed that the sons of the great self-made men had been spoiled for leadership. Lorimer at the *Post* hit this theme repeatedly. In one of his earliest alarms, "The Old Man's Son," he wondered how the son who parts his hair in the middle and hangs around the golf links all day and the town all night would be taken seriously in the "battle of business." Indeed he would not, and rich business leaders, Lorimer assured, were realizing that their sons (and all aspiring executives) still needed some form of self-made seasoning that the traditional route of business apprenticeship afforded but that the modern trust could no longer supply.[94]

Such concerns about the sources of new leadership in a corporate America were pregnant with racial anxieties related to fears of the overcivilization of native-born, middle-class men. The magazines, however, rarely typed their readers in racial tones. While overtly racial references, such as the term *Anglo-Saxon*, were uncommon in these magazines, they did surface in subtle but powerful ways and with enough frequency for one to generalize that editors and writers considered their readership—the implied "we" or "American," to be broadly of northern and western European descent. Consider, for example, a telling editorial in the *Post* titled, "Why is the Anglo-Saxon Disliked?" The editorialist considered both the British and Americans to be of this type, as he observed that the rest of the world resents their prosperity and the character traits that have occasioned this success. "We can subordinate passion," the author opined, "and we can elbow aside the amenities," where as the Italian (as one alternative example) cannot cool his "hot heart."[95] The concerns voiced by editors like Lorimer regarding the softness of American youth, may be viewed as freighted with racial anxieties that exacerbated the crisis of the clerk and the generational crisis of leadership. Did "we" (meaning American, Anglo-Saxon) still possess the character traits that foreordained dominance? Many like Lorimer worried that the next generation of native-stock, white Americans was growing soft, an increasingly common fear in an age accepting the assumptions of Social Darwinism. To make matters worse, from a racial point of view, not only was the model of the self-made success trajectory jeopardized by the corporate setting, the ideal itself was disturbingly colorblind (or racially neutral).

The ideal of the self-made man formed in a period of relative ethnic homogeneity in the United States. As this concept emerged during the early to middle nineteenth century, most native-born American men and immigrants came from northern and western Europe. The issue of slavery and the Civil War only further solidified a generic "whiteness." This notion of a homogenized "whiteness" vanished with the dramatic influx of new immigrants from southern and eastern Europe in the late nineteenth century.[96] This "notion," coupled with the growing acceptance of Social Darwinism and its assumed racial gradations, placed great strain on American democratic traditions of inclusion. Americans faced the prospect of (supposedly) inferior immigrant men taking advantage of relaxed citizenship requirements to exercise their franchise. More deeply problematic, though, was that these immigrants could lay claim via the democratic ideal of the self-made man to social and economic legitimacy. If they worked hard, persevered, and thus exhibited character, why should *they* not rise to positions of authority as well? Certainly Americans would uphold the traits of the self-made man model of personal advancement as generically ideal. White Americans, North and South alike, embraced Booker T. Washington's notions of African American advancement, which were well within the parameters of the self-made man model. Yet even when successful in the South, African Americans faced the increasing legal parameters of Jim Crow. The new "white" immigrants would face few, if any, strict legal barricades to social assimilation or to economic power over other Americans.

Nothing in the magazines' slight alterations to the attributes of the self-made man for a corporate America would lead us to conclude that this revised vision of business success was undertaken directly to bolster native-born white men's claims to continued superiority. No articles explicitly stated the unspoken "this is how you can make it over those Italian immigrants working the same jobs." In the 1890s, articles, editorials, fiction, and advertising rarely inserted overtly racial terms or characterizations that denoted any obvious gradations of competence or fitness based on race. And too, the magazines rarely discussed immigration. This began to change during the first decade of the new century, however, signaling a growing awareness of racial tensions regarding the new immigrants. *Collier's* and *Cosmopolitan* sounded shrill alarms after 1905. Both were most concerned with Japanese immigrants and the continued alien presence of Chinese on the West Coast.[97] As early as 1906, though, a *Munsey's* short story registered anxiety about the new Italian immigrants. In Edward Boltwood's "The Old Neighborhood," a New England mill owner considers selling out to a "Woolen Trust," giving up his benign paternalistic control over his largely Irish workforce and company town. The owner's mind is changed when his young son is kidnapped by "three dago-complexioned men," the very type of new immigrant (along with "Polanders") that the trust planned to hire in an expanded operation. After his loyal Irish workers hunt down the "ginnies," he decides against selling out.[98] *Collier's* offered similar concerns about Italians in a 1912 article featuring the experiences of a female settlement-house worker. She lamented that the Italians she served were little more than slaves in the United States, "for the same reason that the negro was, because they cannot maintain their freedom in competition with the dominant race." The author described this college-grad settlement-house worker as possessing a "scientific wisdom," so that such an article exemplified both the level of concern and the pseudoscientific assumptions that informed the growing discourse.[99]

Still there can be little doubt that the presence of these new immigrants heightened concerns over competition in the workplace. Such pointed racial anxieties about immigrants showed up in "What Is an American," a four-part series run by *Collier's* in 1912. The series exemplified the wide dissemination of Social Darwinistic assumptions and fears regarding race and culture. The author not only viewed all native-born Americans as Anglo-Saxons, he saw the oncoming hordes of eastern and southern Europeans as of an "utterly different race stock."[100] The fear of racial and cultural pollution and of the imminent decline of the Anglo-Saxons pervades these articles. The first two articles dealt with how immigrants (and capitalism) were fundamentally altering the workplace and displacing native-born Americans. He contrasted Anglo-Saxon Americans with "wops," "dagos," and "Polanders," all of the latter groupings characterized as "filthy" and "servile" in nature, breeding indiscriminately, and caring only for money, unlike earlier Anglo-Saxon immigrants who came for the "higher ideals" freedom of worship and to improve the nature of work.[101]

The *Post* rarely touched upon immigrant issues and, when it did, maintained a surprisingly open and hopeful tone.[102] Still, the *Post*'s 1910 short story, "One Way Out: A Middle Class New Englander Emigrates to America," sounded similar alarms, aimed squarely (and tellingly) at the problem of WASP overcivilization in the world of business. The main character (the New England WASP) began the story as a comfortable high-level clerk. Dreaming of the job above him, he become complacent and finds himself fired and displaced by the ambitious young man below him. Even before this shock, the middle-aged clerk had worried about the education and toughness of his own teenage son, growing up "soft mentally and physically" and "chattering about Harvard, not as an opportunity, but as a class privilege." The boy lacked "initiative and energy," a classic statement of overcivilization. His epiphany came when his building's maintenance man, an Irish immigrant, revealed that he had saved enough money to construct his own tenement building as an investment and was sending two of his children to college. He added that "Pasquale, the bootblack" (an obvious reference to an immigrant) earned as much as he ever had as a clerk.[103]

The lesson, of course, was that like other complacent middle-class WASP Americans, he had lost the competitive edge, that old pioneer spirit. The immigrants now seemed to possess it, and the remedy for this New England family would be to start over in America as if they were immigrants. They moved in to the Irishman's tenement building, surrounded by Italian immigrants. The entire family then regained their resiliency and competitive spirit. The boy became tougher due to street life, but he was also able to visit art galleries in the city and rub shoulders with the city elite at the high school. The wife economized at home, while the father learned the contracting trade as a laborer by day and attended classes on masonry at night. The father then taught himself

Italian, gained the trust and respect of his co-workers, and parlayed this into his own contracting firm, becoming successful in short order.[104] While far more generous to the new immigrants than many other stories in these magazines, we understand that once this typical WASP New Englander adjusted his attitude, he naturally rose up to a position of authority over his immigrant neighbors and co-workers. As with "What Is an American," the problem that native-stock Americans seemed to face (according to "One Way Out") was not really the immigrants, but the WASP's own debilitating willpower. The problem was softness or complacency. Clerking jobs and manufacturing (piecework) could no longer supply the old level of disciplined work-education, nor could it offer the traditional route to advancement. These articles, then, not only captured the sense of general cultural and racial crisis felt by many middle-class Americans but also the related anxieties regarding success and manhood in a rapidly changing America.

The remedy offered in each story remained decidedly traditional — self-help and willpower. But would these traits truly be enough in the face of challenges due to the shifting nature of work and the new level of competition from immigrants? Where would the aspiring young business man get his training in manhood? Where would he be able to mold his character if not through sweeping the office or shop floor? Where would he learn the breadth of business and worldly knowledge if not by soaking in the day-by-day lessons of the masters he labored under? Where could the aspiring young man forge all of these qualities of ideal business manhood for a new age that the magazines celebrated — scientific training, genteel polish, yet old-fashioned grit and fortitude? And how could such opportunities effectively be cordoned off and made safe for those holding the most "promise" of rising to positions of authority, those of the "right" background and racial stock? Even if not so clearly articulated, these were the questions reverberating through the pages of these magazines at the dawn of the modern age. The changes set in motion by the rise of corporate capitalism and the arrival of fresh new immigrants inevitably threatened the ideals of self-made success. The new media, with their collective fingers on the pulse of these changes and vitally concerned with connecting with their readers, scrambled to articulate solutions that would resonate with their reading public. By the first decade of the century the solution to this conundrum was already being forged and heralded in the very same magazines that championed the self-made man, and the answer would be found in a surprising place.

2

The College Curriculum and Business

Reconceptualizing the Pathways to Power in a Corporate World

In 1895 *Munsey's Magazine* asked a question that would seem rather silly today, "Should Your Boy Go to College?" But *Munsey's* was, in fact, raising a very serious and telling question. The article presented the subject not for the benefit of the elite but for the "practical men of action." The author had in mind the people who read *Munsey's*, people whose sons looked toward business careers and whose families had limited means and thus asked, justifiably, "whether or not those four years might have been better spent."[1] Only a few short years before, it would have been absurd even to raise such a question to American men reared in the self-made tradition, but Munsey very early on in his editorship (the magazine began in 1893) must have sensed the unease over opportunities. Like the other mass magazines that arose in the 1890s, *Munsey's* knew their readership. Their readers were not the wealthy upper class who took the old literary monthlies, but a new aspiring group, primarily engaged in business, looking both to the past and to the future for guidance and inspiration. George Horace Lorimer, editor of the *Saturday Evening Post*, had these same folks in mind when he asked the president of Princeton to pointedly address "Should a Business Man Have a College Education?" Such articles peppered the new mass periodicals, and they hinted at a massive reconceptualization of the place of college in the lives of American men.[2]

Despite strong reservations about the curriculum at colleges, despite lingering doubts about the college graduate's fitness to start at the bottom, and despite the reluctance to give up on the self-made man, the answer that these magazines gave their readers to "should your son go to college?" was a resounding yes. Businessmen, railroad men—these were the rising professional-managerial class (a new middle class of white-collar, corporate-oriented businessmen) that the magazines arose alongside and they had never considered college necessary, but times were changing fast. In almost every instance where these magazines asked, "should your boy go to college?" the issue revolved around the new responsibilities of the businessman as a leader, business' need for good men, and (implicitly) concerns about the new paths to success. The "crying need at the top of the ladder," proclaimed a *Cosmopolitan* writer in 1901, "is for men with resourcefulness, executive ability and courage to assume responsibilities;" or "men who can act as lieutenants," as one industrialist quoted in *Collier's* noted.[3] Those self-made critics of education, according to former President Grover Cleveland in a featured *Post* article on the value of college education, failed to recognize "the extent of the revolution in the conditions of success." Enterprises were no longer small, stressed Cleveland; they operated on a vast scale.[4] A new order had dawned, and the magazines would now designate college men as the lieutenants-in-training—men who would, "solve the riddles of nature and push forward the electric chariot of the world's commerce."[5]

But what exactly did these editors and contributors have in mind when they posited the college graduate as the ideal business leader (a new hero) for the modern age, and thus collectively trumpeted college as the new route to success and upward mobility? Exactly what kind of leader and what kind of college? A ubiquitous frame of reference arose in many articles that one might label "the businessman's lament"—old businessmen pondering missed opportunities or their own insecurities. Laments like this often commented on the wish for scientific training with the ever-increasing pace of technical change in a rapidly industrializing America.[6] Still more comments expressed a longing on the part of self-made men for the broad knowledge that a liberal education supposedly imparted.[7] Most typically, though, writers and commentators recognized the benefits of both scientific and liberal training. As one New York manufacturer interviewed for a *Collier's* piece stated, he (not able to attend college himself) envied "the men who had been able to gain their technical mastery while at the same time qualifying themselves as members of a community in which literary accomplishments accounts for something."[8] And nearly all such laments linked broad college training with the necessity of visionary leadership in a new age, so that they combined an ideal self-image (scientifically trained and traditionally cultured) with the issue of professional leadership and authority.

These laments, in essence, portended the definition of a new ideal man, a new model for success and manhood in a changing world, with college playing the essential role and with the new middle-class magazines acting as forums for mass dissemination. Magazine editors, writers, and contributors pondered something far more than just curricular reforms. They were in effect spearheading a reconfiguration of national myths and cultural narratives, the accepted archetypes of masculine success, power, and authority.

Despite the rise of graduate and professional studies within true universities and the development of the modern liberal arts curriculum in the late nineteenth century in the United States, colleges and universities remained fairly marginal institutions to most Americans, particularly to American men. Higher educational institutions in the United States enrolled only 5.1 percent of the male college-age cohort in 1900 (and only 6.2 percent by 1910).[9] Football was an increasing curiosity, but until the curriculum could connect to demonstrable practical benefits, until its importance could be interwoven into the cultural narratives of male identity, colleges would remain marginal institutions. Moreover, the correlation between college and success blossomed out of altered cultural perceptions as much as direct practical utility; specialized courses accounted for only a small percentage of coursework around the turn of the century when enrollments began to rise at colleges and more graduates entered into business. Most graduates, even those going into business, received a broad, liberal education.[10] The new mass magazines of the middle class essentially undertook this cultural project of redefining the benefits of college education, reworking them within a new matrix of American manhood and business success ideals.

A careful examination of these magazines uncovers a wide and searching discourse on the potential benefits of a college education in articles and editorials. And this discourse was intertwined with the magazines' efforts to address their readers' concerns over an evolving corporate world that called for the adaptation of cherished notions of power, authority, advancement, and manhood. The aspiring middle-class American man of the late nineteenth century clung to prevailing notions of success that stressed male autonomy and independence, and that through work, one acquired many of the key elements of character. Yet these men hired as corporate managers or white-collar employees, even when well compensated, faced the reality that their working lives failed to live up to the traditional conceptions of self-made manhood. How could one forge character and toughness as an accountant in an office? Exacerbating such pressures were the increased presence of women in offices and the growing challenge of virile immigrant, working-class men in the workforce. The prevailing thought was that middle-class WASP men should be superior to the immigrant men they managed—but were they up to the challenge?

As scholars of American masculinity have articulated, American men (the middle class in particular) created new avenues to cope with this "crisis of masculinity."[11] But the most critical reformulation of college in popular culture, the one upon which the other elements (sports, fraternities, etc.) rested, was the positing of the college curriculum as an ideal training for success in the new world of business. The resulting vision of a college education's advantages, championed by the magazines, constituted a unique educational vision. Overall, the magazines endorsed curricular reforms, particularly scientific, proto-professional, and presumably practical courses that fed the professional consciousness of those engaged in commerce and industry. But many of those writing for the magazine, quite often the same ones calling for reforms in the curriculum, also drew upon traditional, "cultured" arguments for college education when describing the ideal American businessman. The new leaders of America would require the breadth of the liberally educated traditional professional, especially if a new sense of regard for the public weal was to be infused into the industrial age and if claims to leading civilization forward were to be realized.

Finally, as middle-class cultural spokesmen re-envisioned the college curriculum to support a new ideal businessman, they simultaneously worked to neutralize threats from the growing enrollments of women and from the possibility of racial "others," particularly those potentially "white" new immigrants, those from eastern and southern Europe. Women in college (or female college graduates) would be posited as better-educated helpmates to their college-educated husbands, and immigrants of any sort remained conspicuously underrepresented in the developing new narrative of middle-class, white masculine authority, although that rhetorical democratic door would remain open.

We cannot dismiss the revision of college education's curricular benefits that took shape within the cultural forum of these magazines, either as the creation of academics bent on increasing enrollments or as the workings of a hegemonic capitalism intent upon molding pliant employees.[12] Indeed, the process was much more nuanced and complex. The conception of the ideal education for the future businessman that formed in these periodicals reflected a cultural negotiation, which in many ways only the magazines could have accommodated. Magazines had to reflect their audience and the needs of capital while also offering ideal visions of American business and society to strive toward.

In seeking to confront issues facing their archetypal readership, these magazines fashioned a new vision of the college-educated businessman that clearly merged and drew from traditional *and* modern conceptions close to the hearts of their middle-class readership. With the thrust of curricular changes in colleges as inspiration and the developing need for broad-minded, public-spirited leaders of great corporations as a guiding progressive principle, a new route to ideal business manhood took shape in the pages of these new and critical national middle-class forums. Shifting economic imperatives and curricular changes may have fueled this new ideal, but only the magazine editors and writers fully articulated this vision and disseminated it far and wide, intimately interconnecting a coherent vision for the first time and on an unprecedented national scale. These magazines did not rationalize a changing reality; they actively participated in shaping curricular ideals that point to the vital way that college education would be used to refashion and bolster WASP, middle-class claims to authority and leadership.

Making the Liberal Arts Manly

While paeans to the self-educated clerk coexisted in these magazines with anxieties that such opportunities waned, the magazine editors, beginning in the mid-1890s, spearheaded a mass rethinking of Americans' visions of business success involving college education. *Cosmopolitan* magazine under the editorship of John Brisben Walker launched the earliest salvo aimed at transforming higher education to fit the demands of his readers adjusting to a new age. As one of the first magazines to revolutionize the industry, *Cosmopolitan* achieved an early feel for the pulse of changes in American life. Walker championed advertising, science, and technological advancement, and the greater efficiency of the trust or corporation. And while *Munsey's*, the *Post*, and *Collier's* certainly ran articles exploring and encouraging changing attitudes toward college education, Walker's *Cosmopolitan* initially led the way.[13]

In the spring of 1897 Walker penned the first article in a series he planned to pursue called "Modern College Education." In this inaugural piece, Walker bluntly fired a broadside at the defenders of the classical curriculum, "men who are steeped in tradition" residing "within cloistral walls." Walker considered Greek and Latin as mere ornamental knowledge sustained in the curriculum out of blind adherence to tradition. He likened the typical American college's classical training to sending out a raw recruit for battle "minus sword or gun."[14]

The educational establishment needed "to step aside from beaten paths" and consider the education suited for the modern world.[15] These were typical, indeed somewhat sedate, indictments of the classical curriculum and its impracticality for the active man, and it indicated the recrafting necessary for the liberal arts college to become accepted by the average American, especially the businessman.

Walker invited leading college presidents and professors to respond, and respond they did, with defenders of the classics and liberal culture offering some of the most eloquent (and telling) articulations of the benefits of the traditional liberal arts. College should not be the "sum of all things," but rather through culture it would impart "a knowledge of the best things."[16] "Large of intellect, noble in affections, sound in ethics," these were the results of a liberal education according to Western Reserve University's president Charles F. Thwing, and he and other apologists also took pains to highlight that such an education bred "no stinted ascetic," but strong leaders of men.[17] Yale president Arthur Hadley defined his students (still taking a largely prescribed curriculum) as being "among the best examples of manly culture and cultured manhood to be found anywhere in the world."[18]

Certainly these contributors to *Cosmopolitan*'s debate cast a liberal education in elite ways, but they purposefully used language and concepts that invited readers in this new medium to identify themselves as worthy of such an education. They described it in masculine terms, yet also tinged with an appealing genteel image, seductively allowing readers to use their own judgments and imaginations regarding whether they (or their children) might fit this mold.[19] Other articles in the *Cosmopolitan* series, such as "What is a Gentleman?" and "What Men Like in Men," utilized language very similar to that wielded by Hadley, Thwing, and the other defenders of the classical curriculum.[20] Indeed, despite the criticisms of its editor toward the classics, *Cosmopolitan* did not shrink from encouraging their readers to identify with culture and learning, as Walker's interest in the arts and education further demonstrated.[21] The impassioned and seductive characterization of the liberal arts graduate that emerged in *Cosmopolitan* was not radically new. In fact it reflected an evolution within academia and American culture, which had been unfolding for some time.[22] It indicated a new trajectory for liberal culture's appeal among the expanding middle class the magazines reached, and similar characterizations poured across the pages of the other mass magazines, as well, aiming with increasing precision at the generic businessman.

How did a liberal education foster business success? College disciplined the mind. Again, the 1895 *Munsey's* article probing the question of sending sons to college was the first in such a magazine to articulate the advantages of the college man in detail. According to the mayor of New York, Colonel Strong, not specific knowledge but "rather his instruction in the art of the best and quickest way of attaining knowledge" and the developed capacity for "original thought and investigation" proved the college man's greatest assets. "His increasing broadness of vision, the greater extent of the resources at his command," the mayor continued, "will equip him [the college man] to contend with the exigencies of life, and to grasp the business problems that will confront him with a sure hand, a clearer head, and more ready determination than his brother," who had left school for business.[23] The *Saturday Evening Post* editorial "Culture and Success" observed that "colleges are not primarily designed to teach a man to make money, but they teach him to measure his mental powers and make the most of them." When the college graduate then turned his "disciplined faculties" to business, he was likely to succeed.[24] Naturally, the college man would seem to be at a great disadvantage, having lost years to the lad who started as an office boy, reasoned Princeton president Francis Patton in "Should the Business Man Have a College Education?" Nevertheless, "[t]he Power which comes as the result of a liberal education will soon show itself," asserted Patton, "and some day the opportunity will arrive for the university man to reveal the advantage which he has over the man who left school to go into the office" due to his "trained powers." Liberal education, in other words, equipped the aspiring businessman not only with keener mental powers but also "ready determination," attributes formerly monopolized by the self-educated, self-made man.[25]

Advocates linked liberal education firmly to the building of manly character as well, an attribute long held as the most critical indicator of future success. As one *Post* writer argued, "a college man wins in life not by virtue of the special knowledge he has acquired so much as by the habits he has formed," such as hard work, punctuality, a sense of duty, and most importantly, willpower.[26] Using martial language, Roswell P. Fowler in *Munsey's* argued that "as the struggle of life sharpened, nothing will more thoroughly fit a boy for the battle of life" than the power of mind and frugal habits learned at college.[27] Another Lorimer favorite at the *Post*, Sen. Albert Beveridge, also utilized martial images to characterize the benefits of the liberally educated. A liberal education, for Beveridge, developed the mind to its highest "efficiency . . . as highly disciplined as are the wrist and eye of a swordsman." In one *Post* editorial, Lorimer too used the term "efficient manhood" to rate the value of a liberal education. It made one "self-reliant," a "thinking toiler," or as Princeton's Francis Patton argued, college bestowed the "franchise of manhood."[28] Such characterizations of the college man directly countered the common stereotypes of the elite, effeminate, and idle college boy, and freely mingled modern ideals of masculinity (such as efficiency) with more traditional self-made habits of character.

Finally, these articles and editorials left little doubt that a college education fostered the ideal business leader. In Charles Thwing's *Post* article "Should Railroad Men Be College Men?" the author interviewed or corresponded with more than twenty railroad officers and presidents. Although many of the correspondents cautioned that the college man must work his way up to leadership positions, college seemed indispensable in their opinion.[29] The railroads needed administrators capable of overseeing unprecedented problems connected to the "public weal," as Thwing himself intoned. For such tasks, the great need was for "the properly and nobly trained mind."[30] Other highly placed railroad officials concurred in this opinion, perhaps reflecting an ideal image of themselves in the process. As another *Post* writer portrayed the issue, "for the successful prosecution of the highest forms of business pursuits a liberal education is indispensable," since the magnitude and complexity of modern business demanded men of breadth.[31]

In short, a liberal education groomed gentlemen to their duties. It imparted a "grace of manner, refined taste, the ability to appear at ease with cultivated people and to appreciate the best that has been said and done," as Patton summarized it, paraphrasing Matthew Arnold.[32] "Contemplation of the sublime," Thwing argued, bred adherence to "only the highest principles." One did not teach Ulysses to make the bow but "to rear men of strength, of self-restraint, who can bend the bow."[33] Perhaps there was a reason Thwing contributed so prolifically to these middle-class periodicals, since his statements simultaneously fed the anxieties and vanities of America's businessmen searching for competent lieutenants (and opportunities for their own sons). For Thwing and for many others, only a liberal education that fashioned cultured intellect and forged character "for the sake of the manhood of man himself," rather than simply training in a skill, could inculcate a love of truth and beauty, instilling a sense of conscience and duty.[34]

Defenders of liberal education in these magazines appealed to and helped foster a new ideal image of the American businessman and the college simultaneously. Advocates of the liberally educated business leader certainly flattered the middle-class businessmen reading these magazines. In no uncertain terms businessmen were told that they were the new leaders of America and that they (or more likely their sons) merited the education of traditional genteel leadership. Such defenders encouraged a reconceptualization of the businessman as a cultured, learned, and socially responsible gentleman, a leader who required a liberal education in order to handle his responsibilities. No doubt some who made this argument nurtured hopes of reversing the rampant materialism of the business world and also harbored progressive ideals of promoting the college-educated businessman as an efficient, service-minded executive. No less significant than this reconceptualization, however, was the infusion of martial language and traditional self-made ideals that masculinized the liberal arts. For the defenders of liberal education, a cultural training did not create the dilettante but forged disciplined manhood and "civilized character," thus qualifying one as a broadly educated yet manly gentleman capable of bearing the responsibilities of leadership while adhering to "sublime" higher principles. Forging genteel leadership had long been the avowed goal of a liberal education in the United States, but now magazine editors and contributors altered their language and pointedly launched their appeals at a new audience.

Champions of Modernity in the Curriculum

The earliest criticisms of a college education printed in the magazines reflected the typical dismissive characterizations of the college man registered by the self-made businessman. These early complaints revolved around two problems—the length of time spent at college (delaying one's all-important start in business), and the useless curriculum. That well-quoted *Munsey's* article noted the comment of a famous banker that three-fourths of a college man's brain was "filled with classical knowledge, dead languages and high sounding unpractical ideals."[35] Similarly, for all its support of the college-educated businessman, the *Post* also ran strong denunciations of the time wasted at college.[36] The aspiring businessman who went to college devoting four of his most active years to college study would have to "unlearn" this useless knowledge "when he goes into the practical world."[37] One 1903 *Post* editorial attacked collegiate "educational frills," charging that the pursuit of Latin and Greek represented a desire for superiority and "ornamentation." Only the "lusty, alive hustler" maintained a foothold, and the colleges had to recognize this and drop "their beloved, moth-eaten trappings of mediavalism [*sic*]."[38] In the 1906 editorial "The Dead A.B.," Lorimer argued that the "archaic bachelors degree" should be replaced by a certificate that stated plainly the work performed by the student and what "actual value" it provided for particular jobs.[39]

Part of Lorimer's evident concerns stemmed from the oft-repeated indictment that the idleness of college life bred luxurious habits rather than frugality.[40] Lorimer frequently published editorials and articles lambasting the Eastern colleges as bastions of elite snobbery and luxury, while praising what were termed the "freshwater colleges" of the Midwest, where real men and women of character could still be found laboring for a true education.[41] Lorimer and the *Post* also found in the Midwest another form of educational institution, the state university, which provided a model of collegiate curricular reform that dovetailed with that magazine's and the other middle-class periodicals' notions of what a modern college program should be like.[42]

Often in magazine articles, editorials, and fiction, writers recognized little distinction between a technical college graduate and a liberal arts college graduate. A college man was a college man was a college man, with the same haughty demeanor or charms depending on one's perspective. Articles that touched upon the newly complex demands of industry and commerce, however, increasingly mentioned the specific benefits of technical or "practical" collegiate courses, introduced with a quickening pace in the nation's Midwest and land grant colleges.[43] An 1899 *Munsey's* article on the profession of railroading, for instance, highlighted the benefits of a "first class engineering school." The author emphasized the advantages of scientific training but considered such studies no less effective in forming character and self-reliance, which he considered the main goals of a college education.[44] After 1900 the *Post* in particular championed the new technical and scientific courses of study as educational training in step with the changing times. One editorial in the College Man's issue of October 1900 proclaimed the dawning century, "The Golden Age of the Engineer."[45] Exploring a similar theme one month later, the article "Dividends Paid on College Parchments" informed readers how entire graduating classes from technical schools were finding immediate employment in the railroad shops and in the great new industries across the land. The article predicted that "the next generation will see the whole industrial system of the United States . . . directed by men of higher education, technically and professionally trained."[46]

Indeed, one of the *Post*'s 1901 College Man's issues triumphantly celebrated the rise of professional and technical programs at the nation's colleges and universities, and connected this phenomenon with the great economic forces shaping the United States. Each of the five articles on college programs in this single issue focused on new professional or scientific subjects. "The Young Man and the New Force" looked at electrical engineering. The director of Cleveland's Case School of Applied Science remarked in "The Value of Technical Education" on the incredible demand for its graduates and insisted that, consistent with the dictates of liberal education, the Case School educated broadly to fit men to adjust to and to rise in their "new professions." Another key article in this issue described the new School of Commerce at the University of Wisconsin, which proposed to teach business just as an engineering school prepared the future engineer.[47] Articles such as these reinforced the perception, as an earlier *Post* article had declared, that a "New Era in Commercial Education" had dawned. The modern corporation needed men "in these modern days . . . sharpened by knowledge and strengthened by specialization . . . drilled, skilled, and educated."[48] Such articles helped to establish that new scientific university programs would provide the educated men to meet this need. In the technological college man's number, Francis B. Crocker noted that in the development of the new scheme of business (the corporation), "technological knowledge is beginning to be more and more to the advantage of the men who seek the great positions in these corporations."[49]

The magazines urged their readers to associate a university education with the status of being an up-to-date, trained professional and linked such identifications squarely with corporate organization and modern business practice. The magazines collectively rejoiced in higher education's new scientific curriculum as evidence of the new era and prompted their middle-class readership to connect developing notions of professional pride and expert status with a modern, scientific college education. In articulating the new associations of higher education and science on one hand, and university training and modern professions on the other, these magazines played important and largely unappreciated roles in helping to guide developing conceptions of professionalism in America.

One example indicated the full development of the concept. Writing for the *Post* in 1911, business expert and writer Roger Babson's "A New Profession for the Young Man" outlined the need for a new university curriculum that he termed "Economic Engineering." This novel program would, he believed, fulfill the need for "practical men," those who could be called upon to lead the great corporations and who combined scientific principles and the problem-solving technique of engineering with knowledge of economics and how the world functioned. Hardly alone, such an article not only took for granted that higher education had grown more technical and practical, it also fused the image of the modern professional businessman with this reformed notion of the university as an agent of scientific authority.[50]

Forging a Hybrid Curricular Ideal

Even such calls for university-trained professionals in business, however, linked their vision with the university's long identification with leadership, an image the magazines forwarded regularly as well, and one connected implicitly with the broadening powers of the liberal arts. Babson's ideal courses mingled the physical sciences, mathematics, and special business courses such as bookkeeping and banking with history, modern languages, and economics, cautioning that from his own experience and conversations with executives, a strictly technical engineering preparation, while valuable, proved far too narrow. Such men typically remained employees rather than administrators.[51] The fact that these magazines simultaneously offered their readers two very different and opposed visions of college's utility (liberal culture vs. science and practicality) to choose from proved quite significant. Yet as Babson's ideal program demonstrated, the magazines did in fact perform a far more significant and unheralded cultural task: they promoted a novel vision of college that combined these two extremes with the emerging corporate businessman (a new icon) firmly in mind.

For example, Walker's series on modern education, in addition to the eloquent defenders of the classics, included many collegiate reformers as well (David Starr Jordan of Stanford and Daniel Coit Gilman of Johns Hopkins), men who supported the legitimacy of science in the curriculum. In essence, such reformers simply reworked the notion of liberal education, expanding the definition by dropping Greek and Latin and adding the sciences, modern humanities (recent literature and history along with modern languages), and social sciences.[52] The reformers differed from the classical defenders in their conception of what should be included in a liberal education. Both Gilman and Henry Morton (the president of Stevens Institute) advocated a split curriculum, a combination of old and new subjects. Morton depicted the split curriculum at Stevens, what he termed a "liberal technical course," as the ideal liberal education uniting an "efficient technical training" and "liberal culture."[53] Neither would discard entirely, however, the traditional belief that a liberal education was critical for character and morals. Their intellectual co-mingling of the modern and the traditional in a new liberal arts formula perfectly captured the current of the times and the temper of the popular magazine that straddled the line between the modern and the Victorian ages.

Just how the magazines actively endeavored more directly to shape higher education in the image of their readers may be viewed with the launching of Cosmopolitan University (a free correspondence school) in 1897. Conceived by *Cosmo* editor John Brisben Walker, Cosmopolitan University not only pushed a democratic re-envisioning of higher education—bringing college-level instruction to the "many who have the aspiration, but are deprived of the opportunity"—it championed a reworked idea of modern liberal education. Elisha Andrews, the school's president, remarked that the present college curriculum tended to produce a "classically educated prig," a "gentleman of leisure." "The substitute [education]," he cautioned, "must not be a school of technology," but a "seminary for liberal learning;" or a "broad and liberalizing education rather than one for earning a livelihood."[54]

Cosmopolitan University courses included several areas of vocational study. The breakdown of "departments" and courses reflected mostly conventional academic subjects—Wisdom, Science, English, Modern Foreign Languages, Citizenship, Arts, Pedagogy (the unconventional were Life and Accomplishments), but Walker also threw in a department of Business Preparation with courses in organization and accounting.[55] A single student might spend years taking all these courses, but this curriculum reflected what Walker and his associates believed a modern liberal education should include. Courses that prepared for a vocation while acquainting one with the modern world were offered in conjunction with more traditional courses in the humanities (art, literature, history, and philosophy), intended to form character and ethics. All this ideally would be accented by courses in "voice culture" and manners designed to instruct middle-class aspirants in the ways of genteel society. Periodicals like *Cosmopolitan* essentially had been instructing their readers in a similar fashion through their articles and fiction from their inception.[56] Like the other middle-class magazines, *Cosmopolitan* attempted to encapsulate the ideals and tastes of the new middle class. The magazine encouraged the arts and literature; they ran features on culture. But they also proved enamored of science and progress, the modern corporation, and technology.[57] Now, an ideal college curriculum crystallized the overall educational project of the magazine—to uplift readers culturally and intellectually as well as to help them negotiate the modern world.

Walker's vision, in fact, proved too popular. Overwhelmed by more than twenty thousand applicants in 1898, Cosmopolitan University succumbed in December of that year.[58] Walker sustained *Cosmopolitan*'s interest in reforming college education, however, by continuing the modern education series.[59] Throughout his editorship, Walker's and *Cosmopolitan*'s criticisms of higher education revolved more around a reconceptualization of the average American, who—to Walker—was the middle-class man who read *Cosmopolitan*. Through the medium of his magazine, Walker endeavored to guide his readers toward an ideal vision of themselves—simultaneously revolutionary in that this vision included a college education and that this popular vision of college education did not resemble most colleges. After 1900, the mantle of leadership in this endeavor transferred to George Lorimer at the *Saturday Evening Post*.

As with *Cosmopolitan*, Lorimer's enthusiasm for college education was predicated on the rise of new potential students and a reforming curriculum. Year after year and despite the occasional reform-minded criticism, the *Post* continued to celebrate the changes sweeping America's colleges—new students and new courses. The *Post* commented on the rising enrollments and trumpeted the improving caliber of the freshmen (no longer the effete snobs of the past).[60]

And it ran a gushing editorial saluting the graduates of Harvard and Yale who intended to go into the business world, their numbers for the first time outstripping those planning to enter the traditional professions.[61] Lorimer's *Post* trumpeted "The Broadening of the Colleges" and "The Modern College Man." These new students enrolled in the "special departments," and were taught to be experts, but "the idea of all-around training was not abandoned" and the "Modern College Man" was still imbued not only with a "capacity for work" but with an "interest in the better things of life."[62] Lorimer applauded and cheered the new students and the mixed curriculum that seemed to signify his conception of what the ideal education should be.

The editor did not carry the torch of educational reform alone. The *Post* recruited some of the same academics as did other magazines—David Starr Jordan, Charles Thwing, Henry Morton of Stevens Institute—to voice support for both curricular change and the vision of the college educated businessman. In his "The College Man's Advantages in the Coming Century," Jordan argued that college should train for a specific end and instill scientific method, but that it should also allow the graduate "to see things which lie beyond his trade."[63] Nonacademics, too, penned articles on this subject as well, targeting the businessman specifically. Russell Crittenden's "The Practical College Course for Young Men" concurred with Jordan's arguments. College should train for some definite end but should also "afford . . . a broad foundation." "Narrow specialization in the education of the young man," wrote the author, "while perhaps fitting them early in life for moderately remunerative positions, is to be deprecated as lacking those essential qualities that produce broad mental development, of the kind repeatedly reported to be desired by businessmen." Too narrow a training was not truly practical. The best preparation arose from a combination that included "a broad and liberal education."[64] Some might not have realized their participation in helping to shape a new curricular and business ideal, but nevertheless a steady barrage of writers in the *Post* championed the benefits of a reformed college curriculum while firmly connecting this new idea of college with the ideal, modern executive.

No group of articles in the *Post*, however, represented that magazine's hardy promotion of a combined liberal and modern curriculum better than John Corbin's series "Which College for the Boy?" which ran throughout most of 1907. This major series reviewed some of the nation's top colleges and universities. By itself the series reflected the *Post*'s increased attention to the supposed demands of readers for knowledge on the burning question of where to send their sons, a phenomenal indication of the changing views of education in relation to potential success, but also of the self-perception of readers promoted by the magazine. And, significantly, the series came down squarely for a mixed curriculum that avoided the two extremes of either too much culture or too much science or utilitarian studies. For example, Cornell University perfectly captured the mix of traditional and modern values. Corbin noted that "the ideal at Cornell [was] to turn out specialists who were also men of liberal culture—able thinkers, writers, and speakers, efficient men among men." "Breadth of character and depth of culture go hand in hand with utilitarian training," highlighted Corbin. He reveled not only in this ideal curricular mix but also in the astounding beauty of the campus, and, more impressively to Corbin, the simple living displayed by the devoted students, many of whom he noted received financial aid—a truly democratic university.[65]

The universities of Michigan and Wisconsin received similar if less detailed praise, though Wisconsin's excessive utilitarian bent seemed to bother Corbin. Moreover, Corbin judged Harvard too "German" with its free elective system and the University of Chicago still somewhat unstable.[66] The one university that rivaled Cornell in his estimation (and for similar reasons) was Princeton. Whereas Cornell perhaps tilted more to the side of science and the practical, Princeton leaned toward the liberal arts. Princeton had resisted the worst excesses of the elective system and adhered to a prescribed liberal arts curriculum for the first two years to "discipline the mind and enlarge sympathetic imagination." Juniors and seniors were then allowed to specialize, but Corbin intoned, "first and last the college cultivates not science but the man." Moreover, Corbin preached that due to its liberal education Princeton and colleges like it across the nation needed to effect a spiritual uplift through their students, who constituted the future leaders, so that the nation as it grew did not lose its soul.[67] Princeton and Cornell received glowing praise as institutions that offered the ideal education for readers of the *Post*. Both institutions combined a democratic ethos that included modern, specialized offerings with elite surroundings and traditional, genteel ideals of education such as forming character, intellect, and cultural breadth.[68]

Still, the *Post*'s stance on college education always must circle back to the editor's seemingly vacillating position and what it represented. Lorimer's editorials were capable of a misty-eyed veneration of liberal education, which he thought cultivated "civilized character."[69] He could, on the other hand, blast caustic barbs at collegiate snobbery and the impracticality of the classical curriculum (recall his aforementioned "Dead A.B."). One could best characterize Lorimer's most consistent thought on the subject as a hybrid educational ideal that united a reworked and updated liberal education with modern "scientific" subjects in order to live an active life. His editorial, "A Liberal Education," in charting his own list of possible areas of study, harkened back to Walker's Cosmopolitan University breakdown. His list included an ability to think and write in English, "knowledge of the history of democracy and the emancipation of man," knowledge of mechanisms of business, or "how commodities [were] produced, distributed and consumed," and a knowledge of taxation. He considered "a man with such an education would be both competent and cultured."[70]

Lorimer even defended higher education from the attacks of the hypothetical "practical man," who still scoffed at colleges "as a kind of parlor institution where rich men's sons play football, wear fraternity pins and discuss Ibsen and sociology." Lorimer derided the overzealous practical man for thinking so and thus overlooking the science used in business that colleges and universities advanced. It seemed that only the college graduate possessed the patience and knowledge of "investigation and experiment" to push science forward and help business.[71] In the 1904 editorial "Silk Purses and Sows' Ears," he commented on the vast changes in the curriculum and its new utility in fashioning businessmen. He stated that "a generation ago the so-called liberal education was regarded as a mere ornament of life," its classical culture and "unapplied mathematics" useless to "the business man." The university, though, had since become broad enough "to include preparation for useful life in every sphere."[72] And Lorimer would continue to defend higher education as the new route to business advancement and opportunity.[73]

Lorimer's intellectual odyssey regarding the benefits of a college education touched upon common longings, reservations, and demands voiced by many Americans during those years, and perhaps best reflected the multidimensional lens through which many Americans looked at college hoping to define themselves. They could see college education as snobbish, elite, and frivolous, and thereby glory in their own self-education and advancement. Or, they could harbor longings for the supposed cultivation and breadth they wished for and hoped to give their children, seeing in college identifications a way to become cultured. And they could look in the pages of *Cosmopolitan* or the *Post* and demand that education fit the needs of the modernizing, "scientific" world in which they took pride. Consequently, they might revel, as Lorimer did, in the modern democratic development of American colleges and universities—so different from European models, but which were now a growing source of genuine national strength. But one cannot ignore that all these characterizations coexisted and blended together, principally in the *Post* and *Cosmopolitan*, but to some degree in all of the magazines.

The discourse in these magazines on the benefits of the American college curriculum to a certain degree paralleled the fermentation of academic debate on the subject then occurring. College presidents and professors were them-selves reaching a fuzzy consensus when characterizing the curriculum in the first decade of the new century. They might still use terms like mental discipline that recalled the defenders of the classical languages, but they more often em-ployed a term that recurred in the magazines as well, mental training, which reflected the infusion of science and disciplinary specialization into the curric-ula. Graduates would be problem-solvers. But academics in their speeches, just like the discourse in the magazines, retained a reverence for liberal culture for its promising breadth and notions of character formation.[74] What was critical about the magazine discourse was not necessarily the novelty of this consensus regarding the college curriculum but rather the medium itself and who it tar-geted. This media catapulted a vision of college into middle-class male identity and authority through sheer volume and scale.

Imagining the Education of the Ideal Businessman in Advertising and Fiction

Naturally, the attitudes of editors and contributors toward education and its in-creasing relevance to readers emerged most potently in magazine articles and editorials. These magazines, however, were conceived as total packages, in-structive and entertaining, with advertising and fiction as integral features. Both Lorimer and Munsey defended advertising as an educational force, a teacher of commerce and civilization, to paraphrase Lorimer.[75] Advertisers intended to sell products, but the most successful products were those that resonated with the lifestyle, anxieties, and longings of the new middle-class readers.[76] Though in slightly different ways, advertising and fiction attempted to both reflect and guide readers, offering lessons on how to live and construct their lives. Not sur-prisingly, certain evolving assumptions regarding the place of college education in readers' lives entered forcefully into both fiction and advertising.

The largest, most numerous, and most potent ads that pertained to edu-cation and success remained those related to correspondence and business schools. These ads definitely advanced the association between trained, expert knowledge and success on the job, even as they often pointedly disavowed the necessity of formal higher education.[77] Beginning around 1902, however, some correspondence schools began to purposefully cultivate collegiate associations by either directly claiming their programs were college level or by creating ads with key words or images that at least conjured such an association.[78] The International Correspondence University, the most conspicuous example, not only appropriated the term "university" but launched an impressive ad cam-paign in 1904/5 utilizing many images of academia in support of a "higher" business training. In actuality, the university supplied no bachelor's degrees. All of their courses were in fact vocationally oriented—accounting, banking, commercial arithmetic, foreign commerce, U.S. economic history.[79] Proprietary business colleges (schools that normally taught bookkeeping, etc.) also began tailoring their programs to the increasingly accepted dictates of modern corporate success. By 1908 and 1909, the Peirce School (a business college) ads emphasized Peirce grads being leaders owing to the school's combined "general education [and] technical training in commercial subjects."[80] Though clearly not pushing the notion of a college-educated business man in such ads, correspondence and business schools nonetheless altered their language to fall in line with the idea of a broader training while they continued to link education generally to scientific authority and quasi-expert status.[81]

But what about culture? The most remarkable aspect of this insertion of college education into the formula of business success and middle-class manhood revolved around the embrace of liberal culture. It legitimized the modern executive as a true professional: he had received the traditional education of genteel leadership, carried the same respect for higher principles, and thus would run his business with vision and with the public weal in mind. Advertisers offered a wide array of products and programs to enable a person to become cultured. Increasingly, though, references to the busy man of affairs and specifically to acquiring liberal education rather than simply culture crept into the ad copy, and sometimes into the same ads.[82]

No programs or institutions that advertised in the periodicals, however, represented the endeavor to distill a liberal education for the busy American better than Dr. Charles W. Eliot's Five-Foot Shelf of Books, which became well known as the Harvard Classics. Collier and Son Publishers sought and received Eliot's (and Harvard's) participation.[83] Enthusiastically marketed and quite popular, the Harvard Classics have been recognized by scholars as a watershed in the project of disseminating culture to the masses, part of the transition to a consumer-oriented, middle-brow culture.[84] But the program's significance in the transforming meaning of college has been less appreciated. Certainly, the Harvard Classics were offered as an alternative to college attendance. Fifteen minutes a day and one could acquire "the essentials of a liberal education." This was hardly the first collection of books or program of reading offered as a route for readers to acquire culture. Nor was it the first to use the term *liberal education*. It was, nonetheless, the first to utilize a marketing strategy that traded on the prestige of an institution and its famous president to legitimize its cultural program.[85] Even a few years prior to the Collier's venture, it was hardly necessary to bolster a cultural product's authority through association with an institution. This said as much about the rising acceptance and prestige of college as it did about the increasing desire for culture generally by the American public. Touting colleges as the new ideal location for Americans to receive the benefit of liberal culture was a relatively recent development and one intertwined with the magazine's role in popularizing this shift in perception for the businessman.

The fact that Harvard and especially Charles W. Eliot were exalted as icons of liberal education must be considered even more significant. Certainly Harvard was the oldest and most well known of American colleges. But under Eliot, Harvard had also become famous for its reforms, the most critical of which was the elective system. Eliot believed in a student's free will to choose the studies that would benefit him most and prepare him for his life's vocation. He accelerated the introduction of scientific and specialized courses at Harvard and discarded the prescribed Latin and Greek. Charles Eliot loomed as the high priest of modern higher education, celebrated as the champion of practical utility over classical learning.[86]

Eliot was far from a radical with regard to the curriculum, though. In fact, his vision fell in step with the rather vague and all-encompassing ideal of a liberal college education that took shape later in the middle-class magazines. At Harvard Eliot had in effect redefined liberal education to include the sciences and specialized subjects. And this included "something of what has been done and thought in the world."[87] Eliot disavowed narrow vocational pragmatism as well as classical learnedness at the undergraduate level and advocated a combination that prepared one for usefulness while also imparting a learned breadth.[88] The new middle-class magazines had endorsed educational reformers like Eliot. It seems quite natural, then, that a magazine publisher and an educational reformer should join forces to launch a commercial product offering the promise of becoming liberally educated. Each had pioneered a new definition of liberal education to fit shifting times.

The ad copy and the editorial promotion of the Harvard Classics hit the same themes—the same mixture of respect for Arnoldian liberal culture and for broad knowledge as a base for useful action. For example, a *Collier's Weekly* editorial announcing the new project contained several references to the value of liberal culture. But this set was for "sensible men and women" and not for "pedants," who remained devoted to ideas "built upon Greek and Latin." Only what Eliot deemed "most useful" made the cut.[89] And large ads followed suit. "The Five-Foot Shelf" was for the millions "busy doing the nation's work— professional men, office men, farmers, salesmen, mechanics." The volumes would provide classics of literature "essential for a liberal education" that formed the foundation for one's intellect, "the foundation of the world's thought and achievement."[90] These would not be just old classics, then, but also works on modern subjects. It appealed to the longing for an acquaintance with liberal culture and to the modern sense that such an education still needed to be useful, calibrated for active Americans. Eliot's vision of a liberal education dovetailed with the vision that took shape in middle-class magazines, and now the two worlds merged in a common commercial promotion prominently advertised in the pages of middle-class periodicals.

Though the first to neatly market the growing prestige of a college education to magazine readers, Collier and Son Inc. was hardly alone.[91] Ads for the Mentor Association intensified the play upon hidden anxieties regarding a lack of culture and liberal education. Spread usually over an entire page, their ads asked, "Have you ever envied the culture, the wide familiar knowledge" of those who have traveled or who possessed a "liberal education?"[92] The Mentor Association claimed to have sprung from a meeting of businessmen at a club, each lamenting his lack of time to acquire a broad cultural knowledge. The ads that expanded on these founders' concerns noted that the businessmen had realized that knowledge meant power, and they desired to "know about the important things of the world—foreign lands, famous books, great men and women, the great achievements of history." They supposedly pooled their money to hire an editor to prepare periodic lessons delivered twenty-four times a year, which contained (according to their ads) six essays from authorities on art, literature, history, and geography, along with reprints of famous paintings.[93] Now they invited others to join the "better class of Americans [who] have been growing more interesting, more cultivated and more refined."[94]

The emergence of Eliot's Five-Foot Shelf and the Mentor Association signaled the wide currency of the new, educated, businessman ideal. They also indicated how deep the imagined benefits of a college education had been implanted in the American matrix of both masculine identity and business success. These enterprises owed a great deal of their success to the fact that they hit a nerve, and they tapped into the anxiety of not living up to a new ideal, one cultivated in the pages of the national periodicals. Being a cultured man had long been honored, but now the examples bombarded readers weekly and monthly from these magazines, and were tied more powerfully than before to a college education. Together these ads reinforced the redefinition of the businessman as a highly trained, scientific professional, but also broad-gauged and cultured enough to fulfill high executive positions. The ads drew a closer association between the qualities of a redefined businessman and the imagined benefits of a modern college education endorsed elsewhere in the magazines.

Magazine fiction, too, increasingly utilized college-educated characters, and in such fiction one may see the full development of the college-man amalgam—the evolving set of assumptions surrounding the connections between ideal male attributes and college education. The earliest magazine stories involving college characters in a positive light focused on college life or sports. Most stories that intertwined college and business settings or characters neglected the issue of curricular change—it simply was not a driving force for plots. But the subject did surface often enough to reinforce the developing consensus surrounding the benefits of college worked out in other elements of the magazines—emphasizing a character's broad, liberal education, his culture, or what might be termed a generic intellectual prowess that college education imparted.

When authors specifically explored the issue of how the college man's education potentially affected business, they focused on his creativity and rational, efficient, and "scientific" solutions to problems. H. K. Webster's "The Matter with Carpenter" offers one of the earliest treatments of the subject. One problem with the college man often cited by employers was the graduate's impatience with menial tasks, which led to inattention to details and poor work habits: college boys expected to rise too fast. Webster addresses this issue with the tale of Carpenter, daydreaming of past college gridiron glory, unhappy with his job as a draftsman. Enduring the knowing snickers of noncollege draftsmen when late from lunch again, Carpenter is called into the boss's office. But the boss moves Carpenter out of the monotonous job of drafting and into research and development, where he excels.[95] Carpenter's story highlights the connection between college education and modern thinking that was both creative and efficient.

At the turn of the century, another brave new world for businessmen was advertising, and Richard Walton Tully's *Cosmopolitan* short story, "Love and Advertising" perfectly captures what ideally the new college man could offer the business world. Tellingly, the major subtheme of the story (besides love) centers on the traditional business antipathy toward the college man. At the insistence of one of the old German partners, the candy manufacturing firm in the story had steadfastly refused to hire college men, and for the latest advertising campaign, amid sinking sales, had gone with a graduate of a practical advertising course. The firm's "American" partner, however, and an old college man himself, acquiesces to the wishes of his daughter to hire her recently graduated beau, Tom Brainard, as an advertising assistant. Facing the axe due to his lack of support for the current campaign, young Tom mounts a spirited defense of the college man, arguing that most so-called college men who failed in business were little more than drop-outs, unfinished products of the college experience. The daughter prevails upon her father to give Brainard the chance to run the campaign while the firm's partners take a vacation.[96]

Young Brainard's campaign quadruples sales, but it is his explanation of his thinking and, again, his defense of the college curriculum that stand out conspicuously. Tom explains that freshmen rhetoric led him to see that the firm's "practical" ad man was attempting two incongruous things—selling chewing gum and being elite. Elite people do not chew gum, Brainard observes. His economics class taught the laws of supply and demand, and his "analytical research of original authorities," "deductive logic," and "psychology" classes provided the knowledge of how to create the demand (where the potential market lay and how to access it). Tom then outlined how his old college connections supplied the talent for his new campaign. One classmate, now a bohemian opera composer, wrote up a catchy tune for the gum, "My Lulu Tulu Girl." Another classmate in a social settlement (where, "those dagoes worship him") supplied the organ-grinders to disseminate the tune, while the dancer-wife of his former college football trainer also sang the tune in her act. Another classmate, now a professor, supplied a scientific explanation of the gum's benefits to the digestion of food. Brainard's character potently demonstrates the superior vision supplied by his modern liberal education. His was not a professional course of study, but a mixture of modern science and traditional classes that render Brainard the ideal manager and ad man. He combines penetrating analysis with breadth of vision to solve problems.[97]

Distinction between what type of college curriculum a particular character attained before arriving in business was almost nonexistent. In fiction, when a business-related character had been to college, what seemed to matter was that college had prepared him for leadership. This proved true even when stories specifically mentioned a business character's technical or engineering background. Most often such a background marked him as middle-class (as opposed to a wealthy background), perhaps as technically competent, but most importantly as a manager of some variety.[98] When authors increasingly utilized collegiate references, even in passing, for their business-related characters, the characters were not clerks but salesmen, managers, or men on the rise—a new professional, managerial class with advanced educated skills and a broad vision.[99] The portrayal of college's benefits in magazine fiction paralleled in descriptive form the arguments forwarded elsewhere in the magazines, though with less clarity. In fact, fiction authors seemed to boil down the benefits of college into the most agreed upon elements—a combination of liberal culture, intellectual sharpness, creativity, and leadership.

Fashioning Cultural Barriers

In magazine fiction, the refashioning of college as a component of modern American leadership clearly contained certain racial and gendered assumptions about who writers and editors envisioned benefiting from college and filling new positions of authority in American society. Consider the lead characters in the two stories featured in the previous section. Both Carpenter and Tom Brainard were unquestionably WASP, and both sported love interests; yet in neither story did the author deem it of sufficient importance to note if the women had been to college. Recall, too, Brainard's offhanded remark about his classmate in the social settlements, surrounded by worshiping "dagoes." Such a reference points to one of the subtle ways that fiction shaped implicit assumptions about who could see themselves in college and who should not, who were leaders, and who were followers. Of 160 short stories integrating college references or college-educated characters (read for this study), the vast majority (154) may be categorized as WASP or "old stock" immigrant. College-educated women in magazines form a special case that will be discussed later in this chapter, but in only one short story, for instance, did an independent college-educated woman run a business, and this was an upscale escort service.[100] Such omissions speak volumes. In other words, as magazine editors, contributors and authors reconceived the importance and purpose of the college curriculum in their positing of a new success narrative for middle-class men, they did so guided by relatively established ideas of what type of American would go to college and rise in the emerging corporate world, thereby shaping powerful cultural parameters.

This is not surprising, given that the magazine editors and publishers conceived their readership as primarily male and middle class. Overtly racial language entered into these magazines' discourse with surprising rarity, but in enough instances for one to understand that publishers, editors, and writers assumed their readership to be primarily WASP or at least "old stock" immigrant. A handful of telling Anglo-Saxon references in conjunction with the curricular debate reinforce such broad assumptions. In an inaugural address article expounding upon the grand design of the endeavor, Cosmopolitan University president Elisha Benjamin Andrews argued that such a university venture (a correspondence university) arose from the fact that many Americans "of the best Anglo-Saxon stock" but including some "extremely intelligent people of foreign parentage" were left in need of higher educational opportunities.[101] No articles or editorials dealing with the college curriculum ever pointedly referenced the idea of immigrants as students, and particularly of new immigrants as a distinct type, even when the articles dealt with students working their way through college. Similarly, in the articles covering the growing immigrant problem of the era in these magazines, college as a potential form of assimilation never received mention, while grammar school education was referenced.

When the subject of racial "others" and college education did arise, it tended to implicitly reinforce the distinctive elements of the American college curriculum then taking shape in the pages of the periodicals as a distinctively "white" endeavor. Booker T. Washington's article on Tuskegee Institute in *Cosmopolitan* and one impressive article on the Carlisle Indian School in *Collier's* emphasized the appropriately practical thrust of the curriculum at these institutions. Tuskegee graduates were shown learning modern bricklaying techniques and practicing with the latest farming implements, while the *Collier's* article lauded the Carlisle graduates going back to the reservations to become farmers, armed with their modern training.[102] Hayden Carruth's light short story in *Cosmopolitan* (on a missionary's attempt to run a college for Indians) ended supporting the denigrating notion that it was pointless to teach an Indian about high culture since it would fail ultimately to cultivate their characters—the Indian students in questions, while they could recite poetry beautifully, succumbed to temptations to steal and drink at the first opportunity.[103] Such treatments of the educational aptitudes of American Indians and African Americans, in themselves exceedingly rare, highlights on one level that while these magazines pushed practical and professional reforms in the America's colleges, there were assumed racial gradations of utility. On another level, this assumption sharpens the important distinction magazine contributors and editors placed on the role of the liberal arts as a key element distinguishing the college training they advocated for their typical WASP readers.

A handful of short stories do feature non-WASP college students or graduates. Although the small number of exceptions tend to "prove the rule" regarding the racial assumptions informing periodical writers on the topic of college students, they offer some tantalizing hints as to how American magazines allowed for possible access to emerging opportunities as they molded the evolving narrative of middle-class success. Surprisingly, two separate stories focused on Asian characters (one Japanese and one Chinese), significant because Asian immigrants in general had attracted some of the most vitriolic attacks in these magazines. Three additional tales featured immigrants from northern and western Europe (Scandinavian, German, and Irish). In each of these examples, the curriculum studied at college by these characters elicited scant mention, except that the Japanese college student (in Japan) won an oratory contest, thus reinforcing the ideas of college and culture as manly, as it defined the Japanese within that circle of acceptable manhood.[104] "The Efficient Salamander," a humorous tale by Montague Glass, however, took on both the subject of curricular relevance in the new world of business and the new immigrant in America as a college man. Glass was a regular *Post* contributor with stories exploring Jewish ghetto life, and particularly Jewish businessmen, all written in an American Yiddish dialect. "The Efficient Salamander" leaves the nationalities implicit, but Glass's typical subject matter and the dialect makes it quite plainly Jewish. Salamander is the family name of the building-owner from whom two garment-shop owners rent their manufacturing space. Salamander threatens to raise the rent unless his son, a recent college graduate, receives a manager's job. The college man, Philip Salamander, had pursued commerce as a course of study (focusing on "ziontific management") because it seemed less strenuous than law or medicine. Glass paints Philip as a typical nouveau-riche college sport, worried more about "wearing neat but serviceable clothing" to look the part of a manager rather than actually working. To everyone's shock, however, on his first day he immediately diagnoses several efficiency problems in their shop. The rest of the tale revolves around love and proving himself a hard worker, but the most significant aspect is that a Jewish immigrant not only graduated from an American college but also proved the professional worth of the college curriculum (he only mentions having taken one class in scientific management).[105]

As magazine writers and editors busily reimagined the accepted cultural narratives of success for their central readership, their implicit racial assumptions formed de facto cultural filters regarding what types of Americans could imagine even going to college. Although powerful filters indeed, they were imperfect, as the handful of short stories like "The Efficient Salamander" attest.

Virile immigrant men did pose a challenge to WASP manhood, but more on a symbolic level. Few new immigrants enrolled in four-year colleges or as yet vied for positions of authority in the world of business. The new woman of this era, however, offered multiple challenges to American men both symbolic and real. Female college enrollment was skyrocketing around the country in this period, eliciting severe consternation. At the same time academics and cultural spokesmen in the magazines endeavored to "masculinize" the college curriculum, the increasing enrollments of women threatened (and helped inspire) the entire project. Not only was the new woman on campuses in increasing numbers, her mere presence threatened to feminize the image of college, as David Starr Jordan, president of Stanford at that time, openly discussed in one article on the topic.[106] These magazines' collective treatment of the coed proves quite revealing. Recall that these magazines, intended for a general readership, were aimed primarily at men; compared to the *Ladies Home Journal*, few articles directly addressed the issue of college for young women. But how they dealt with the issue, as with racial others, illuminates the various ways editors and writers as cultural architects used the notion of the woman in college to support the re-envisioning of the college curriculum as part of the ideal new route for forming middle-class masculine authority. They turned a potential threat into a reinforcing subordinate, the new woman into a new helpmate.[107]

One finds surprisingly few articles, editorials, or short stories that offered cautionary notes about young women going to college. One editorial in the *Post* (written by a woman) worried that the new woman of the era who went to college too often eschewed marriage for a career, raising a fear of *race suicide*, a term first used by Theodore Roosevelt and made famous by early psychological researcher G. Stanley Hall, who made only one appearance in these periodicals.[108] To the degree that they specifically addressed the issue, the magazines generally endorsed and even championed the new woman and her college attendance, often quite enthusiastically. Both *Collier's* and the *Post* ran positive articles on highly professional and academic female presidents of women's colleges. The *Collier's* article discussed the Bryn Mawr president's research on women college graduates that directly countered Hall's well-known warnings of race suicide—the theory that college-educated women would not have enough children to counteract the rise in immigrant births, thus creating a deficit in control and culture of "old-stock American WASPS." The readers of these magazines were all assumed to share a vision of vigorous existence in modern America, and the college-educated woman fit well within this overall vision.[109]

Magazines did not give the increasing enrollment of women in college anywhere near the same level of attention they gave to the issue of men in college. When they did pointedly address the topic, however, all of the magazines assumed a positive and encouraging position. Informative articles celebrated the new development much as the magazines did for men. Articles, like the 1899 *Post* story "Women's Colleges" or the 1901 *Munsey's* article "The Girl Freshman," noted the growth of enrollments, informing parent-readers of the new possibilities for their daughters. Women's sororities received positive attention in *Cosmopolitan's* 1897 piece on men's fraternities, and the *Post* even offered examples of women working through college in their article on "How Modern College Students Work Their Way Through."[110]

A central issue was not just women's presence at college, but rather what they studied. Were they preparing for new professions and thus charting new roles in society, or were they sticking to traditional areas such as teaching and "domestic science," or cultural refinement? Naturally, Lorimer at the *Post* weighed in on the issue and unequivocally told his readers to "Send the Girl to

College," again basing his opinion on the reformed curriculum, which allowed women, like men, to train for an active role in society. Nathaniel Butler, writing for the *Post* in 1910 intoned, "on a priori grounds there can be no good reason for not giving [women] the same education as men, if she wants it." *Cosmopolitan* offered perhaps the deepest discussion of the topic with its two-part exposé on women in college, "The Crusade Invisible" and "Away from Ancient Alters," in 1910.[111] In classic exposé fashion, author Harold Bolce sensationalized the fact that professors at the universities of Chicago and Michigan taught women to doubt biblical authority, and indeed "all forms of authority." Good "girls from Christian homes [go] to study in institutions in which the Bible is not taught," Bolce warned. Ultimately, however, Bolce's series celebrated the increasing numbers of women in college and their studies as revolutionary but positive. College women were "evangels of a new era."[112] They were being led away from traditional authority in order to live in and reform the present; they were in fact "the vanguard of a great spiritual movement" hoping to "clear fields for efficient service to mankind," a classic expression of the Progressive Era's secularization of faith.[113] Most tellingly, for all Bolce's warnings of radical, nontraditional thought, the types of service he expected these female graduates to render remained decidedly traditional—as teachers, wives, and mothers. Indeed, Bolce's conclusions echoed arguments forwarded by Lorimer and Butler, in that the chief benefit of the college-educated woman would be as a better wife and mother, especially so that the intellectual gap between the college-educated husband and his wife would not grow too wide and foster problems in the marriage.[114]

In fact, only one article in these mainstream magazines directly addressed the female college graduate's career options. "Magic Wands and Stepping Stones" in *Collier's* offered practical advice to the woman graduate, but even here the author argued that the chief reason for self-support was so that one did not have to "marry the first man who asked." Coverage of the new women of the era in college most often focused on the social side of the woman in college.[115] Overall, then, when these magazines tackled the potentially threatening new phenomenon of women in college, they emphasized the social nature of the experience. Even when exploring curricular issues, the articles and editorials ended up endorsing the college woman, but casting her studies and roles in a very traditional manner.

If these magazines failed to give the burgeoning enrollments of women their due editorial attention, that was not the case in their fiction. More subtly but more potently than articles and editorials, fiction in these predominantly men's periodicals crafted an image of the college girl that was indeed traditional, thus offering visions for women that were at once modern (going off to college) and yet nonthreatening to men.[116] One does find numerous stories revolving around a woman's college or coed experience. Similarly, many stories feature a female character with a college background, usually as a love interest to the male lead, so that the female in college or as a college graduate formed a conspicuous presence. Her presence in fiction is overshadowed by her nonmatriculating sister, however. Most commonly one finds no reference to college in the intellectual pedigree of the female love interest to a college man or male college graduate in these stories. For instance, the upper-middle class, lead female characters in *Munsey's* "Whose Fruit is Dreams," and *Cosmopolitan's* "The Case of Helen Bond," are noted only as women of obvious good breeding with no educational credentials mentioned, even though both stories involve college professors as love interests.[117] Another *Munsey's* story focusing on society women in a "college town" never mentions a college background for any of the young women.[118]

Even in fiction where female love interests did receive a college background or where the story focused on college-educated women, their roles more often than not ultimately conformed to traditional patterns, almost always centered on love and marriage. For example, Robert Herrick's "Mother Sims" in 1900 follows two nontraditional coeds, as they explore college life—one a widowed housewife, the other a school teacher, both after culture. They display genuine intellectual curiosity but do poorly in classes, with the older housewife-widow finding a professor to "mother," and the school teacher marrying another professor. Similarly, the first-generation college girl in "Memoirs of a Co-Ed," pledges herself to serious study (in part to counter the warnings of her mother's friends), only to end up dropping a procession of courses and finding love. *Munsey's* serialized novel, "The Lion and the Lamb," features a female college professor (of music) at an all-women's college as the love interest to a recent Yale grad engaged in coal mining. But the author never develops this element of her character, emphasizing instead the deepening romance and business intrigue— her professorship simply marks her as supremely cultured and refined.[119] If acquiring "Culture" was an acceptable curricular endeavor for the woman in college, one *Post* story, "When Culture Comes In at the Door," fired a comic cautionary note, even for this seemingly acceptable line of study in college. Here, an overly proud Bryn Mawr graduate refuses to marry a wealthy polo-playing suitor of inferior intellect, and in the end settles for an even duller cousin.[120]

Of all the magazines, *Munsey's* fiction presented the most consistent offerings focused on women in college, and some of the most positive. In particular, three stories in 1908 (two by the same author, Martha Wheeler), were the only ones throughout all the issues that revolved around college women, which involved absolutely no love interests and emphasized college life and study. Perhaps the greatest championing of the college girl came in Dorothy Canfield's "A Quiet Path to the Pierian Spring." This storiette in *Munsey's* captured the whirlwind excitement of opening day at a woman's college as the girls signed up for clubs, plays, athletics, and classes. Centering on the arrival of the chosen leader, a parade of classmates request her to captain the basketball team, to take the lead in a play, and to occupy the first chair in the violin section. The girl, Annette Walker, is described as "tall [and] athletic . . . with an alert, aquiline face," and is accompanied by a cabbie carrying skis, golf clubs, a violin case, tennis rackets, a pair of snowshoes, and a letter sweater. In a comic twist that tweaked common misperceptions of women, the author has Annette reveal that she could come back to college only after convincing her mother that her nerves were frayed as she prepared for her "coming out" in society and so needed the restful retreat of college life to recover. In Annette's character we see the all-around, modern "new woman," as college girl—active and academic. But even here, her college pursuits remain traditionally cultured.[121]

Such stories, focused exclusively on women and with no love interests, were conspicuous exceptions. In these predominantly men's magazines, writers tamed the potential threat of the college-educated woman by configuring her primarily in traditional modes. She would, of course, be the partner to her college-educated husband in a brave new world.

Conclusion

Did the magazine treatment of college education start a stampede to college campuses? Can it explain why corporations increasingly began to hire college graduates and promote them into management? Were editors like Walker and Lorimer responsible for curricular reforms on the college campuses? Not completely. People chose to go to college or decided not to go because of a variety of influences. Owners, corporate boards, and managers made decisions on hiring without consulting a magazine, and many college administrators and faculty pushed curricular reforms without having read debates in the magazines. But the mass magazines brought the concerns of the WASP middle class, the big businessman, and curricular reformers together in an unprecedented national forum, and focused all of these voices toward a vital issue for all—how to achieve success in a changing world. The power of this medium eludes direct measurement. Unquestionably, though, it possessed a power to set agendas, to conjure and promote ideals and values its editors and contributors deemed important, and it did so on a vast new scale. The explosion of collegiate expectations in America during the twentieth century is fairly incomprehensible without understanding how the magazines encouraged a rethinking of the college curriculum in conjunction with a reworked vision of the businessman and his new route to success.

These middle-class magazines promoted curricular reforms in the nation's colleges, but the overall reformed vision of the college curriculum (and its benefits) that developed in these magazines represents much more. It offers a window to view how the mass magazines facilitated a much deeper transformation—fashioning a new powerful cultural narrative of masculine authority and power. On one level, one does witness the cultural formation of popularly accepted notions of the ideal college education, a unique American hybrid. This hybrid vision blurred the extremes of American higher education, neither utilitarian nor wholly devoted to liberal culture. The vision that evolved in the magazines sought to combine utility and science with liberal culture, and this vision seemed more inspired by the needs, demands, and wishes of the middle class (as perceived by the magazines) than from academic reformers. The issue of fashioning a new type of businessman for a new age permeated and informed the entire discourse on curricular reform, so that the American embrace of higher education as part of the formula for success in no small part took shape largely filtered through the pages of these magazines.

On a deeper cultural level, the curricular re-envisioning orchestrated in this media forum arose only as part of a much broader and more significant transformation. The reformed vision of a college education and the ideal of the college-educated corporate businessman were informed by and in turn helped articulate the values of an emerging middle-class masculinity. Through a revamped, manly liberal arts, the aspiring businessman could forge Victorian virtues and lay claim to genteel leadership qualities—breadth of vision and character—that rendered him a worthy heir to the self-made man and also a promising new captain to chart business' more socially responsible course. Through higher education's increasing linkage with science, the new corporate lieutenants could establish themselves as modern men, proud of their association with the forces of change, the promises of efficiency and abundance. The new vision of college education united the potentially discordant streams of masculinity and business success. Through a college pedigree, one could now simultaneously cultivate Victorian virtues, aspire to genteel culture and leadership, as well as a modern identity, thus perfectly capturing the hybrid identity of the middle class itself—longing for both traditional and modern images of self.

Part of the potency of this re-envisioning of the curriculum for middle-class men emanated from the formation of powerful gender and racial barriers built in to this new cultural narrative of authority, though even here one also sees the potential for future meritocratic "whiteness." How the magazines collectively posited the purpose of college education for women and racial minorities, including new immigrants, placed their curricular vision of college for middle-class men in stark relief. Women college students and graduates, a very real potential challenge to men, were depicted positively but mainly as worthy consorts and teachers in a new America—their curriculums remaining based on acquiring "culture" or appropriately feminine professional training. "Scientific" professional study thus marked middle-class men as distinctive compared to women, while this along with the civilizing liberal culture acquired at college together served to mark them as superior in comparison with African Americans, Native Americans, and immigrant others. Refashioning the curricular benefits of college essentially facilitated the creation of new WASP, middle-class models of authority, new pathways to leadership. Even old-stock immigrants (German and Irish) received only marginal recognition as potentially worthy college students. This emerging cultural narrative defined new tracks to power and simultaneously limited assumptions on who should have access to such avenues to power. But exceptions—potential meritocratic cracks in the barrier—did indeed exist. New immigrants like Philip Salamander ("The Efficient Salamander") could partake of the same "white" narrative of authority via a college education and a management position. The same medium that erected such potent cultural filters could also plant the seeds of their potential demise.

The college curriculum was undergoing reform. Businessmen and manufacturers were discovering the value of educated and technically skilled individuals. And many Americans increasingly wished to improve or safeguard their family status by sending their sons to college. But these developments cannot fully explain the voluminous discourse touching upon higher education and business in the middle-class periodicals. In fact, the discourse itself helped to articulate and disseminate these changing impressions, informing popular attitudes. These magazines functioned as integral forums of negotiation where evolving meanings and identities were hammered out in the process of cultural transformation. The twentieth-century view of higher education in America as both an opportunity and a sorting-machine was formed out of that process as much as by college presidents or corporate policies. In other words, the magazine discourse on college education and business success did not just reflect or rationalize a changing reality; it was an active part of constructing new ideals, erecting a new avenue to power and authority for WASP Americans—creating a new WASP hero to replace the dying self-made businessman—with college as the essential new ingredient. It is refreshing that the same cultural capital barriers erected to cordon off opportunities for WASP men could also serve as the entering wedges for eventual claims to meritocratic advancement in America. Eventually women and minorities, and especially "new immigrants," could easily envision themselves within this new cultural narrative, advancing through college to authority and power.

3

Athletes and Frats, Romance and Rowdies

Reimagining the Collegiate Extracurricular Experience

I n October 1899 the *Saturday Evening Post* ran its first College Man's number, an issue devoted to highlighting aspects of American college life and to attracting college-age readers. While two editorials addressed the benefits of the college curriculum ("Shall I Go to College?" heartily endorsed a college education for its broadening effects), most of the issue's contents celebrated nonacademic elements of American college life. "Presidents as Fraternity Men" recounted the achievements and exploits, the brotherly bonds, and loyalty to alma mater of numerous American presidents down to the contemporary occupant, William McKinley (Sigma Alpha Epsilon). Jesse Lynch Williams's "The Great College Circus Fight," detailed the humorous and raucous antics of college days, featuring the football team's captain. Unmistakably, the college man as athlete and, in particular, the football player took center stage. Another contributor to the issue emphasized football's unique manly benefits to the college man—how it built "higher and more 'manly' qualities" than any other game. It developed character. And in a vivid depiction, Arthur Hobson Quinn's story "The Last Five Yards" captured the heroic toughness of the game, the romantic pageantry of game day, and the almost spiritual love of alma mater as the hero summoned all of his will to win the big game for Penn on the final play.[1]

Reforming the substance and image of the college curriculum proved to be only one facet of college life that demanded a makeover in order to erase the unmanly, effeminate, and overcultured stereotypes long associated with the college man. Curricular reform indeed rendered the college a more fit place to nurture a new professional-managerial leadership for the corporate world. Nevertheless, many more attributes contributed to conceptions of American manhood other than education and intellectual prowess, even if linked directly to future business leadership. If the American college was to be established as a truly appropriate place for one to acquire the intellectual skills and breadth to take up the reins of corporate leadership (the new vision of American masculine success), then the entire image of the college experience required transformation into a fitting manly preparation.

From the earliest magazine treatments of college as a possible new route for advancement, the endeavor evolved alongside and was intimately related to a multifaceted reformulation of the college man and the college experience. Nothing symbolizes this better than the cover art for the 1899 College Man's issue (see fig. 1). It features two collegians each gripping the other's shoulder with one outstretched arm in fraternal solidarity. One wears an academic cap and gown, an arm laden with books, eyes turned toward heaven. The other, staring resolutely ahead at the future and clad in football gear, solidly grips a football. In the background stands the gated quad of the college, the foundation upon which each has formed his manly character. The cover graphically illustrates how the ideal college man now united two heretofore antagonistic ideals of American manhood—the cultured, genteel scholar and the resolute, courageous, and vigorous man.[2] But as the contents of the College Man's issue indicate, the college experience could be constructed in a variety of ways to satisfy other masculine longings. One might nurture fantasies of heroic success on the gridiron or simultaneously forge discipline through team play—building the character honored by the self-made ideal or the loyalty and team ethic demanded of the corporate world. One could indulge in the rowdy fraternal bonding of college pranks and fights or imagine college fraternities and the bonds of alma mater as an opportunity to connect with an imagined elite— instant pedigree and tradition. As the *Post* exemplified, the magazines acted as critical cultural forums that spearheaded a reworked, image of the college man and college life, newly charged with multidimensional possibilities to satisfy the contradictory expectations of American masculinity.

In no uncertain terms, the transformation of the college man was intertwined with a broad shift in masculine ideals that occurred in the late nineteenth
and early twentieth centuries. With the swift advent of industrialization and ur-
banization in America, all men (but especially elite and middle-class men) faced
a withering barrage of challenges to accepted Victorian constructions of ideal
manhood. The increase of permanently subordinate, white-collar occupations
pinched the opportunities for the self-made man to rise to control his own business. One's work in increasingly sedentary, bureaucratic business environments
drained the vigorous competitiveness and camaraderie out of most business
and professional experiences. Combine this with the closing of the frontier (and
the chance of self-made rejuvenation in the mythical West), an increasingly
leisured and material life that seemed overcivilized and soft, hordes of vigorous
immigrant males, and finally, the entering wedge of women into the once exclusively male worlds of politics and the office, and middle-class American men
found that their traditional routes to self-made identity and success faced severe
strain.[3]

Naturally, American men, especially those from the middle class, longed
to confirm their manhood in accord with dictates of the traditional self-made
man (Anthony Rotundo's masculine achiever), even as they adapted conceptions of masculinity to compensate for and to align with the emerging corporate and consumer-oriented world they inhabited.[4] American men responded
to these challenges in a variety of ways, and scholars have excelled at detailing
how traditional and more modern conceptions of being manly coexisted in this
transition. The traditional Victorian ideals of toughness, honesty, sobriety, piety,
and self-control remained honored but reshaped into new patterns. The rise of
organized sports in the U.S. grew in no small part out of the muscular Christianity movement. Originating in England in the 1850s and then picked up with
enthusiasm in the U.S. later in the century, the movement embraced physical activity, bodily strength, and competitive sports to nurture a new Christian manliness in the hopes of energizing Protestant churches worried about the feminiza-
tion of religion and the enervating effects of urban life. Eventually linked with
broader anxieties over racial fitness and culminating with Theodore Roosevelt's
cult of the strenuous life, muscular Christianity preserved much of the traditional Victorian "character," while introducing more modern elements exalting
the masculine passions, needed for the increasing fires of competition.[5] Additionally, men joined fraternal associations (lodges and clubs) as never before,
sought the outdoors or the American West for manly regeneration, and many
even embraced the once suspect working-class, urban sporting life of gambling
and saloons, all in a quest for rough male-bonding or for a brush with more

Figure 1. The cover illustration for the first College Man's issue of the *Saturday Evening Post*. This image captures the two sides of the ideal college man—tough and cultured. *Saturday Evening Post*, 28 October 1899.

virile and seemingly authentic experiences.[6] Similarly, American men revered new fictional heroes, such as the cowboy, the athlete, and Tarzan, figures that celebrated such traditional ideals as freedom and individual heroics, while the same men indulged in the new fantasy of a reassuring primitive masculinity.[7] The evolving masculinity ethic preserved Victorian notions of autonomy, perseverance, and self-control, but did so in altered forms that also facilitated a more therapeutic, consumer-oriented venue for experiencing and displaying masculinity.[8]

Despite the superb insights on the shifts in masculine identity, the full significance of the rise of college education as an element of this transformation has remained woefully unexplored.[9] Gail Bederman has suggested that native-stock American men during this time felt pressured to reconstitute their masculinity in order to affirm their contributions to civilization as well as to assert their primitive masculinity in the face of numerous racial challenges.[10] A college education proved wonderfully suited to fulfilling these conflicting impulses and longings. In a consumer-oriented medium such as mass magazines, where multiple identifications could be and were promoted simultaneously, college attendance proved a marvelously malleable experience, easily freighted with often contradictory meanings and identifications. Owing to this cultural flexibility, the college experience would acquire a new significance in American culture and a multifaceted potency for the middle-class American man.

Nowhere were all the shifting notions of being masculine so interwoven or intertwined with an idealized representation of college life as one would find in these magazines. which fashioned a multidimensional, civilized-primitive college man for their prime readers, WASP men. This culturally constructed vision of the college experience derived its appeal from how it offered a cultural bulwark, an instant identity (through college) that could shore up their masculinity and racial superiority. This new vision of college played a critical and unheralded role in adapting new ideals of masculine authority in America.

The College Athlete as a Civilized-Primitive

Historians have long noticed that in the latter years of the nineteenth century, conceptions of ideal masculinity underwent significant change, tending toward a glorification of the male passions, a tendency drawing from the influence of Darwinism, to define core masculine attitudes as harkening back to an aggressive, more primitive level.[11] Victorian spokesmen urged participation in sports as one of the principal ways to reinvigorate a declining sense of manhood in a rapidly changing and challenging world. The muscular Christianity movement, the glorification of an aggressive, martial spirit, and the rise of sports

clubs all exemplified this trend toward a new celebration of masculine passions.[12] The athletic contest emerged as a new way to forge martial virtues as
well as Christian character through competition and physical exertion since the
old potential proving grounds (such as the frontier) had, supposedly, vanished.[13]

The editors of the magazines certainly followed suit. At the same time that
Munsey's, Cosmopolitan, Collier's, and the *Post* pondered "Should Your Boy Go
to College?" these magazines, like much of America, became enthralled with
athletics and the vein of passionate masculinity. Lorimer at the *Post* ran many
stories aimed at improving the health of the American man.[14] Similarly, nearly
every issue of any one of these magazines contained at least one short story of
international adventure, war, or a biography of a military figure.[15] The ads also
offered numerous products to invigorate one's health, or biographies of military men, Captains of Industry (depicted as conquerors), or world history compilations with illustrations that almost always seemed to depict martial scenes.[16]

College became an ideal site where middle-class men could fulfill these
emerging ideals. *Munsey's* ran some of the earliest stories on college athletics, and
they focused on football, running one story on the Harvard team and one on
"Athletic Yale" in 1894. Yale reigned supreme on the college gridiron during the
1890s, and *Munsey's* highlighted this prowess and the discipline it required,
noting admirably that it took "long training and much practice."[17] *Munsey's* continued to devote some attention to college football in later years, featuring a
poem on the Harvard–Yale game in 1896 and in 1898 printing the pictures of the
captains of the Cornell, Princeton, Harvard, Yale, and Pennsylvania squads.[18]
Beginning in the late 1890s, *Collier's* supported a regular sports department—
the only one of the periodicals in this study to do so—and lavished the most attention on amateur athletics (despite its growing popularity and respectability,
boxing was almost never covered in any of these magazines). In the spring *Collier's* reported on golf and yachting (genteel sports) but focused most of its attention on collegiate track, baseball, and rowing events, offering dynamic photographs of meets and races.[19] Their sports coverage expanded in the fall during
football season. *Collier's* featured none other than Walter Camp (famous Yale
gridder and coach, and ceaseless enthusiast) as their field reporter and colum-
nist. Long articles each week informed readers of this new and exciting sport
with accompanying photographs of the big games.[20]

During a time, then, when the athlete increasingly became an esteemed
public hero, these magazines offered the college athlete as a new icon; one that
could, most importantly, satisfy two contrasting longings of middle-class men—
to appear rugged but also gentlemanly. Camp's *Collier's* article of the Harvard–
Yale game, for instance, coupled lessons on gentlemanly play with action shots

of Yale's goal-line stand.[21] Several covers of the *Post*'s College Man's issues boasted heroic illustrations of college athletes. One sported two colossal figures of college rowers, one displaying the Harvard *H* the other the Yale *Y* on their uniforms, with the two crews racing in the background. On another issue, a football scrimmage raged across the cover, and a third pictured a heavily muscled track man poised for the hammer throw.[22] And recall the cover illustration mentioned earlier in this chapter—the scholar and the determined football hero, linked together—that symbolized the ideal new college man. As with the coverage of the Harvard–Yale game and the exhorting of gentlemanly play, the setting of the college easily united the apparent extremes of aggressive athletic competition and the training of gentlemen.

While efforts to use sports to remasculinize Christianity had been occurring since at least the 1850s, something else lent new force and anxiety to the championing of sports in these magazines. The lessons of Social Darwinism, well absorbed in the cultural mainstream by the 1890s, caused many WASP spokesmen to lecture with renewed vigor about the dangers of "overcivilization." Rugged sports, martial virtues and an emerging respect for primitive impulses seemed the perfect competitive antidote for a beleaguered WASP manhood. And while many in the colleges, like William James and others at Harvard, upheld college as manly, just as often the college man was castigated as a model of overcivilized manhood, with magazine characterizations often reinforcing such popular notions. But Social-Darwinistic anxieties about one's manliness swirled with concerns about contributions to and identification with advancing civilization as much as worries about physical and racial fitness.[23] What separated men of supposedly superior and inferior racial stock, according to the widely accepted developmental theory of G. Stanley Hall, was that a WASP man could harness both primitive impulses and civilized traits. In racially superior men, the primitive urges vital for successful competition lay just below the surface of the consciousness, imprinted from the race's earlier evolutionary struggles. These latent impulses could be easily rekindled through such things as athletic activities. Inferior races possessed the same primitive urges, but lacked the higher governing ideals of civilization.[24] The history of American culture during this time brims full of efforts to cultivate one or the other "sides" of American masculinity (the primitive or the civilized). Something was truly changing when the middle-class magazines elevated the college athlete as the perfect manly embodiment of disciplined physical strength *and* virtuous character, the man to carry the race forward.[25] And that something emanated from the fact that college proved the perfect site, physically and intellectually, to simultaneously form *both* sides of an evolving American masculinity.[26]

The *Post*'s "Athletics and the Future of the Nation" article in 1900 exemplified the subtext of racial and gender anxieties that now propelled the college man as a solution to the psychic crisis. Like many other writers, Eugene Lamb Richards first warned that "culture carried too far polishes all the force out of a man, all his vitality spent." Richards preached the need for "body-brain work." He linked this to traditional Victorian self-discipline, character, and will power, and used the outstanding Yale crew of 1860 as living exemplars. All of this crew were still alive, while of the top five scholars from that class, only one still lived. More telling, though, in a section titled "The Source of National Power," Richard's connected the need for such men to historic evolutionary struggles. "In all races which have shown power . . . the main sources of that power have been physical," and he went on to cite the Greeks and Romans. These peoples combined regimens of physical culture and martial games while also advancing civilization. He then discussed how "the English" maintained their empire through vigorous athletic competition and, finally, connected this racial stock to the first settlers and present racial makeup (and vitality) of the United States. As America looked to advance civilization, as heirs of Greece, Rome, and the English, Richards implied that college athletes like the Yale crew of '60 offered models for emulation.[27] The clear lesson was that if America was to advance in the Darwinian world-struggles ahead, the college man as athlete must lead.

Other articles cited classical authors, and in their championing of athletics extolled the need "to cultivate . . . sobriety, cleanliness, self-reliance, temperance and moderation," but as Richards's article indicated, by 1900 mass middle-class magazines began celebrating college as a special location where the athletic, moral, and intellectual instruction could be integrated, a source of national and racial strength that could move civilization forward.[28] In a 1901 article titled "The Making of the Perfect Man," *Munsey's* offered up the athletic college man as the new supreme ideal. The doctor writing the article first quoted Aristotle on the need for balance in life, and then preached that the brain and the physique must be developed in proportion to obtain "intellectual, moral and physical virtue." Numerous pictures of ideal physical specimens (all college men) accompanied the article—a Yale Phi Beta Kappa gymnast; a Yale football halfback, "who is also a high-stand man in his class;" another with a "high-stand" record was a pole-vaulter. These WASP scholar athletes not only represented an ideal, they were contrasted with immigrant athletes—an Irish-American boxer, "shoulders and torso . . . developed out of proportion" and the famous German-born bodybuilder Eugen Sandow, who "would make a poor show in all around athletics."[29] The native-stock American college men represented ideal proportionality, linked to esteemed Greek ideals and Western Civilization. The immigrants reflected an unhealthy imbalance.

Overtly racial references proved rare in magazine coverage of college football, but as the "game of college men" it more than any other sport reformed the image of the college man and integrated college athletics squarely within the evolving matrix of masculinity.[30] The nature of the game in that era—the minimal equipment, the massed plays to gain a five-yard first down, and the brutal nature of the play (no forward passing until 1909), exacerbated by lax rules—lent itself naturally to the swirling issues and concerns surrounding the evolution of American masculinity.[31] Football seemed the perfect primitive tonic, the moral equivalent of war, to impart core lessons of manhood, explaining why upper-class men concerned about the overcivilization of American men (and particularly the ruling class), such as Henry Cabot Lodge and Theodore Roosevelt, so passionately embraced and defended football.[32] The discourse on football unquestionably was constructed to respond to the prevailing racial and masculine anxieties of native-stock American men. Constructed first by the nation's major metropolitan newspapers, middle-class magazine coverage of college football would build on various narratives for understanding the game. Beginning in the 1880s, metropolitan newspapers developed distinct narrative tensions in their coverage of college football that charged this very obscure game with issues burning through American society, thus helping to catapult the game into national consciousness. Writers created rugged individual heroes, yet also celebrated the scientific efficiency and teamwork necessary for victory. Reporters celebrated both the toughness required of football and also the brains behind the scenes—the team captains or managers. Such coverage transformed the game's popularity almost overnight, and American men grew accustomed to interpreting football in seemingly incongruous ways—a game linked to Victorian traits of the self-made man and individual achievement, yet one also inculcating the values necessary for the interactive corporate world.[33]

Magazines then hammered these narratives of football and masculine identity into shapes that more specifically addressed the longings and demands of their middle-class readers, and they did so in more pointed fashion than newspaper coverage of games. To be sure, *Collier's* still reported on key games. And muckraking exposés, particularly after the fatalities in the 1905 season, arose (in *Collier's* and *Cosmo*) arguing for abolishment or at least rules changes to make the game less brutal and less professionalized. But even the game coverage and the exposés almost always circled back to or emanated from the key point—how football related to a young man's life preparation. Most distinctively, dozens of articles and editorials pointedly addressed the importance of the game for American men. *Collier's* ran at least one such article or editorial per year; the *Post* ran about one positive article per year; *Cosmopolitan* only ran one such endorsement, but *Munsey's* published long, informative articles explaining the game as well as its significance for American men (and society)— four articles in the 1890s and three more in the first decade of the twentieth century. Although many complained of football's extreme violence, no sport rivaled college football among magazine writers for nurturing the manly qualities of Victorian character. According to one *Post* writer, football stood for "learning by doing." It taught a man "self-control and to take punishment without flinching." As a team sport it encouraged "the exercise of higher and more manly qualities than any other game," since one worked together along with teammates rather than individually toward a goal. Furthermore, facing sharp competition, the college football player received praise only when truly deserved, so that it promoted meritocratic striving.[34] In another *Post* article, the novelist Owen Wister, renowned for Westerns such as *The Virginian* that celebrated the masculine passions, singled out the college football player for special inclusion within the sacred circle of the "natural, wholesome man!—the man who thinks straight, feels straight, and acts straight . . . the man of action."[35] Magazine writers celebrated college football as a "gentleman's game with scientific rules," yet one where these gentlemen—with photographs of Ivy League team captains to reinforce the proper image—also learned to be "honorable, tough and team players."[36] The promotion of modern, corporate ideals mixed freely with the celebration of rugged manhood and the notion of forming traditional gentlemen.

Additionally, magazine writers more pointedly amplified a theme not critical to newspaper coverage of the college football player—that of the virtuous scholar-athlete, a civilized-primitive. Articles on athletes or football players often were peppered with references to Aristotle or classical writers quoting honored ideals of virtue.[37] In praising "A Sound Mind in a Sound Body" in a 1904 *Post* editorial, Lorimer perhaps best captured this uniting of competing manly Victorian ideals such as toughness and culture in the figure of the college man. Lorimer first warned against a "false view of athletics," that winning was the most important thing. True college athletics, wrote Lorimer, was a means, not an end. The college athlete enriched his "manhood" through sports, but he was "primarily the scholar, the thinker, and the gentleman."[38] Whereas throughout the nineteenth century, the rugged side of Victorian man and the cultured side had often been at odds, the new ideal man exemplified by the college athlete seamlessly united the two in a new vision promoted with great vigor by the editors of middle-class periodicals.

Although enthusiastic about college athletics (especially football), magazine writers did not explore the full range of developing masculine connections, as did fiction writers for the same magazines. Fiction writers were able to more fully develop characters and themes, so that the lessons took on a much sharper detail than one would find buried in the description of a football game in newspapers or even in magazine articles on the importance of football.[39] The first (and earliest) theme to predominate in college football magazine fiction celebrated the college football athlete as a great individual hero—a man of honor and physical courage in the face of danger, who displayed gentlemanly character while still exhibiting manly, aggressive prowess. The second theme revolved around what might be branded a new corporate mentality, stressing loyalty to the team over the individual; the third narrative theme highlighted the passionate side of those who played the game, reveling in the viciousness of the sport that functioned both to satisfy a fantasy of individual heroics and to posit college football as a potential opportunity for forging manhood in a changing world. Quite often these themes intertwined in the same stories, and together they indicate how such stories encouraged new definitions of masculine success and promoted college as a new location to cultivate such idealized identities.

Although stories drawn from each of the magazines make an appearance, the preponderance of examples come from the *Post*. The *Post* ran four stories that featured gridiron action from 1899 through 1902, and later would publish five in 1909 alone (by contrast there were only a handful collectively between *Munsey's*, *Collier's*, and *Cosmopolitan*). Perhaps this is most appropriate, since that magazine under the editorship of Lorimer worked the hardest to engage the average American man. Due to Lorimer's personal distaste for sports, the *Post* declined to cover actual football games, except for some passing commentary, leaving such coverage to *Collier's*.[40] But the *Post* contained by far the most stories that dealt exclusively with the football tale prior to 1920, incorporating graphic and romanticized accounts of battle on the gridiron with appropriately martial language and imagery. In the 1890s, football fiction remained within the realm of juvenile or working class literature—*The Police Gazette* or *Frank Leslie's Illustrated Weekly*. The penetration of such fiction into the middle-class magazines reflected the growing importance of the college man's game for American masculinity. Even though these stories were often set in an Ivy League locale, their lessons were universal and interlaced with some of Lorimer's (and the middle-class's) favorite themes, such as democratic opportunity, anti-elitism, and rising through character, grit, and merit, while simultaneously celebrating Victorian character and a rugged masculinity.

Arthur Hobson Quinn's "The Last Five Yards" touched upon nearly all of the basic elements this genre of stories excelled at portraying—conjuring romantic, martial images of football combat, love of alma mater, and striving to succeed. Quinn's story opens with the main character, Franklin Smith, as a senior at the University of Pennsylvania, dining with his family and fiancée, Dolly, on the Friday night before the big, final game with Princeton. An illustration of Smith in padded football sweater stitched with the Penn *P* adorns the first page.[41] Dolly had grown jealous of her boyfriend's devotion to football, even as Frank protested; "I'm doing this not for myself, but for the University."[42] She argues that her father, also a Penn graduate, would have given up his cricket for her mother. The author seems to use Frank's prickling at the comparison of football and cricket, however, to highlight the difference between the old, unmanly, and elitist sport of past collegians. And Dolly remains unmoved even after Frank's grandfather toasted Frank, noting that Frank had been called "to show his manhood in the service of the college."[43] Dolly quickly comes around, though, amid the pageantry and emotions of game day—flags flying, fans cheering. The story follows the action of the scrimmage up and down the field, flowing to the climax when Frank enters the fray at quarterback in the waning moments of the game. First, he leads a goal line stand and then (in the days long before one-way players) directs the winning play. He catches a lateral and races the length of the field, only to be tripped up at the five "his ankle gone," and crawls across the goal line as the men of Nassau pounce on him. The final touching scene has Dolly tending to Frank in the hospital while the Penn student body serenades college songs below the window (incidentally the author thought it unimportant to note the educational status of Dolly).[44]

Such heroes upheld ideals of loyalty not only to alma mater but also to higher moral principles, directing their physical and leadership talents toward a loftier goal than self-gain—some of the very traits that champions of liberal college education endlessly forwarded elsewhere in the magazine when touting college for the future businessman. Such characters graphically personified the emerging magazine image of the ideal college man—rugged yet principled, exhibiting the stamp of character—the masculine ideals of late Victorian manhood. In "The Last Five Yards" the theme of corporate loyalty (ultimate loyalty to the team over self-gain) did make an appearance as well. That the great college football hero exhibited manly grit, determination, and fortitude was a given and pointed to the fact that he had earned his status.

While these stories always implied the meritorious rise of the hero, a very prominent set of stories by one author in the *Post* placed the ideal of self-sacrifice and hard-won success at the center of his stories. James Hopper was a leader in college football fiction prior to 1920, second only to Owen Johnson (*Stover at Yale*), contributing at least seven such stories (and some short serials) from 1904 through 1912. A former college football player, Hopper was a boyhood friend of realist author Jack London and remained in his close circle of friends. Hopper brought not only the literary realist's attention to detail but also London's elevation of the primitive, even brutal side of the sport.[45] Hopper excelled at capturing the thrill, excitement, and violence of turn-of-the-century football. Yet, unlike London's unrestrained primitivism, Hopper's tales contained parallel themes. His stories all focused on characters that must prove themselves or rededicate themselves in order to redeem their self-respect and their proper place on the team—it was not just about the hero's primitive toughness. For example, one of his earliest stories features an unlikely hero, a senior long relegated to the scrub team, who saves the day in the big game. The hero of "The Idealist" stuck through four years of football practices as a scrub due to his love for alma mater, even when at first ridiculed by fans as a "girlie." He wins the grudging admiration of the student body and team, though, for his fortitude and finally earns his chance. Perhaps overdramatizing the moment but depicting a gripping gridiron scene, Hopper wrote of the hero, "rising lithely and casting off his sweater in the movement, [he] stepped out upon the field . . . across the trampled ground, calm, grave-eyed, as if to a sacrificial rite."[46] Then with only a few minutes left, "thrilled in an ecstasy of resolution," Thane (the hero) hauls in a fumble, breaks free, and stiff-arms opponents to stand beneath the goal post "erect and serene."[47] The one-time effeminate collegian had proven his manhood.

Hopper emphasized the importance of traditional manly qualities. Through sheer perseverance his long-struggling scrubs not only proved their worth physically, they exhibited their superior force of will. Hopper depicted college football as the ideal training ground for young men to develop the rugged qualities necessary for success, where "girlie" young boys could regenerate themselves and prove their manhood. In one of his last *Post* stories, however, Hopper altered the equation. In "The Redemption of Fullback Jones," the senior star fullback has grown complacent. His uninspired play against a weaker Amherst team one week before the big game prompts his coach to bench him. Jones contemplates quitting over the indignity, but listens instead to the advice of his roommate, Midge, a senior scrub. Midge lectures that Jones's problem is that he has never played scrub, where one plays for the love of the game, learns to take licks, plays with heart—and never surrenders. Instead of hitting a brick wall, a metaphor Jones uses to describe his play, Midge argues that playing the scrub line fosters a belief that you can indeed break that wall.

Hopper then describes two days of viscous scrimmages, with Midge calling the signals for the scrub line in practice, handing the ball repeatedly to Jones who grinds out punishing yardage. Led by Midge and Jones, the scrub line actually scores on the varsity. Jones has learned his lesson and regains his old form in the big game; Midge proudly tells his teammates that even though he was not playing, his reward was watching Jones succeed.[48]

Although seemingly all of the action-oriented college football tales involved some degree of love and loyalty to alma mater, self-sacrifice, and the martial glories of football, Hopper's stories enshrined such themes with particular intensity. And more so than most, he emphasized that while talent was important, proving one's merit and true character through loyal perseverance in the service of the team in the end counted for more. All of his characters had to toil up through the ranks of the scrub team, learning the true measure of physical toughness and mental fortitude before claiming righteous glory.

In an era excited about the promises of industrialization but bothered by the giant trusts, their secret deals, unrestrained individualism, and the specter of diminishing opportunities, Hopper's numerous football heroes championed democratic openness and meritocratic opportunity. The football team represented the ideal corporation—a place that preserved the promise of individual glory, but where such glory could only be achieved only through an efficient team effort. Similarly, through the toil of practice in another of Hopper's stories, the hero's team worked "as one man."[49] Hopper and other authors in this genre stressed the efficiency of the team effort as well as individual glory—very progressive, middle-class, corporate ideals.[50] Furthermore, many commentators at the time praised the democratic effects of football, and in each of these stories, the heroes deserved their status as leaders.[51] More significantly, though, Hopper's popular and long-running stories exalted the reward of sacrifice and proven experience: the scrubs earned their place on the varsity, their sacrifices ordain their heroics. But in "The Redemption of Fullback Jones," the scrub's reward was even deferred, transferred to the glory of another and the success of the team. In tune with the shifting imperatives of the business world, the authors of these stories offered lessons geared toward the emerging corporate world that resonated with and celebrated the values of the new professional-corporate middle class who read the magazines.

Nevertheless, these tales offered college football as an ideal new location to fulfill virile masculine dreams of forging a regenerated aggressive manhood, as well as a venue for exhibiting individual heroics. The football stories suggested a new site for testing and forming manhood, filled as they were with images of physical extremes and combat. For instance, Owen Johnson's "Varmint" (a series depicting the young Dink Stover's start) describes how for Stover the "phalanx of bone and muscle coming toward him [a flying V formation in early football] roused only a sort of combative rage, the true joy of battle."[52] Johnson also paints Stover in the final goal-line stand "trembling like a bloodied terrier, on edge for each play, shrieking."[53] And like Hopper, Johnson excelled at depicting the violence of football. He details Stover leading the interference (blocking): "Dink swept around for a smash on the opposite tackle, head down, eyes fastened on the back before him, feeling the shock of resistance and the yielding response as he thrust forward," to gain a first down.[54] Or in the last installment of "The Freshman," Hopper shows the hero, Carter, on the field "full of proud fury."[55] Before the game Carter rose from the locker room speech of his varsity hero "muscles tense, with eyes flashing, and within his breast a convulsive desire to weep and kill."[56] Here were gentlemen who could match the masculine passion and vigor of any immigrant worker or fantasy cowboy.

Hopper and Johnson were only the two most prolific contributors, but all other college football tales offered similar details of manly, martial combat. Perhaps they functioned for some simply as a virile fantasy. Or perhaps adult male readers fantasized about their sons going to college to play football in order to form their manhood, to gain the masculine experience that the bureaucratic business world or the comfortable, overcivilized suburb no longer supplied. The critical point, though, remained that these stories revolutionized the image of college at the very time that the idea of going to college received increased attention as an important new route to authority in the business world. In effect, football legitimized college as a place to form traditional manly character on the sports field while indulging male fantasies of proving one's passionate masculinity through the combat of the scrimmage. Character, self-sacrifice, courage, and willpower mixed with more modern ideals of rugged, passionate masculinity, all in the service of alma mater and the success of the team (a corporate value) and all while sustaining the promise of individual heroism and glory.[57]

Unquestionably, the football tale in these middle-class magazines was part of that broad literature in America at that time, like the Tarzan novels or the Western, that provided vicarious models of manly, primitive regeneration.[58] But we should not overemphasize the college football player's primitive attributes. After all, the football player was in college, and these football tales did not occur in a vacuum. The college sports narratives in magazines constituted a vital element of the turn-of-the-century discourse on American masculinity that reconstructed the middle-class American man as simultaneously civilized *and* aggressively masculine. Pressed by economic and social change (especially the arrival of immigrant men), many native-stock, American men felt pressured to reconstitute male identity around 1900, to affirm their contributions to civilization but also to assert their primitive masculinity, especially through sports. It is an important point to emphasize that the vast majority of the college football players celebrated in articles or depicted in fiction were conspicuously WASP. Naturally, national mass magazines participated in this discourse (indeed were a critical element of it), and the college athletic hero stood as a perfect new masculine ideal. He stood either directly or implicitly as the embodiment of the masculine civilized-primitive, with racial assumptions of superiority constructed within this concept. Numerous contrasts between the civilized manner and the primitive violence exhibited by various college athletic characters could be noted, but the more fundamental and telling contrast remained that these were college men, depicted at some of the most celebrated seats of learning in the nation, rejoicing in the combat of sport. Certainly competitive sports built Victorian character, but in a far different manner than the ideal celebrated only a generation before that posited simply hard work, morals, and self-restraint. The aggressively masculine hero who was also a college man implied a perfect combination of the primitive and the civilized, and nowhere was his superiority championed more than in the middle-class magazines.

Instant Tradition: Conjuring the Idyllic College Experience

Despite the currency of the college athlete, especially the football player, as a popular icon, American colleges never lost their elite associations in the magazines. In fact, while many articles and stories re-formed the college man as an aggressive hero, magazines concomitantly enhanced the image of college campuses as seats of high culture and sophisticated manhood. And this too also contributed to the growing appeal of college life and the college man as a new masculine model, augmenting the "civilized" associations connected with the ideal college man. For example, as groundbreaking periodicals *Munsey's* and *Cosmopolitan* shared a fascination with the elite of Europe and America. Every issue contained at least one article on a European royal family (Kaiser Wilhelm being a favorite) or on America's East Coast elite. As much as these magazines celebrated the modern marvels of the United States, they also seemed transfixed by elite lives, perhaps a reflection of the uncertainty within their new bourgeois readership.[59] Linked to this fascination with elite life and occurring at the time that their editors began noticing and endorsing college athletics, the magazines simultaneously ran articles, replete with illustrations or engravings, that upheld the identification of colleges and universities with the elite of the world in revered citadels of distinction and learning. Articles such as "Picturesque Oxford" (1899) in *Munsey's* and "Where English Lawyers Are Made" (1900) in *Cosmopolitan* primarily featured the exquisite illustrations of the distinguished architecture—quadrangles, gates, and Gothic towers.[60] Such universities as Oxford, the article in *Munsey's* noted, "maintain their ancient prestige, yet lead in the path of learning."[61] Another typical *Munsey's* article on the subject, "Universities of Europe" (1901), filled with similar illustrations of European university architecture, reverently described the history of various institutions.[62]

Images of impressive, awe-inspiring European universities reinforced the general impression of colleges and universities as hallowed places. These magazines' depictions of the college environment as prestigious, however, were not limited to Europe. Americans had their own hallowed academic grounds, and the magazine editors seemed to take a new pride in their lustrous existence. *Munsey's* ran an enormous article on "The Expansion of Our Great Universities." Full of rich photographs, the article featured shots of venerable (though often newly built) Gothic towers and campus scenes—Columbia's famous domed library, a beautiful view of the Harvard Yard, and Princeton's Nassau Hall—while the text detailed the new scientific curricula and luxury dormitories that signaled progress.[63]

Frequent articles explored college life, academic personalities, and seasonal collegiate events much as the magazines covered American high society and elite lifestyles.[64] *Munsey's* printed a photo-article on "College Rooms and Their Traditions," with more than a dozen shots of resplendently adorned Harvard and Yale dormitory and private boardinghouse rooms.[65] *Cosmopolitan* covered the "premier rowing regatta of the world" as the oarsmen of Oxford and Cambridge competed against the gentlemen of Yale and Harvard, a major social as well as athletic event. Photographs captured the carriage of the Yale coach and other elegant spectators sporting Yale pennants.[66] *Collier's* regularly followed occurrences at the elite schools, such as elections of new presidents and new buildings, and also ran pictures of the graduating classes as if the magazine were the nation's society page.[67] Such stories unquestionably strengthened the association between these schools and the privileged elite of American society, part of the world these magazines offered as models for emulation.

Cosmopolitan, the *Post*, and *Munsey's* also delighted in informing their readers of college fraternities and exclusive eating clubs. In long, informative articles, these magazines described details of these intriguing and elite institutions. *Cosmopolitan's* 1897 article on the subject played on the mysterious, male-bonding side of these organizations, complete with illustrations of secret symbols and accounts of midnight ceremonies, but the article also lavishly described the newly built fraternity houses and offered numerous engravings.[68] A *Munsey's* fraternity article of 1901 even outdid *Cosmopolitan*'s, with detailed illustrations of houses from the "ancient" Skull and Bones at Yale to newer houses at the University of Minnesota. They also printed reproductions of fraternity keys from many prominent houses, the symbols of privileged membership.[69] With the images of noble architecture and impressive fraternity houses, such articles highlighted collegiate traditions, romanticizing the college experience. Other articles directly cultivated the elite, cultured side of the college man. *Collier's* "The College Man of Yesterday" (1902) described the traditional college man as a "gentleman [whose] . . . character very largely determined the character and history of the American people," as teachers, preachers, and influential leaders. The author, George Hoar, still believed that the college man was entitled to inscribe "gentleman" after his name.[70] Other articles emphasized the same romantic ideal of the college gentleman. Not only stories of college athletic glory, then, but a myriad of other articles in the magazines presented American colleges in an idealized and highly attractive form, promoting middle-class readers to think of college in particular ways (privileged and genteel) and inviting readers to perhaps see themselves or their children in this exciting new environment.

Articles performed such cultural work in the magazines but, not surprisingly, so did fiction. The earliest fiction in middle-class magazines that employed college settings and characters, in fact, helped to establish some standard frames for conceptualizing college life that bolstered a romanticized genteel tradition. Of course, college football stories offered the most glamorized and exciting pictures of college. Such tales irreversibly tied cheering fans, crashing bodies, and heroic action with college life. But they also romanticized the loyalty to alma mater as in Hopper's "The Idealist" or Quinn's "The Last Five Yards," promoting a sense of belonging to something special, instantly connected to an esteemed tradition. The opening lines of "The Idealist" captured this romanticization: "the long shadows of the autumn evening were creeping slowly across the campus," during the last practice before the big game when the team would "go forth to battle for the college."[71] Football was a new sport and truly few of the nation's colleges in 1900 qualified as old, but such football stories, in particular, created an attractive generic image of college as long-esteemed and beloved seats of tradition. While newspaper reporting of the spectacle of the big Ivy League games might have helped familiarize readers with such occasions, the magazines went farther. They did not report; they conjured an ideal and invited readers to imagine themselves at such revered seats of learned culture and tradition.[72]

College football stories, though the most popular, were hardly the only ones forging a popularized romantic image of college life. Charles Macomb Flandrau penned two long-running serials in the *Post* revolving around college life, "The Diary of a Harvard Freshman" and "Sophomores Abroad." "Diary" detailed the first year of Tommy Wood.[73] The stories reverberated with comic accountings of student activities—moving in, worried mothers, registering for classes, tight money, flunking exams, pranks, and class fights.[74] These tales contributed to forging and popularizing the folklore of college life, but Flandrau's serial also offered scenes of an idealized image of college. Flandrau captured the breathless excitement of Tommy's first day in the marvelous world of Harvard, capped by Duggie (the captain of the varsity football team and Tommy's boardinghouse mate) advising young Tommy on the finer points of Harvard life—proper vocabulary, clubs, teams, musical societies, crews, and papers. When Duggie notes what he loves best about Harvard, Flandrau paints a romantic word-image of living "on the Yard." "In May and June the morning and evening views from your windows are different from and more beautiful than anything in the world," as the glee club sings under the trees.[75] In a later installment, Tommy himself, despite his academic troubles and reputation among the faculty as a sport, has come to appreciate Harvard. Tommy comments that he never tired of "looking up at the stained-glass windows and the severe portraits." It all seemed "so academic . . . [possessing] a calmness and dignity."[76] Most readers of the *Post* or *Munsey's* would never go to college, let alone Harvard, but fictional idealizations of college such as Flandrau's helped establish the expectations and imagined vistas of college life for a rising group of Americans awakened to new possibilities and longing for the stamp of traditional gentility.[77]

Conjuring picturesque college vistas was not limited to Harvard, though. In fact, most stories that used collegiate settings or that made reference to collegiate pasts for characters simply traded on the established expectations of what college must be like.[78] Arthur Stringer's "The Professor of Greek," presented one of the best examples of college-based magazine fiction that utilized word-images of idealized college vistas and illustrations to conjure a romantic view that was vital and modern yet also very traditional. The lead illustration of a campus scene and an opening word-picture of the campus established a traditional image of college: "It was a clear day in November—a day intangibly melancholy in aspect, yet keenly exhilarating in effect. About the wide campus of the University of Elsewhere the yellow leaves blew in ragged lines and ever narrowing circles, while over the half-bare trees that fringed the West . . . an amber-colored sunset glowed through broken clouds, flaming above the fine

lacework of the maple and elm boughs, burning over the old gray college buildings and the dormitories and the library with lights already twinkling from its
serried windows."[79] An accompanying illustration attempted to capture the
scene as well, as the professor went out for his afternoon walk.

While evoking romantic images of college, the central point of the story
contrasts the staid and reserved professor with the students he meets on campus.
As he walks, the professor criticizes college youth for their failure to embrace life,
culture, and knowledge like the ancient Greeks. Modern youth, he thinks, are
too bookish. That the professor in truth characterizes himself is driven home by
his encounter with cheering students accompanying their triumphant varsity
team. The scenes emphasize the vitality of the gridiron heroes, modern Greek
warriors attended by admiring underclassmen. Like squires to Greek heroes
shredding their armor, "willing freshmen proud of the honor, stripped each
man of his moist jersey," clouds of steam "drifted up from every pair of stalwart shoulders." One running back, in an obvious reference to his superior
manhood, even took off a brass plate worn to protect two broken ribs.[80] The
story combines traditional campus scenes and the modern vitality of student
life. While obliquely critical of the professor's passive life, it posits the college
youth of America as the new Greek heroes—whole men, like the ideal Greeks,
who unite action with a respect for the contemplative life via the college experience. The story perfectly captures a romanticized conception of the American
college, at once reverent with tradition and yet surging with modern heroes,
who themselves embody the best of past and present.

Many American colleges were indeed fairly old, but magazines had only recently begun their infatuation with the college man, focusing America's attention on the subject. Much like the new universities used Gothic architecture to
create the instant image of tradition, so too many magazine short stories alongside articles and advertisements (see chapter 5) fostered and popularized the
idealized conceptions of college life, permeated with assumed traditions for
their readers.[81] While the proliferation of articles and fiction on the new phenomenon of college-going opened up middle-class magazine readers to a new
possibility, that possibility was presented in a highly romanticized form. Word-
images and illustrations evoked elite associations and encouraged a very attractive view of college life. The content of the stories often celebrated modern masculinity, but always in ways that retained connections to cherished conceptions
of genteel, civilized manhood. Such tales established enduring expectations
and perceptions of what college should be like and how attendance could mold
ideal self-perceptions. Through the college experience, the reader might imagine not only instant identification with a genteel tradition, but also a feeling of

connectedness, a part of a special, intimate community that could satisfy long-ings for such associations absent in modern life.

Raucous and Titillating: Democratic Visions and Parameters

Although articles and fiction with their romantic imagery cultivated the vision of American colleges as prestigious locations, they were not depicted as beyond the grasp of Americans. Just as these new magazines brought a world of once upper-class ideas, culture, and consumable reproductions into the realm of de-sire for their readers, so they rendered the elite college more accessible in the imaginations of their readers. The juxtaposing of articles featuring the impres-sive facades of collegiate buildings and the hallowed confines of the quad with the sporting images of the college athlete only broadened the spectrum of col-lege's appeal and a new sense of accessibility. But often in the same article, while the illustrations or photographs portrayed an elite association, the text either directly celebrated the democratic nature of American institutions or indirectly contributed to a reimaging of the college as a more typically manly rather than simply elite place. *Munsey's* "Expansion of Our Great Universities," for ex-ample, characterized the expansion of "social progress" and differentiated American institutions from those in England due to the fact that here a "poor boy" could work his way through to an education and become "a leader in political and social life."[82] And naturally, the author's articulation of this demo-cratic ideal in American higher education flowed alongside the article's accom-panying half-tone illustrations of traditional collegiate settings—Princeton's Nassau Hall, the Gothic Blair Hall (with tower and gate), Harvard Yard, an im-pressive vista of Cornell with majestic campus buildings framing a picturesque lake.[83]

The middle-class magazines, then, continued to invoke the genteel and privileged image of American campuses while stressing the increased democ-racy and meritocratic opportunity of American institutions. In fact, true to the self-made man's traditional suspicions of formal education, many magazine commentators pulled no punches in attacking the snobbishness and elitism of many American colleges. The presence of nouveau-riche students with their cosmopolitan lifestyles and corrupting habits remained the principal criticisms coupled with the waste of precious years and the uselessness of the classical curriculum.[84] Former President Grover Cleveland, a man who earlier had writ-ten a lead article in support of college education in the *Post*, worried in a 1905 article that American institutions bred only a feeling of pompous superiority.[85] *Post* writer John Corbin in "High Life and Higher Education" warned that the influx of wealthy students and increasing luxury indeed seemed to corrupt the necessary austerity of campus life, an opinion echoed in the *Post* editorial "The Gentle Art of Snobbery."[86]

Easily the most caustic blast at the perceived aristocracy of American higher education came from Owen Johnson in the five-part *Collier's* exposé, "The Social Usurpation of Our Colleges." Johnson surveyed Harvard, Yale, Princeton, and the fraternity system nationally, and ridiculed these institutions for allowing themselves to be captured by a social elite, who cultivated luxurious habits, received no exposure to the average American (whom they will presumably lead later in life), and did not learn the power of disciplined study. Although these were hardly novel charges, Johnson's critique was rooted in the assumptions of Social Darwinism, as he warned that the failure to perceive these problems would ultimately weaken the nation in the looming international commercial struggle for supremacy. It proves quite telling, then, that this author of the Dink Stover tales, who helped fashion the college man as the new masculine ideal to lead America, criticized colleges not simply out of some latent populist anti-elitism, but rather out of a sincere belief in the vision of the college man as a potential source of national and racial strength.[87]

Despite such recurring alarms, magazine writers still found plenty of healthy democratic forces within American colleges. Editorials in the *Post*, for example, cautioned that while Eastern schools languished in the mire of luxury, "Freshwater Colleges" (as D. K. Pearsons dubbed them), worthy of support dotted the country.[88] In small colleges and state universities in the Midwest, one could find "humble institutions" still imbued with a "pioneer spirit" and "the vital breadth of high moral purpose," a healthy atmosphere of "democratic learning."[89] In a later series on higher education, John Corbin highlighted the democratic spirit that existed even at Princeton, its "organized democracy" rivaling the democratic environment prevailing at midwestern universities like Michigan and Wisconsin, which he also spotlighted.[90] Others commented, however, in what would become the typical argument, that while rich students, luxury, and inattention to studies existed at most institutions, one could usually find the democratic spirit rising through the land due to a combination of factors — the increasing practicality of the curriculum, the camaraderie of athletics, and the presence of more and more self-supporting students.[91] Corbin even cautioned that at Harvard a spirit of democratic acceptance emerged once the sons of the South and Midwest made it into a club, usually via success on the athletic field.[92]

One very telling aspect of the myriad articles on American colleges and college life, even those detailing elite campus activities and lifestyles, hinged on

the fact that they were almost always highly descriptive, the tone that of a reporter informing a curious readership eager for details. The author of *Cosmopolitan's* "College Fraternities," for instance, described some major fraternity
houses on each campus, the process of selection (how alumni often wrote in advance of promising prospects from their area), and the types of men who joined
at the various schools.[93] College seemed an exciting new possibility that articles
on college athletics and elite college fraternities made accessible for the first
time. And many of these writers advised parents about college by offering a
"how-to" guide to going to college. The *Post* wrote about "The Age for Entering
College," and "Furnishing a College Room."[94] The most frequent topic in this
genre of articles, though, focused on (just like today) paying for college. Here
again, the emphasis was placed on the democratic ideal of working one's way
through school, chiefly in order to counter the temptation of luxury, sloth, and
the multitude of accompanying bad habits present at college, but also to let parents know that this was quite common. "Earning an Education" highlighted
that roughly half of all college students paid their own way and that all things
being equal, such students emerged better for it.[95] Articles like "Through Harvard on Fifty Cents," "How to be Self-Supporting at College," "How Boys Earn
Money," and "Financing a College Education" advised parents and students
on the types of jobs available for working students as well as affordable housing
and scholarships.[96]

   This "how-to" genre of articles reached its peak with John Corbin's
"Which College for the Boy" series of 1907. Corbin traveled around the country to investigate the nation's top institutions in order to give *Post* readers an
accurate picture of such institutions as Harvard, Yale, Princeton, Chicago,
Michigan, and Wisconsin. He lavishly detailed the type of curriculum offered,
the dominant clubs, sports, and student activities, as well as the nature of the
students drawn to each institution, all accompanied by photographs. These
articles seemed geared to satisfying a desire to learn more about these newly
esteemed schools, again part of the middle-class magazines' indulging their
readers' fascination with elite activities, at the same time encouraging a feeling
of knowing familiarity. The title of the series said it all, "Which College for the
Boy?" This once exclusive and privileged endeavor (going to college) was posed
as a choice most readers would soon face. The articles prompted readers to
think of themselves (or their children) circulating in the rarefied circles of college life they read about, even as Corbin's articles also informed them of how
these schools increasingly aligned with more democratic and meritocratic values. Corbin's articles, for instance, focused most upon the shifting nature of the
curriculum. Recall that he reserved his greatest praise for those institutions

(such as Princeton and Michigan) that combined the best of traditional liberal culture and practicality, again much as the middle-class liked ideally to imagine themselves. Similarly, he favored Michigan and Princeton for their heterogeneous student body. One could find sons of laborers, clerks, and farmers fully accepted in clubs and activities.[97]

Corbin's series functioned on multiple levels. It reported "nuts and bolts" information about institutions, reassuring parents that many institutions possessed a democratic spirit. He seemingly provided such information to allow parents to make informed decisions about college. Like all the "how-to" articles, it democratized the colleges while still upholding their privileged associations and encouraging readers to view such an opportunity as accessible.

Writers and commentators in these magazines, then, both reflected and guided emerging middle-class attitudes regarding the colleges. They struck a tone at once critical of older elite associations yet fascinated with them, all while straining to characterize American colleges as now democratically open. Nothing caught these currents better than Wallace Irwin's bitingly humorous series in the *Post*, "Shame of the Colleges." Irwin traded on Lincoln Steffens's muckraking *Shame of the Cities* and fashioned these comical pieces as exposés of collegiate misdeeds. Playing on stereotypes, Irwin dubbed notoriously undemocratic Harvard the "Gentleman's Trust." In contrast Yale was the "Democratic Machine," churning out graduates from raw freshmen through the cogs and wheels of Yale's educational factory (perhaps a jab at their adherence to a prescribed classical curriculum), all to a ceaseless "rah, rah, rah," that could be heard for miles around New Haven.[98] Irwin followed Yale with a look at Princeton, "Frenzied but Unashamed," in which he lampooned Princeton's reputation for overzealous commitment to sports. Classes were taught by cheers, and faculty rejected for mediocre yelling. Irwin launched his most stinging arrows, though, at Rockefeller's "Self-made Antique," the University of Chicago, where "John D" strove to make "Oxford or Bust" and attempted to help sell the university through a winning football program (legendary coach Amos Alonzo Stagg caricatured as Coach Wagg).[99] Irwin's barbs reverberated with democratic themes. Even though these depictions at times seemed quite critical, such humor nurtured familiarity; it brought once elite institutions and their pretensions down to size, and it heightened the sense of college as a new American phenomenon.

Irwin's humor may have rendered the college experience more conceptually accessible, but its rough image of college life (rowdy club activities, sports, and the hyper-extracurricular) also made it, again, more suitably masculine. Even the informative articles on college life that assumed the posture of tour guide into the lives of an upper class usually sustained the rehabilitated image of the campus as a new manly training ground. In the *Munsey's* article on college rooms, for example, one sees objects that suggested masculine vigor—a row of beer steins on a mantle, crossed fencing swords, and team photos mounted on the walls. Moreover, such manly décor also seemed to cast these college rooms (once the retreats of effeminate grinds) into manly dens, retreats for men to bond and properly recharge themselves.[100] The articles highlighting the fascinating, elite world of college fraternities also described the secret world of pranks and hazing, the rituals of brotherhood, and the "fierce strife" of campus competitions, where men formed lifetime bonds.[101] These articles, then, established fraternities not only as exclusive societies but also as manly clubs, not at all unlike the fraternal organizations sweeping through America to satisfy men's longings for solidarity, brotherhood, and rough male bonding.

Articles in the *Post, Cosmopolitan,* and *Collier's,* also ran stories that depicted an even more masculine side of college life that complemented the rehabilitation of college through sports. Class fights and raucous pranks had long been a staple of college folklore. When they had noticed such behavior, highbrow magazines had condemned such barbaric, un-restrained activity.[102] But as middle-class Americans and their magazines became infatuated with college life, stories of college fights, pranks, and other adventures worked alongside tales of football action, to reconstitute and masculinize the image of college. While some articles and editorials attacked hazing, most accounts were light-hearted even as they exposed the rough side of college life.[103] "Early Influences: Reminiscences of My School Days" and "College Pranks," as well as the fraternity articles, recast college life as full of fraternal bonding, heated scholastic and athletic rivalries, interclass fights and pranks, plus the close comradeship formed out of such "strife."[104] "College Pranks," for instance, detailed such typical college feats as stealing the bell clapper, and relayed accounts of duels and the many infamous class fights that had long been traditions on college campuses.[105] In fact, football would be accepted at many schools because it rerouted such violence and directed it for the honor of alma mater rather than splitting the school apart.[106] These articles painted a unique new image of college life— privileged yet manly, full of rowdy comradeship and competition to educate the "whole man."[107] Much in the same way that the embrace of once working-class sports, such as boxing, during this same period reflected a middle-class infatuation with the more "real" or authentic world of the urban sporting lifestyle, stories of raucous college antics (once reviled) offered a campus underworld as an appropriate (and relatively safe) alternative for the middle-class American to match the rowdy sporting life of the urban working class.

A variety of magazine fiction added even more vivid color to this reformation of the college as rough and gritty. "The Crime of '73," for instance, published in a *Post* College Man's issue, comically chronicled one freshman class intent on breaking tradition and provoking the sophomores by having one of their class walk with a cane—a presumptuous usurpation of maturity on that campus.[108] Charles Macomb Flandrau and Jesse Lynch Williams also incorporated repeated accounts of pranks and hazing into their numerous tales of student life at Harvard and Princeton.[109] Flandrau's Tommy Wood, for example, garnered an instant reputation at Harvard by running from the sophomore class carrying the head of a statue in a (supposedly) time-honored game called "the king's head."[110] Stories of bold pranks and hazing merited a whole installment of Williams's "Letters to a Kid Brother at College" series, when the brother awoke to a bear in his bathtub after a long night of partying.[111] Fictionalized accounts of college fights and hazing simply made the college man seem tougher, his life fun and rowdy, adding to the manly rehabilitation of college life, while also marking the college experience as unique and formative.[112]

Nothing exemplified the ability of humorous college fiction to simultaneously criticize college life while qualifying the experience as something unique and special better than George Fitch's long-running and highly popular stories of adventure at ol' Siwash. As a writer Fitch belongs in the same category as George Ade and other prominent midwestern writers such as Booth Tarkington. Fitch's brand of writing was similarly realistic, or at least cast in a down-to-earth style—one of the reasons, no doubt, that Lorimer's *Post* ran his stories for so many years. Fitch graduated from Knox College, the same small Illinois school that would produce Carl Sandburg. The fictional Siwash resembled Fitch's alma mater, and some of the material may have been partly autobiographical—although that would have made Knox one boisterous place indeed.[113] But the adventures, pranks, and high jinks he situated at Siwash seem more drawn from (and in turn contributed to) the evolving popular impressions of college life the magazines enthusiastically portrayed. The college students' overzealous devotion to athletics and the problems this engendered were a common theme. Siwash, for example, recruited a huge working-class, immigrant Norwegian to enroll and play football. The recruit, Ole, was characterized much like a Forrest Gump—lovable but not too bright, needing explicit instructions on the football field.[114] Another story poked fun at the then-still-controversial figure of the paid college coach (in this case Coach Boast). The boys faked a funeral in another installment in order to get the president to suspend classes so students could sneak off to attend a school baseball game.[115] But most of the stories recounted parties and pranks—sophomores trying to ruin the freshman formal dance or sneaking a foulmouthed parrot into the chapel organ pipes.[116] One story detailed a wild fraternity rush party filled with drinking and singing as well as raucous initiation rites.[117]

On the surface, the image of college portrayed in the Siwash stories seemed to cast college life in a negative light. Accounts of drunken students, fraternity parties, overzealous devotion to athletics, and even the uselessness of the curriculum surfaced repeatedly and seemed to reinforce calls for collegiate reforms.[118] Yet in the end, Fitch's tone was sympathetic to college life, his characters endearing, and his messages often upheld common arguments of the benefits of the college experience. Fitch was overtly critical of the classical education of Siwash, for example, but intoned that what he termed "applied deviltry" taught one creativity and leadership, making up for any deficiencies in the curriculum. Fitch's recurring master of "applied deviltry," Petey Simmons, obtained a top management job immediately upon graduation due to his organizational skills and imagination.[119] Fitch's narrator also upheld the character-forming value of football, even under the ministrations of the cussing and insulting Boast, and even though he never advanced off the scrub line to play a varsity down.[120] Most of all, though, Fitch depicted college life as full of fun and camaraderie, where men formed lessons and friendships that lasted a lifetime, an argument that had long been a central theme for proponents of college education.[121]

Much of the explicitly college fiction in these magazines mimicked the 1890s *Harvard Stories* and *Yale Yarns*.[122] Such tales of pranks and hazing served the critical function of introducing college life to the middle class, of democratizing college without losing touch with its elite appeal. But Fitch's Siwash stories evidence a much more profound evolution. Siwash was not Harvard; her alums were not wealthy bond salesmen. They were in fact common, nondescript businessmen who toiled in the office.[123] Most of the stories took the form of a man (Fitch as narrator) reminiscing about his old Siwash days. In one, the narrator turns toward his classmate, who worked beside him in the same office eight hours a day, and asks, "how can I be the same guy who climbed sixty feet to get the bell-tower clapper?"[124] The Siwash stories posited college experiences and friendships as the greatest times of one's life. Though not the Ivy League, Siwash was a sacred place full of its own traditions and the seat of nostalgic fantasy. But the stories also solidified a parallel image of college life adapted from the middle-class fascination with urban underworld—a world full of aggressive masculinity, rough friendships, and morally questionably behavior. Along with the other magazine treatments of this once unseemly side of college life, Siwash helped to legitimize college as a safe outlet for such passions, to sanitize them, and thus incorporate such experiences as part of the growing process for men. Siwash was everyman's college, and the stories invited average readers to see themselves at such a place.[125]

Painting the college as rowdy helped rehabilitate the college man as sufficiently manly, but another set of stories surfaced that also offered readers a vision of college life full of titillating adventure—a brave new world of sexual fantasy. Evidently the seductive character of the so-called "College Widow" had long been a staple of campus folklore before George Ade's poem and play made her famous.[126] She was typically a local bachelorette, charming and worldly wise, who lived close to campus and year after year bewitched a new crop of undergraduates. Ultimately, however, she cut a pitiable figure, living with a soiled reputation and forever clinging to the retreating shreds of youthful beauty. To the young men reading the *Post*, though, she must have seemed an enchanting enticement, a titillating symbol of the romantic adventures potentially awaiting them at college. The *Post* ran several short stories conforming to the college widow genre, for example, "Miss Maria's Fiftieth: The Romance of a University Town" in 1898 and a 1907 story, "Puppy Love: The College Widow." [127] Although these tales might have worried some parents, such tales undoubtedly helped color the campus as a place of amorous adventures that potentially challenged Victorian sexual mores for the young male readers of the *Post*. Advertisers even tried to cash in on (and in the process promoted) the sexually charged symbol of the college widow. Advertisers regularly offered sports scenes and (believe it or not) illustrations of college women to entice young men to request a clothing catalogue, and in 1909 the Rosenberg Brothers offered illustrations of "the College Widow."[128]

Stories of love on campus, though, were not limited to risqué accounts of college widows seducing underclassmen. Most magazine fiction in general contained a love subplot, so obviously authors worked them into college stories as well. And coed campuses, much like offices that were throwing men and women together in a new setting, were naturally intriguing locations of liberated sexual dynamics, charged with new possibilities.[129] Magazine fiction capitalized on both. With regard to coed colleges, for instance, "Memoirs of a Co-Ed," explored this relatively new phenomenon. The freshman coed begins the story recalling her mother's "prudy" friends advising that she attend an all-female school. The young coed swears to devote herself to school and not boys, but the story details the breaking of that oath as she is swept up in the excitement of campus life.[130] Certainly, coed colleges had existed, but in the late nineteenth century, women flocked into colleges. By 1900 they made up 40 percent of enrollments.[131] At the same time the numbers of male college students were on the rise, so that more and more young people were thrust together in a (relatively) liberated environment. In the nineteenth-century colleges' mostly male environments, the local college widows provided, perhaps, the only opportunities for sexual adventures, but now the rising number of coeds rendered the college campus a hotbed of romance, as George Fitch, dubbed it in "Cupid—That Old College Chum."[132] Such stories contributed to the reconceptualization of college life in American culture, another element in magazine fiction that cast college life in an exciting new light, one charged with quite un-Victorian sexual energy.[133]

Calls for more democracy on campus, depictions of raucous activities, and the inviting possibility of romance depicted in these magazines seemed to paint the college experience in a more democratic hue. Yet the democratic visions also subtly worked to establish racial and gendered parameters as well. The immigrant as football hero, proving himself on a team, held out democratic possibilities for inclusion or "whiteness." Walter Camp's yearly All-American selections, for example, remained quite free of racial overtones even as Carlisle Indian School greats, such as Jim Thorpe, earned recognition, a fair treatment that stood in stark contrast to the often blatantly racist themes in newspaper coverage of that team.[134] George Fitch's depiction of Ole the Norwegian football hero in his numerous Siwash tales, however, played on the otherness of this immigrant, even while his presence at Siwash could be seen as democratic inclusion. Ole Skjarsen, "came to Siwash to absorb learning from the fullback position," and in one telling story, Fitch notes that while Siwash loved Ole, they did not accept him in a fraternity. Ole's clothes were ill-fitting. "He regarded a fork as curiosity," while "his language was a head on collision of Norwegian and English." Fitch always wrote Ole's speech in a hard, childlike dialect. Ole cut a comedic figure, accepted at Siwash but obviously out of his proper element in college. Similarly, another humorous writer for both the *Post* and *Collier's*, Wallace Irwin, penned a highly popular series in *Collier's* titled, "Letters from a Japanese Schoolboy," which played on the theme of an alien's take on American culture. Irwin too wrote this in a thick dialect, and one letter followed a Sidney Katsu, who tried Harvard for a semester, and discovered through his attempt at "feetball" how to be a "mollycoddle" (a term loaded with effeminate connotations).[135]

One short story did surface that supported a broader notion of "whiteness." *Munsey's* "Under the Banyan" in 1900 reinforced on one level the emerging characterization of the college man as sophisticated and privileged. The college grad in this story dresses well, plays college songs on his banjo, and exudes a polished air. The intriguing element, however, is that this Yale man is one-quarter Chinese. He is expected upon graduation to don the traditional garb of a mandarin and serve as a Chinese diplomat, but he chooses instead to enter business and remain "American" in Hawaii.[136] With the exception of the Yale man in "Under the Banyan," when immigrants or minorities received inclusion in the manly college experience, they were still seen as distinct and "other"; thus they could cut comic figures that cast the normal "white" college students in stark relief.

Unlike minority or immigrant men, thousands of women were flocking to American colleges during these years in record numbers, and this development was hailed as healthy and democratic. Articles like "The Girl Freshman" in *Munsey's*, "Women's Colleges" in the *Post*, and "Court Circles at Wisconsin" followed the same format as the "how-to" genre of articles for men. "The Girl Freshman" was typical. The author, Alice Katherine Fallows, intended the long piece to be instructive, to put "parents who are thinking of sending their daughters, and the daughters themselves" at ease about the "breaking in" process of the first year. She describes the whirl of social activities at places like Smith and Mount Holyoke, meant to assimilate the freshmen and allow them to bond with their new classmates. Forrest Crissey's "How Modern College Students Work Their Way" even contained a couple of paragraphs on the various jobs—housekeeping, stenography, typing, and babysitting—that he found college women performing in order to earn their way.[137]

Nevertheless, as with articles covering men going to college, often the very same articles contained messages and visions that invited readers to see the newly accessible college experience as privileged and loaded with special traditions—instant connection with a sacralized past. The Fallows article, not only informed but offered rich descriptions of the "Lantern Ceremony" at Bryn Mawr and the "Tree Day" costumed march and ceremony at Wellesley, rituals that rendered the girl freshman as part of a distinct and sacred circle. Illustrations of such ceremonies or photographs of the majestic campus vistas accompanied the descriptions in this and similar articles. In all this they replicated the mixture of democratic and genteel visions offered in articles focused on men's college experience, as in P. F. Piper's "College Fraternities." That article, in particular, provides evidence of how the woman's college experience, while promoted, was envisioned along strict gendered lines. Piper carefully noted that sororities did not promote the same masculine qualities, such as competition, as did the male fraternities. Instead, "the tendency has been to accentuate and to develop the truly feminine side of their natures," with opportunities to decorate their sorority houses with "handsome painting, sculpture and dainty-needlework." And the house table offered plenty of practice in "the domestic arts." So even as magazines rendered the college experience, with all its instant pedigree and tradition, more democratically open for women as for men, the coverage was careful to paint the experience as one that only enhanced the traditionally feminine. College would not "masculinize" American women.[138]

Tales of college widows, campus coeds, and rowdy pranks indeed democratized the image of college alongside articles and editorials that asserted that most collegiate institutions were meritocratic and open to new students. But they also did much more. Stories of fraternal ritual and bonding, along with tales of college fights and pranks, rendered college more ruggedly masculine. Accounts of romantic adventure and raucous campus antics refashioned the college experience in ways that aligned with the middle-class man's broad new fascination with the gritty, un-Victorian urban sporting culture, drawing the college experience tightly within the national discourse that was altering notions of appropriate middle-class male activities. However, the same articles that seemed to open the college gates (at least conceptually) to more Americans also worked to establish definite parameters and limits. Racial minorities were viewed as an oddity as were potentially "white" ethnic immigrants; the presence of women in college, while often celebrated as a sign of healthy democracy, served mainly to reinforce rather than masculinize traditional female traits, and more often functioned as a titillating and alluring aspect of the revamped college experience for men.

Theodore Roosevelt and the New College Man: The Complete Civilized-Primitive

Certainly changes occurring independently on the college campuses (the rise of collegiate sports and fraternities) and the influx of nouveau-riche students with their more cosmopolitan lifestyles drew the attention of these periodicals. Students and faculty were the ones casting about for new venues for proving manhood, for rough play, and for sexual adventure. But the magazines focused on and amplified these various campus experiments, and injected them into a national discourse. Their coverage invested the college experience with multiple layers of meaning for middle-class American men, constructing parallel narratives of being masculine that a college detour might ideally satisfy.

One prominent set of articles and fiction, however, went farther by uniting these parallel representations of collegiate masculinity. Beginning in 1899, several articles appeared that profiled the college days of presidents and other leading politicians. "Presidents as Fraternity Men" in the *Post* and "College Days of the Presidents" in *Munsey's*, for instance, reported on this critical period of these presidents' lives long ignored by biographers.[139] The writer in *Munsey's* pointedly addressed this issue. A "conspiracy of silence" had existed among presidential biographers, "by which our Presidents have been pictured as a succession of poverty stricken and uneducated boors." "The self-made man is worthy of the highest regard," he continued, "but . . . [the Presidents'] lives shouldn't be altered to fit this ideal."[140] Three quarters of the nation's presidents had gone to college, but in the nineteenth century especially, college had been linked to aristocracy. Presidential hopefuls had typically suppressed their college associations, as the author noted, playing up log cabins and self-struggle. That aspect had begun to change, and new presidential pride began to generate interest. President McKinley wore his SAE pin during his inauguration ceremony and Theodore Roosevelt sent an inspirational telegram to his Harvard football team before the big Yale game in 1902.[141] This "conspiracy of silence" regarding presidents' collegiate experiences reflected both the powerful attraction of the self-made ideal and the commonly held biases against college education, but its end signaled the shifting perception of college that the middle-class magazines facilitated and encouraged.

Like many of the articles describing college and fraternity life (but in a more pointed fashion), the profiles of the presidents and politicians communicated a multifaceted vision of the college experience. "Garfield: Man of the People" focused on the president's days at Williams College. Garfield reportedly achieved a high rank of scholarship, wrote poetry, and participated in the religious life of the college. The author of this profile cautioned, however, that Garfield was not an overcivilized college boy. He debated at Williams (a very manly competition before the days of football), and though religious he "never held himself aloof from the society of intelligent and vivacious sinners."[142] Similarly, the 1900 *Post* article, "The Strong Young Men of the Administration," reveled principally in the college exploits of some among Roosevelt's staff. An assistant secretary of state, who matriculated at Lewisburg College, was described as a studious literary fellow but also a "lover of college sports." The article detailed numerous college pranks of these fellows as well.[143] Albert J. Beveridge, a young senator from Indiana in 1900, became one of Lorimer's favorite political figures in the *Post*. Beveridge's first profile, however, epitomized the new image of college life and the college man. Described as a grind and also a member of a fraternity, Beveridge was no college dandy. He took cold baths and escaped to the woods regularly for exercise. Moreover, in what would become the new self-made ideal, Beveridge worked his way through college.[144] Not surprisingly, Beveridge contributed several advice articles for young men in the *Post*.[145] *Collier's* too found Beveridge's college days irresistible and utilized manly terms, such as "combative mind," to describe the character of Beveridge as a college man.[146]

Nevertheless, these accounts of presidential indulgences and old college pranks were only one part of these articles. They uniformly depicted presidents and politicians as serious scholars, and each one recalled these collegiate experiences in a respectfully nostalgic tone—these were places that left their mark on character. The author of "College Day's of the Presidents" included romanticized depictions of the various colleges the presidents attended alongside the recollections of undergraduate adventure. Kenyon College's "ivy covered stone" and "venerable air" punctuated the author's assertion that her famous graduate, Rutherford B. Hayes, was indeed a "gentleman." Illustrations of the presidents' college fraternity pins adorned several pages as well, adding visual emphasis to the romantic visions of college life conjured by the article. In other words, these articles forwarded a multifaceted characterization of the college experience.[147]

Scholarly yet athletic, cultured and yet manly, privileged yet meritocratic, no political figure rivaled Theodore Roosevelt as the key personality in refashioning the image of the college-educated man. Roosevelt personified a new concept of manhood that embraced not only the masculine, martial passions for which he is well known, but also for combining these with an esteem for scholarship and an appreciation of culture. Roosevelt and many Easterners had become obsessed in the latter part of the nineteenth century with rehabilitating American (especially Anglo-Saxon) manhood—part of the so-called crisis of masculinity. Roosevelt and numerous other champions of the strenuous life extolled outdoor activity to reinvigorate American men and celebrated the American West and sports as ideal activities to achieve their reformation—a regeneration made particularly acute by the rhetoric of Social Darwinism.[148] Less appreciated but no less significant was Roosevelt's role in the masculinization of culture and college. Caring deeply about art and literature, Roosevelt as president promoted American authors and artists. He consistently set a personal example that encouraged embracing the arts and learning, by inviting writers and artists to the White House.[149] The press frequently publicized this Renaissance man in the White House and, as one contemporary judged, Roosevelt's personal example "did much to encourage the wholesome notion that a manly man might be serious in purpose in his college days without becoming a prig."[150]

The subheading of a *Munsey's* article on Roosevelt from 1901 describing him as "a scholar and a gentleman, a brave soldier . . . the author of fifteen books and the father of six children," perfectly captured the ideal combination of qualities Roosevelt stood for and by association helped to identify with the ideal college man.[151] Roosevelt obviously captured the public imagination, and the middle-class periodicals, especially the *Post*, exalted the new president as the ideal man. Virile and athletic, well educated and genteel but also a modern, progressive-minded leader, Roosevelt exemplified what the twentieth-century man should be to meet the challenges ahead. And his college education figured quite prominently in nearly every article praising his virtues. *Munsey's* colossal profile of the dynamic new president, filled with his hunting, ranching, and Rough Rider exploits, also noted Roosevelt's Harvard days where he split his time between "healthy sport and healthy study."[152] Twice the *Post*'s College Man's issue featured articles by Owen Wister, a colleague of Roosevelt's at Harvard, an ardent admirer, and a prominent champion of the strenuous life in his own right. In "Theodore Roosevelt, Harvard '80," Wister recalls his first encounter with Roosevelt as a student working out in the new Harvard gymnasium. Even then Roosevelt exuded fierce energy and charisma. Later Wister records Roosevelt's brief but memorable and gleeful leadership as a fraternity brother presiding over the playful torturing of initiates, Wister among them.[153] In his article, Wister endorses the vision of the college man ideally exhibited by Roosevelt—a man "devoted to manly sports," yet retaining the "character of a college-bred citizen," his mind both "vigorous and highly educated." Moreover, in one subsection headed "Where the College Training Shows Itself," Wister notes the reason why college had become so essential for men to form their all-around character. He states that "the training brought forth certain qualities which all manly men possess, but which must lie largely repressed in city houses and city streets."[154] One *Collier's* article on Roosevelt urged all colleges to reform their curriculum to include physical education and to adjust their outdated subjects in order to direct the intellectual energy of students like Roosevelt, who were vitally interested not in Greek but in the real world.[155] Roosevelt even merited his own issue in the *Post*, as that magazine devoted its full attention to the president and the celebrated aspects of his life.[156]

Roosevelt's ascendance to national prominence as an ideal man solidified the new image of college as a place uniquely fitted to mold the well-rounded, cultured, and yet manly gentleman. The rise of manly sports on college campuses no doubt was the key factor in the transformation of the image of college. But the rise of new male heroes like the athlete and college-educated leaders like Roosevelt—and their subsequent celebration in the media—also masculinized the gentleman of culture or the scholar, and posited the college as the location where such ideal, all-around men were formed. Being cultured was honored in

the past, but the disparate strains of Victorian manhood had never fully recon-
ciled the extremes of being tough *and* being cultured. Roosevelt united them. In
addition, depictions of his raucous fraternity hazing recalled other magazine
accounts of such fraternal antics—the rough world of college men. He put a
final stamp of legitimacy on college as a manly place where leaders were forged,
their character molded through sports, fraternal bonding, and the refining qualities of college education even as the very same experience also allowed for a
healthy expression of the masculine passions—a rowdy, strife-filled substitute
for the American frontier or the rough urban sporting culture.[157]

Magazine fiction also excelled in providing engaging characters that drew
together and celebrated the various elements of the new ideal college man.
While the football heroes who dotted the magazine landscape provided some
of the most enticing examples of the civilized-primitive, many writers created
heroes like Roosevelt, who more pointedly mixed culture, scholarship, and athletic prowess.

Perhaps the finest example emerged from the pen of popular *Post* fiction
author Charles Macomb Flandrau. Flandrau's ongoing serial, "Diary of a Harvard Freshman," chronicled the life of a Harvard freshman, Tommy Wood, and
his many trials. The most intriguing character in the series, however, was Douglas Sherwin or Duggie, the senior football captain. Rooming in the same boarding house as Tommy, Duggie took the freshman under his wing.[158] Duggie
reigned as the ideal college man, a model for Tommy (and all readers) to idolize.
Flandrau never depicted martial scenes of gridiron glory but used Duggie's
identity as a football hero to solidify him as credibly possessing fine qualities of
leadership and manliness and, more importantly, to set up the other ideal aspects of such a leader. Duggie handles his prominence with grace and ease.
Tommy is awed by the army of callers seeking out Duggie at the beginning of
the semester—the Dean, the editor of the *Crimson*, and the crowd that gathers
around Duggie on campus. But Duggie finds time in the evenings to give
Tommy sage advice on being polite and on the finer points of Harvard life.[159]
Later Duggie surfaces at a professor's house party for freshman in order to set
the freshman at ease: later they would be able to talk of things other than football such as literature and history.[160]

Duggie's character fell into sharper relief when he takes Tommy home
with him on a weekend after Tommy fails the first round of exams. Tommy is
astounded by the family's wealth but also their humility. They did not flaunt
their wealth or culture, though in the evening the whole family sat with each
other reading aloud from Emerson, Thoreau, and Hawthorne.[161] Through
the eyes of Tommy, Flandrau conveys Duggie as the ideal civilized-primitive,

college man, "the busiest, hardest worked, and most influential person I ever knew." Duggie might have settled into the life of a sport, but instead he excelled in academics and athletics. He belonged to several clubs, captained the football team, studied hard and received high marks (in the days of the gentleman's C), and he spent most of the year "in training." And as Tommy observes, Duggie was no snob.[162]

Many writers worked similar all-around college men into their stories.[163] In one especially revealing *Post* story from 1912, Holworthy Hall's "Tutoring Henry," the author creates a character that exemplifies the scholar-athlete, but additionally points to the wide currency of the ideal and the appeal of college life longed for by many in the middle class.[164] Henry's big sister, Stephanie, has decided that her brother should go to Harvard, "his advent in Cambridge [she expected] would . . . bolster up the family tree and add a dash of prestige to the dead weight of vulgar fortune."[165] Stephanie possesses an enormous cache of educational leaflets, "the latest football guide, a volume of college songs," and fantasizes about her brother rising "among the fellowship of educated men to give three cheers for the aristocratic place of learning-on-the-Charles—the home of Emerson, Eliot [Charles W., president of Harvard], and the Flying Wedge."[166] Through Stephanie, the author easily mixes images of Harvard as a seat of learning and of manly sport. As Hall wrote, "Stephanie went to sleep with a fat red catalogue under her pillow, and dreamed of Henry playing half-back on the varsity and leading his class in scholarship."[167] He uses Stephanie's character to articulate the emerging ideal middle-class vision of what college should offer and what the college man should be. Unfortunately, as Hall reveals, Henry could not have made "the bean-bag team of an orphanage."[168] Henry's tutor, however, "a thorough gentleman" with numerous degrees and an outdoor sportsman, embodies the collegiate ideal. He simultaneously disabuses Stephanie of her pretentiousness and whips the slothful Henry into intellectual and physical shape.[169]

Hall's story hints at the growing popularity of the collegiate ideal, the associations coveted by the emerging corporate middle class and, while poking fun at longings for collegiate identifications, still confirms the validity of the ideal and the model scholar-athlete hero.[170] It is also worth noting, however, that the story also exemplifies the fine limits of that idea. Though Stephanie obviously esteemed the college experience and obsessed about its social possibilities, she had not been to college. She only envisions it as a hallowed ground of male identity, and particularly for men of a certain class. She saw it as a route for the rehabilitation of a flagging, native-stock, American manhood, represented by her weak and overcivilized brother, Henry. Yet her educational status (did she even attend an academy or high school?) never comes up as a worthy topic in this story.

Conclusion

Celebrations of Theodore Roosevelt, followed by story after story featuring the manly scholar-athlete as hero, provided vivid examples of ideal manhood to magazine readers after the turn of the century. Certainly, these shifts in college life had been occurring independently on the nation's campuses for several years prior to the explosion of middle-class magazine coverage. The magazines did not create these changes but, in fact, did something much more important. They interpreted and disseminated such changes for a new set of Americans, and they injected college education into the recipe for American masculine identity and authority, weaving this revamped vision of the college experience into a potent new cultural narrative of WASP, middle-class manhood in America. Functioning as the critical cultural forum for the American middle-class, the mass magazines fastened upon the notion of going to college owing to the ease with which a college detour accommodated the various and often antagonistic currents of evolving masculinity, issues at the center of their male readers' swirling anxieties.

The college experience, quite simply, could be used to assuage many of the parallel longings and desires of middle-class men in a changing world, to unify so many of the discordant urges and ideals of evolving American masculinity around the turn of the century. Magazine writers celebrated the college athlete, particularly the football player, as a new post-Victorian hero. The athletic contest instilled all of the essential features of self-made manhood—toughness, courage under fire, perseverance, and (of course) character. Football especially also allowed for the constructive indulgence of the male passions, part of the more modern embrace of primitive masculinity and martial urges. Concurrently, team sports taught the requisite corporate values of teamwork and self-sacrifice. College was simultaneously recast as a safe place to accommodate a brush with some of the urban sporting culture experience. Raucous pranks, fights, and other manly strife, offered rough male bonding, while the magazines also characterized the campus as charged with a new sexual energy. A few years prior to this, such indulgences were derided as immoral and unhealthy, but now the middle-class magazines incorporated them via the college experience into an acceptable (indeed important) aspect of male college life.

Still, magazine authors cultivated American colleges as citadels of sophistication, sites to forge the refined elements of character and gain a civilized polish. Magazines posited college as an experience through which men could gain a sense of connection with something special and become part of an instant tradition and the superior upsurge of Western Civilization. Yet while depicted as a privileged place, college was also characterized in decidedly middle-class fashion. In other words, campuses allowed for meritocratic opportunity. Finally, the magazines offered numerous idealized heroes who united most of the emerging collegiate associations of the college experience. Scholar, athlete, fraternity man—these heroes were capable of violent action and raucous behavior yet remained refined, dignified gentlemen. The college experience as constructed by the magazines conveniently sustained cherished concepts of traditional manhood, while it allowed for the embrace of more modern notions of masculinity. Collectively, then, the magazines fully articulated this reworked image of college life, incorporated the college man into a new formula of ideal masculinity, and disseminated these new ideals on an unprecedented scale. It forever altered the image of college in America, but also played an unheralded yet critical role in facilitating shifts in masculinity as well.

Unquestionably the magazines served as chief conduits in a cultural refashioning not only of college but of middle-class male identity, pointing the way to shore up opportunities to buttress a flagging sense of virile, democratic, native-stock American manhood. The vast majority of college students or college characters in this magazine discourse were implied or directly noted as WASP or old-stock immigrant, so that the open invitation for readers to identity with the college experience in certain ways also served to reestablish racial barriers in a cultural setting. Women too, while encouraged to attend and while playing a major role in sexually energizing the college campus, ultimately functioned more in a traditional roles as helpmate and consort (or even just as sexually enticing extracurricular attractions of college life). While inviting readers to see themselves in new ways via the college experience, the magazines' cultural reconstructions of that experience and college manhood were fashioned with the particular needs and longings of native-stock American men firmly in mind.

Still, while these new intertwined narratives of the college experience bolstered native-stock prestige (simply by establishing college as a new avenue to desired identifications), immigrants do make enough of an appearance in the narratives of the college man (such as Ole at Siwash and the Chinese-American in "Under the Banyan") to offer hints at the potential pathways through collegiate identities to middle-class "whiteness." The cultural reconstruction of college, fashioned as it was initially to establish new class, gender, and racial parameters of cultural capital, could also furnish the cultural basis for inclusion, if one conformed to the emerging conceptions of middle-class experience in college—if one could be the college man.

One must not lose sight that this recrafting of the image of college and the college man occurred as these magazines wrestled with changes that drove the need for such alterations in masculine ideals—the shifting world of business. Undoubtedly the college man and the college experience were retooled to align with and facilitate evolving ideals of masculinity arising out of the dawning corporate age along with the racial and gender challenges of a modernizing and urbanizing America. Once created, the idealized, all-around college man transformed quite naturally into the model business leader of tomorrow in the pages of middle-class magazines, bringing with him the unique combination of masculine qualities that preordained his success.

4

Horatio Alger Goes to College

College, Corporate America, and the Reconfiguration of the Self-Made Ideal

Throughout 1906 Wallace Irwin led *Saturday Evening Post* readers on a delightfully humorous fictional tour of America's most prominent and prestigious campuses. Purporting to expose the truth behind these colleges and universities in mock-muckraking fashion, Irwin outlandishly magnified the well-known traits of the schools and their students incorporating twists on muckraker themes drawn from contemporary politics. For instance he exposed the gentleman's trust at Harvard and the democratic machine at Yale, trading on each institution's stereotypical student depictions. One of his most memorable and telling characters, however, he discovered at Princeton. Touring the campus Irwin encountered the "self-supporting student" on the steps of the library, "reading a volume of Xenophon which he held in his right hand, while with his left he sold socks, suspenders and collar-buttons to the passing undergraduates." The enterprising young man guided Irwin through his typical day. From five to seven in the morning he washed dishes, followed by two hours of cutting hair and tutoring on Goethe and Schiller. The balance of the morning he drove a grocery team for deliveries and then waited tables during lunchtime. He devoted his afternoons to "giving lessons on dancing and painting, filling teeth and sawing wood," with his evenings and spare time given over to study, recreation, and "devotional exercises."[1] Irwin fastened upon several of the common features that constituted the ideal self-supporting student. A newly minted cousin of the nineteenth-century self-made man, the student Irwin crafted seemingly captured all of the evolving characteristic elements of an ideal man for the new age—cultured yet vigorous, collegiate yet hard-working, learned yet enterprising. The *Post* ran numerous articles and fiction that nurtured such stereotypes, but Irwin likely drew from a much broader repertoire of evolving cultural images and ideals.

The self-supporting student was not the only novel creature to evolve from the self-made ideal. Even more significant, another collegiate cousin of traditional self-made lineage formed around the turn of the century. A 1901 *Munsey's* article profiled young Cornelius Vanderbilt, whose life refuted the charge that millionaire's lines lost "their virility within three generations." The day young Vanderbilt left Yale, the article crowed, he worked to improve his engineering and business skills by starting at the bottom, assuming a bench in the "ordinary machinist shops" of the New York Central Railroad. "Shoulder by shoulder with the men on a daily wage," the article continued, "[he] has wrought his way upward through various divisions of the motive power department."[2] A college graduate marked for management learned the ropes and won promotion on his merit, one of the earliest examples in the media chronicling management-track training designed purposefully to emulate the rise of the self-made man in business. While the rich, college-educated sons of the self-made men who built America might have been some of the first to experience the necessity of proving themselves through starting at the bottom (recalling the *Post*'s fictional Pierrepont Graham, see introduction),[3] they represented only the leading element of a new trend.

The years surrounding the turn of the century witnessed the massive corporate reorganization of American business—integrated enterprises, interlocking business structures, and the advent of "professional" managers. These new corporate businesses, however, also met with heated criticism from new breeds of social activists alarmed by the size of the trusts, labor unrest, and the harsh realities of economic change. To meet these challenges many businessmen embraced some elements of what one might term "progressivism." They sought to eliminate waste by enhancing efficiency (the new mantra and supreme ideal).[4] As business, labor, and social historians have noted, hiring college-educated men (particularly engineers) constituted one important element of progressive business practice. This practice aimed at one level to rapidly fill management posts and, on another level, served to gain for management control of the production process from laborers in the name of scientific efficiency.[5] On a practical level we know why corporations began to hire some college-educated men, but college education and, thus, the authority of the college-educated manager were invested with meaning beyond that of simply instilling scientific knowledge and efficiency.[6] What remains unclear is how the concept of going to college became reworked and integrated into the cultural matrices of masculine identity and notions of advancement.

One integral aspect of this interconnected transformation that remains unexplored, however, is the component exemplified by Irwin's character and young Vanderbilt toiling at the workman's bench—the college man reveling in hard labor and rising on his own merits, true to the self-made model. The self-made man remained a key ideal in the American conception of success, with the self-made businessman as the archetype. Mass magazine editors (much like the corporate middle class themselves) retained a reverence for the self-made man, even as they helped to inspire this evolving class to embrace modern corporations and consumer identities.[7] Lorimer at the *Post*, for example, labored to translate the Victorian attributes of the self-made man into the modern age, attaching them to the salesman and manager. Other magazines strove to do the same.[8]

The editors and writers of these new periodicals knew their prime readership—"The Plain Businessman." They understood his longings and anxieties facing a new age. Perhaps both of these new college versions of the self-made man could be seen as ways that the magazines helped the future sedentary manager (assumed to be a native-born, white American)—with his precious few claims to self-made manhood and his notions of virile masculinity challenged by immigrant working men—to construct himself in ways that simultaneously satisfied each demand. He could sustain links to traditional notions of manhood (that he possessed character) by either working through college or rising on the job, emulating his father. And through exhibiting such masculine vigor and energy (perhaps even having played football in college) he could counter the challenge posed by the immigrant workmen he managed.[9] Few immigrants and no minorities enter into these new stories of American business success and opportunity. Functioning as cultural spokesmen for their middle-class readers, magazine editors and writers forged marvelous new models of how to achieve business success that combined traditional conceptions and modern demands all helping to legitimize managerial authority— created as much for the new middle-class businessman as to impress the working class.[10] This evolution of the self-made ideal marks the final, and perhaps most significant, component of the multifaceted re-envisioning of college and middle-class manhood that proceeded in tandem within the pages of middle-class periodicals, helping their readers adjust to a brave new world.

The Working College Student

Just as the question of college for the corporate world loomed as a constant presence from the very beginning as these magazines pondered the place of college in American life, the self-supporting student surfaced early on as a new self-made mutation making the college experience less pretentious. In the magazines surveyed, references (including mentions and features from articles, editorials, or fiction) to the working student as a model occurred 67 times. The vast majority (42) came in the *Post*, which should not prove shocking given Lorimer's already noted interest in both college and opportunity. The *Post* also offered the most articles or editorials (10) and the most fiction (2) that featured or focused on the working student as an ideal. Most references, however, are "mentions," and occurred most prominently in all magazines from 1898 to 1904, in what I have termed the "foundational period" introducing the idea of college and positing it as critical to middle-class identity. Quite often the mention of the working student functioned as an antidote to the perceived wealth and luxury increasingly associated with college, his presence acting in part to reassure Americans that colleges still possessed healthy democratic elements. This proved a powerful recurring theme in *Post* editorials and in a prominent exposé serial by Owen Johnson in *Collier's* in 1912 (see chapter 3). References could also function as a new form of Horatio Alger tales. For example, the self-supporting college years at DePauw and its character-forming aspects always received mention in over a dozen articles spread across the *Post* and *Collier's* covering or penned by Senator Albert Beveridge of Indiana.[11]

Two types of articles bear particular attention, a "how-to" genre focused on paying for college, and the integration of working students into the *Post*'s standard and ubiquitous tales of manly success, occurring almost exclusively after 1905. These articles pointedly prompted the reader to reconfigure not only their accepted notions of who could go to college, but also that it could function as a site where sons looking toward a business career could gain the still-revered lessons of self-made manhood.

Just as editors strenuously sustained the belief in the self-made man, so the magazines applied the same optimism to the self-made student. Opportunities to rise through willpower were the same whether one went to college or dove into the world of affairs. Magazine articles assured readers that if one truly wanted a college education, opportunities abounded to work one's way through, and this method provided the added benefit of shielding the college student from the vices of college luxuries and snobbishness, teaching him to respect hard work and its virtues.

Much like modern advice literature on how to pay for college, the advent of "how-to" articles in the popular magazines—advising parents and students on the various ways to pay for college—signified the increasing popularity of college-going as a new route for advancement that simultaneously preserved self-made ideals. The *Post* ran two separate articles in 1900 advising young men and their parents on the nuts and bolts of working through school, "How to Be Self-Supporting at College" and "Through Harvard on Fifty Cents." Both detailed the many job opportunities and democratic spirit. In "Through Harvard on Fifty Cents," the author assured readers that while Harvard was expensive and known as a "rich man's school," the worthy poor boy could work his way through or find scholarships, graduate with honors, and thereby gain a far deeper satisfaction than the rich boy. The author advised one typical, time-honored route—tutoring the dull sons of the rich. He relayed his own story of arriving in Cambridge with only fifty cents. He secured a loan from a friend of the family and worked in a bookstore, dining and living frugally, spending less then three dollars per week.[12]

In *Collier's* 1902 "The College Man of Today," a Yale professor fastened upon the working student-athlete as the new ideal type, part of the balanced, civilized-primitive that emerged as the principal model that college could supply for leaders of tomorrow. After cataloguing in "how-to" fashion the kinds of jobs available, the professor recounted several stories of scholar-athletes who worked through school and upon graduation received business positions with top salaries. Working ensured they remained grounded, while athletics allowed them access to membership in the top clubs. The art accompanying the article even sustained the civilized-primitive ideal of the modern college man. In contrast to college students of old, pictured as stunted ascetics hunched over a desk, the modern student was illustrated as both an athlete (in crew gear with oar) and a robust scholar (in cap and gown), upholding the manly, civilized side of the modern student and part of the new self-made ideal possessing the proper "sand" in their character.[13]

Forrest Crissey's 1903 *Post* article "How Modern College Students Work Their Way" captured the novelty of "modern students" and the routing of typical rags-to-riches tales through the college gates. Crissey opened by noting that the old-style, self-made student, the poor divinity student cutting wood to meet college expenses, no longer represented the "universal experience of the American boy working his way through college."[14] Instead, he chronicled the tales of more modern American students, such as the son of an immigrant miner waiting tables at the University of Chicago and the athletes employed by Chicago reform politicians to ensure fair elections. Crissey gleefully noted how one freshman athlete not only kept the election fair but "upheld the dignity of his colors and pounded into the sluggers of the First Ward a new respect for higher education"—a shining example of a new hero, the civilized yet manly college man.[15] He also identified several modern enterprising students who exhibited business talent in solving their financial problems. One started a messenger-and-shopping service, while others worked as night clerks in drugstores and hotels. Such characterizations in the popular media masculinized the college experience, rendering it a worthy place to forge character and experience for the world of affairs while it also legitimized college as a more open and democratic proving ground.[16]

For all his examples of democratic working students, however, Crissey (and all the other writers mentioned here) did not mention a single *immigrant* working his way through (although a second-generation immigrant was mentioned). Crissey devoted a paragraph to the working college girl but not immigrants. Such pointed omissions places in sharp relief the assumptions that guided accepted notions of the ideal American college student and that likely informed such writers as Crissey. If the magazines had truly wanted to celebrate the democratic nature of modern college students in America, they certainly could have found some working immigrant students—urban and Roman Catholic institutions of higher education were full of them. But that obviously did not fit their assumptions or purpose. Consider too how one of the "jobs" profiled by Crissey involved knocking heads in Chicago's First Ward to ensure fair elections. It requires no great leap of imagination to conjure what types of Americans (eastern and southern European immigrants) needed such proper discipline administered by upstanding, middle-class college youth. These omissions and references again speak volumes about the assumed racial nature of the readership and the creation of new ideals and collegiate visions for that readership. These were not periodicals, despite their "mass" nature, written for a more proletarian audience, like newspapers, that included immigrants.[17]

While earlier articles labored to cultivate the new ideal, the 1911 *Post* article "Financing a College Education" evidenced the notion as an accepted model. While continuing to offer advice on typical work opportunities, the author championed the self-supporting democratic student as an acknowledged new force in college and American life that helped to explain why Andrew Carnegie had changed his opinion of higher education. Whereas the old, irresponsible college lifestyle indeed produced leisured men unfit for the world of business, by contrast "the self-helping student fits easily into the world of work and wages." The article quoted one university professor who likened the American college to the new battleground of the survival of the fittest for American youth. The article, too, reiterated that even Harvard's clubs were growing less exclusive (with more self-supporting men) as Harvard became more democratic like the rest of the nation's colleges, an argument that reflected more the power of the ideal than any reality.[18]

The evidence of an increasing acceptance of the working student into the pantheon of self-made manhood may be seen in the celebration of the self-supporting college student in articles not focusing solely on college. By the late years of the first decade and beginning of the second in the *Post*, the working student frequently coexisted alongside the more established self-made aspiring businessmen in the regular articles and series focusing on the real-life stories of success. The *Post* ran many such articles on business success, often two or three an issue, the majority of which written by Forrest Crissey or Edward Mott Woolley as parts of ongoing series. One such series, "Getting on in the World," featured letters from businessmen and some professionals on how they achieved success in life, usually noting traditional trajectories from clerk or shop hand. Quite tellingly, the working college man became a presence in the series. One enterprising student began an advertising business on campus to pay for his education; he sold it to underclassmen upon his graduation so that they could follow in his footsteps.[19] A more typical self-supporter worked his way through at the bookbinding trade, repairing library and faculty books.[20] A later *Post* series by Forrest Crissey, "Some Efficiency Secrets," not only reinforced connections between college, science, and modern business efficiency, it now pointed to determined college students as great examples of the self-made spirit. One of Crissey's articles, for instance, highlighted a young apprentice who always found the most efficient way in his jobs. The apprentice, young Billy, had at first failed his entrance exam to the technical college, so he delivered papers in the morning while taking a double load of math and language at the local high school. He also read every evening at the town hall library. Once in college he went to work in the local foundry shop to earn money. He easily mastered new machines and always sought the most efficient technique. Billy combined desire and "scientific" understanding to find the ideal way and was then asked to teach the other workers his method, a perfect illustration of what the self-made college man could do in the work force.[21]

Undeniably, a college education increasingly became a desirable quality, especially for rising into positions of leadership, with magazines helping to establish such expectations. But certain elements commonly associated with the college man, such as the debauched college sport or the effeminate and leisured college classicist, bothered many writers and editors as they promoted college education as a new route to corporate success, just as it must have caused hesitation in many middle-class American parents contemplating their sons' futures. The creation and celebration of the self-made student served to mitigate such tensions. The "how-to" articles on working through college and the celebration of the self-supporting student connected this new phenomenon of college-going with the traditional values and image of the self-made man, even as the connection facilitated modern notions of education, job training, and advancement.

The Working Student in Magazine Fiction

While only a handful of short stories revolved around or featured a working student, the infusion of this new character into the cast of fictional heroes in story plots was significant, as it reinforced the ideal with potent development of such men as only fiction could do. For example, the author of the highly popular *Post* series on Harvard freshmen, Charles Macomb Flandrau, also penned an early short story featuring a self-supporting student. Unlike Flandrau's "Diary of a Harvard Freshman," which contained no working students, his "Kicker Lang—A Harvard Story," centered around two contrasting characters, a hard-working senior tutoring a ne'er-do-well freshman with excessive debts—a common vice attributed to wealthier college students. The freshman finds and "borrows" the savings of the hardworking "Kicker" Lang. Rather than turn in the young thief, Lang rehabilitates the smoking, gambling, out-of-shape boy into a model of collegiate manhood, like Lang himself. The boy learns that Lang had been a star athlete from a rich family until the financial ruin of his father forced him into an austere, monkish lifestyle, working his way through.[22] In the turn-of-the-century volatile business climate, Lang's character and family suffered from a common malady. Many short stories and biographical sketches utilized this subplot of the fallen rich. Yet unlike many of these tales where they were forced to quit school, Lang forged ahead undaunted as a self-supporting student, made more masculine by his association with football at the same time retaining the badge of learned cultivation. Such a character embodied the perfect moral, athletic, hardworking, self-made ideal, but now placed in the college rather than in the mining camp, shop, or office.

If stories featuring working students were potent but few, the increasing "mentions" of such activity in a main character's background proved even more significant. Several *Post* short stories integrated the self-supporting student into plots and characters that focused solely on business success. Like the passing reference to college football days to signify manliness, working through college often entered into the biographical profiles of fictional businessmen. In "My Rich Wife," a mining engineer recalled, "I was glad that I had been dirt poor and had washed dishes to start me on my way through college." This marked the character as a worthy and steadfast man, and exemplified the same fortitude that the character used later to rise in the mining firm (although our hero seemed to conveniently overlook his marriage to the owner's daughter as a possible aid in his rise).[23] Another story in the *Post*, "Keeping Up Appearances," featured a well-to-do college man being dressed down in the office of his self-made superior, whom the college man heartily resented. In the midst of this lecture the college man, a self-described example of shirtsleeves to shirtsleeves, thought back on those college mates who had excelled. One of these successful college friends, in contrast to himself, worked his way through college waiting tables and had started on the varsity eleven as well—both attributes setting the narrator's own apparently wasted college years in sharp relief. This son of the rich had failed to adhere to the evolving dictates of the self-made success model.[24] In these stories and others, being a self-supporting student helped clarify and define the business success that naturally came to individuals who had to struggle in the old self-made fashion. The interesting thing about these stories, though, was that the formative self-made struggle occurred not in the world of business but at the once reviled college.

Not surprisingly, the *Post* published the first serial that fully integrated college and business, with the hero's working-student past as vital in defining his character. David Graham Phillips's "The Cost" possessed some stereotypical college characters but with a new twist. Set in a midwestern state, Dumont, the son of an industrialist, goes off to college following the wishes of his mother that he should receive culture, only to return a typical college sport—drinking and gambling. He ends up taking over his father's business and eventually becomes a corrupt monopolist. His high school sweetheart and future wife, Pauline, also attends college, but for a time falls in love with a new variety of college hero, Hampden Scarborough—the self-made student.[25] A self-made man who hated pretentious elites, Scarborough's father disowned his son when the boy chose to attend college rather than stay on the farm. The boy longs for "an all-around" education and works his way through college.[26] A good student, a champion debater, he even leads the "barbs" in their overthrow of the "greeks" when the latter dominated a literary society, replacing the fraternity men's petty political squabbles with serious intellectual discussion. Scarborough embodies the new ideal, the democratic college man who excels at a wide range of activities.[27] Significantly, however, when jilted by Pauline, Scarborough proceeds through a seemingly requisite cycle of collegiate sin and redemption.

He descends for a brief time into the life of the classic college sport—drinking and gambling and indulging in expensive liquor and clothing.[28] Swearing off such behavior, though, he redeems himself by selling books in the summer to pay for school (which he had financed previously through gambling) and again selling books after graduation, becoming top salesman in the region and then manager.[29]

Although Scarborough decided to forgo a career in sales and management for the law and reform politics, he had proven his merit and fitness in the heat of business competition. Interestingly, the brief foray into the sporting life, too, was depicted less as an example of debauchery than as requisite rite of passage that actually functioned to paint Scarborough as more manly. He was a "manly" drinker and an exceptional gambler due to his "naturally bold spirit."[30] The appearance of Scarborough's character, then, marked a watershed in how mass magazine authors celebrated and fashioned the ideal college man. Scarborough was a naturally democratic leader of sound character, who desired an education and whose carousing, in effect, indicated less a corrupt person than a manly indiscretion, a requisite brush with the un-Victorian but authentically manly urban sporting culture. The story posited that the proper type of college man could excel in business and the real world—again, ideally both civilized and capable of primitive exhibitions of manhood. The fact that he had worked through school served as the foundational example of his masculine worth.

Coinciding with the masculinizing effect of football, college itself now became a potential self-made proving ground. Yet, college education still signified the acquisition of culture, refined breadth, or the modern knowledge increasingly necessary to rise in the corporate industrial world after college. "How-to" articles and advertisements not only upheld college as a real possibility for more Americans, they marked the working student as morally superior to the corrupted rich sons not working to meet their expenses. Through these articles and fictional stories, popular magazines actually wove college into the cultural fabric of American success mythology. They equated the old self-made man with his modern brother the self-supporting college student.

Notable, too, is the dearth of fictional self-supporting college students of an immigrant background. Unlike the articles on self-supporting students, however, where one found no examples of immigrants presented, the magazines analyzed for this study produced two short stories featuring foreign-born or immigrant characters nobly working their way through college. The "Jinrikisha Man" in the *Post* follows the travails of a poverty-stricken son of a Samurai in Japan as he works his way through college pushing a cart taxi (a jinrikisha). Ultimately, he proves his mettle (and his liberal learning) through an oratory

competition. *Munsey's* "Father and Son" featured the generational struggle between a German immigrant father, struggling at farming, and his son, who in-
sists on working his way through college, which the father regards as a waste of
time. In the end the boy redeems his father's fortunes and honor in a struggle
with the telephone company (the modern vs. the traditional conflict mirroring
the generational strife in the story), finishes college, and goes on to graduate
study at Harvard.[31]

On the surface these stories seem to testify to the fact that the new ideal of
the self-supporting college man as an "American" model of success was democratically open. Yet the "Jinrikisha Man" transpired at a safe distance (in a
foreign land), while "Father and Son" involved a relatively accepted immigrant
group in the United States, the Germans. The working student eventually
would prove a very democratic ideal, one that would offer a way for American
immigrants and minorities to lay claims to cultural legitimacy. But judging from
these magazines, that was not the original purpose of the narrative. Originally
the self-supporting student, as a new corollary of the old self-made man, was
constructed to legitimize the college student as potentially manly and worthy in
a traditional sense. And while it perpetuated the ideal of democratic opportunity inherent in the self-made model, in reality it functioned more to cloak the
middle-class college man in the aura of democratic legitimacy. Middle-class
magazines with their myriad examples of working, native-born white students,
in effect presented college to their anxious readers as an experience within the
honored tradition of the self-made man. And simultaneously they crafted that
vision to include only the "right sort" of American—a fascinating way the magazines paradoxically conceived a "democratic" pathway to privileged status for
their readers.

Many self-supporting students no doubt existed on college campuses. Ultimately, however, editors and writers in the popular magazines likely took
some "real life" examples and (what is most important) vastly enlarged their
significance, integrating the tale into the dominant cultural narrative of American masculinity then in the throes of transformation. Magazine editors and
writers fastened upon this trend, magnified it, and helped to define it, giving
it a broader cultural meaning. They crafted the self-supporting student from
the self-made hero mold and thus aided in the formation of a new American
hero.

The Self-Made College Man Goes to Work

An even more momentous change in the notion of American success may be
found with the incorporation of the college man into the up-through-the-ranks

model of advancement. The young man who came from humble origins, hired on as a shop apprentice or office boy or clerk, and then advanced up the accepted ladder to business clerk or shop foreman to manager or owner was the common trajectory of the self-made businessman. The model was readily adaptable, as well, for the emerging corporate, bureaucratic age. One learned skills on the job to advance. Such tales remained an essential part of business lore and the ethic of success. But around the turn of the century in magazine discourse, the college man entered into the equation, bringing the promise of science and cultivated breadth. Owners and managers likely saw an idealized version of themselves in the new college man, the future executive they wished to hire—mentally trained yet cultured, perhaps even a vigorous manly athlete. Football and curricular reforms had masculinized the college man and rehabilitated his image while the self-supporting student potentially fused the college man with the self-made formula. The integration of the college graduate into the up-through-the-ranks scheme of advancement, however, fully allowed the college man to prove himself in true self-made fashion.

As with the self-supporting student phenomenon, the popular magazines reflected and magnified a changing reality. The majority of executive businessmen at this time still remained noncollege men, but a few major railroads and industrial organizations were beginning to experiment with management-training tracks or special rotating assignments for those deemed potential management material. Owners and corporate officers were groping toward an answer to how to find and train managers for the burgeoning organizations in industrial and commercial fields.[32] For a variety of reasons a college education increasingly came to be viewed as potentially desirable, but only a handful of corporations had formal procedures for hiring and training managers, and college men had no monopoly on these positions. Popular magazine articles relayed these shifting beliefs and practices, enhanced their prominence, counted them as proof of growing opportunities, and portrayed them as a new aspect of the self-made tradition for a corporate age.

Not surprisingly, the *Saturday Evening Post* offered the most abundant examples of what one might term the self-made college man. George Horace Lorimer as the *Post*'s editor, led the way in articulating a vision of the ideal education and training of the future business executive. Lorimer's "Letters from a Self-Made Merchant to His Son" addressed the generational anxiety attached to the so-called big man's dilemma—how to train the business leaders of tomorrow. In this regard, college seemed the perfect answer to the crisis of business leadership that many felt as the new century dawned. According to Old Gorgon Graham, though, his son Pierrepont and all college graduates still had to exorcise their faults and prove their fitness in traditional self-made fashion. Gorgon Graham's early letters were filled with lectures on the college man's propensity to expect too much for too little work and to exhibit excess self-pride — to be "chesty." These lessons echoed common complaints of businessmen and offered (not just to Pierrepont) the college readers of the magazine sage advice on how to conduct themselves when hired in the real world.[33]

Most significantly, though, Lorimer in the form of Old Gorgon Graham presented a blueprint for the breaking and training of the college man, the future executive. Pierrepont began on the slaughterhouse floor. He then transferred to billing clerk, salesman and, finally, a district manager over the course of many letters from 1901 through 1903.[34] Along the way he learned the lesson of not looking down upon the immigrant boss who had himself worked up the ranks, but rather to appreciate the Irishman's gruff honesty. He learned too not to waste the company's time writing letters to pretty ladies (he accidentally sent one to a business client who informed Pierrepont's father).[35] Over the course of the articles Lorimer presented 6 separate examples of how not to promote sons prematurely to high business positions, injected as foils to the example of Pierrepont. Pierrepont's friend, Coartland Warrington, for example, had started at the top and worked his way down after his father gave him an interest in the concern. Old Gorgon Graham had informed his son in the first letter, indicating the importance of this lesson for the whole series, that he had to start at the bottom and earn his way up the firm by proving his ability.[36]

Lorimer's highly popular "Letters" series captured the anxiety of many American businessmen as they observed the changes occurring around them. The men who had built industrial America, though filled with optimism and pride in what they had produced, wondered how they would find competent successors? How would they train their sons, giving them the collegiate liberal culture the previous generation lacked along with the specialized training increasingly necessary in the modern world, and still make them tough enough to prove themselves in the self-made mold? Lorimer's answer, though highly illustrative, was not original. Of 108 references (including both features and mentions in fiction, articles, and editorials) to this self-made collegian/up-through-ranks model in the four magazines surveyed for this study, nearly two-thirds (72) occurred in the *Post* between 1900 and 1905, a slightly inflated number owing to the presence of the Old Gorgon Graham series (see table 1). Most references were also merely mentions, but they are highly significant and form the preponderance of my examples. They fall into one of three categories: profiles of businessmen, articles or editorials on opportunities, and advice articles on a career choice, such as *Cosmopolitan*'s "Making a Choice of a Profession." Early on the latter two quite often took the form of articles revolving around the question of college for a business career. Mentions of a college grad working up through the ranks, however, became more numerous in profiles as the years advanced, so that when a seasoning period in the shops was referenced for the college man after graduation, it functioned as an implicit model of advancement for emulation.

A constant refrain echoed through articles reporting on these changes. True to the self-made mold, the college man must begin at the bottom. In "Why Young Men Should Begin at the Bottom," an article that likely inspired Lorimer's Old Gorgon Graham, the former mayor of Brooklyn preached that if any business was to be protected from failure, then those who head it, especially wealthy sons, must begin at the bottom. And while he thoroughly endorsed college education as the best equipment for a mercantile or manufacturing career, again a progressive position, the college man must assent "to be an ordinary apprentice."[37] Similarly, a 1901's *Munsey's* writer, while acknowledging college as the new route to success in business, cautioned the college graduate not to expect to start at the top, as was too often the case, he believed. The writer described one college-educated railroad president who considered himself lucky to have begun as a leveler on a road gang.[38] One technical college president quoted in a 1900 *Post* article commenting on the revolutionized attitude of employers toward "liberally and practically trained" college men, offered a letter from Andrew Carnegie praising two employees who had graduated from the college and had risen to the positions of general manager and plant superintendent. Carnegie and the college president pointed out that these two men had started at "menial jobs," one literally scooping manure.[39] In his 1902 article "Should Railroad Men Be College Men?" Charles F. Thwing, president of Western Reserve University, quoted several top railroad officials who enthusiastically endorsed a liberal and technical college education as particularly beneficial for those advancing to "higher positions." Most of those quoted in the article cautioned that college men must not think they "know it all," and must content themselves to start "at the lowest round of the ladder."[40]

Such magazine coverage captured the beginnings of a transformation occurring in American business regarding college education and the training of management, but the belief in proving oneself by rising remained, incorporated into the evolving equation of success. As one 1907 article in the *Post* observed, for the young man of that day the world had changed substantially from his father's day, becoming "consolidated, capitalized and incorporated." Had opportunities dissipated? Yes, if measured by older standards, argued the author. But typical of the new genre of advice articles, this *Post* writer echoed

Lorimer and other editors in heralding the arrival of the "Salaried Man." The trusts desperately needed good men and scoured the colleges and technical schools for them. If one was willing to work upward from the bottom, the opportunities seemed as grand as ever.[41]

The *Post* and other popular magazines carried numerous articles describing real-life examples of men and companies forging this new model of executive training in action. Like Old Gorgon's son, Pierrepont, some issued from wealthy families, received a college education and yet worked their way up either out of principle or necessity. Recall the *Munsey's* article of 1901 profiling young Cornelius Vanderbilt rising into management after working "shoulder to shoulder" with wage-earners in the New York Central machine shops. Similarly, a 1902 *Post* article lauded the president of the New York Central, who despite wealth followed his liberal education by beginning as a rodman.[42] Many articles detailed the successful rise of railroad executives or industrial managers during the first decade of the century, evidencing both the need for college education and the typical trajectory of advancement from the shops to the top as a vital component of their seasoning. One railroad president described by business writer Forrest Crissey in 1903 as a fiercely proud MIT graduate, rose to his first general manager position at the tender age of twenty-nine, but cautioned that he had earned the swift rise. He reminisced how his summer breaks were occupied by "hard service" on the railroad surveying gangs. Technically, he had earned his self-made stripes.[43]

While the magazines continued to document the rise of noncollege, self-made men in the corporate setting, the trend toward hiring the college-educated man pointed to a definite alteration in the assumption of self-made success that magazines amplified. Businessmen now sought to hire the college man and endorsed a college education in growing numbers. They believed that by definition the college man was more qualified to rise to positions of leadership.[44] Similarly, when B. C. Forbes questioned the innovative bank president Frank Vanderlip on how he chose vice presidents, Vanderlip rattled off many traditionally admirable qualities (frankness, honesty, capable, red-blooded), but added that he preferred college-educated men for their trained minds and "broad gauged" intelligence.[45]

Of necessity, great organizations clung to the idea of training future managers and executives by making them learn the business from the bottom up. This was no creation of the media. Not only did such a practice mirror the rise of the ideal self-made man (and how the managers and owners likely saw themselves), it made logical sense. The ideal manager had to see the big picture. But increasingly, the college man was specifically placed in such positions with the expectation that he would rise. Starting the college man at the bottom would season him and test whether he was tough. This seasoning simulated the self-made trajectory on purpose, both out of tradition and of necessity. Such management trainees, nonetheless, bore only a pale resemblance to the self-made men of old. Scions of elite families like T. Coleman DuPont could be christened a self-made man since the company's nascent management-training track prescribed starting him and other managers at the bottom. DuPont began scooping coal after graduating from MIT, in the best tradition of the self-made man.[46]

The college man, even the likes of DuPont, had to prove himself. These management tracks resembled the old self-made paths to the executive offices for that reason. But to label the college men increasingly hired into management-track positions as self-made men indicated in reality the transformation of that ideal. The magazine coverage of these changes touched upon a very real evolution in the conception of choosing and training executives that was highly complex in its development. But the popular magazines translated these changes into familiar conceptual terms—they utilized the self-made man model. Casting these college-educated managers as newfangled self-made men legitimized on the one hand their authority in a traditional sense. They had earned their way. The articles employed the rugged language of the self-made tradition, further masculinizing collegians long held in suspicion by the business world. On the other hand, while retaining the façade of up-through-the-ranks, self-made mobility, only those supposedly broadly educated and trained enough for the highest levels of management would be allowed onto the ladder. Thus, the self-made man remained a cherished ideal integrated even into the modern conception of the college-educated organization man, constituting a fundamental shift in notions of authority. Magazine articles depicting these shifts interpreted them back to their readers encoded in language at once pronouncing the changes as both traditional and progressive—exactly the way their middle-class readers liked to see themselves. The reworked image of college proved a critical element enabling the creation of this new hybrid manager, allowing him to fulfill, again, so many different aspects of masculine authority.

Magazine Fiction and the College-Educated, Self-Made, Corporate Man

Not surprisingly, the adaptation of the self-made hero to the emerging dictates of the industrial and corporate world left its imprint on the fiction in popular magazines as well. An increasing number of business stories focused on the various problems of the shifting American business scene. Labor unrest, stock speculation, the evil trust, all received attention in the popular magazines either as central features or settings for action or love. Such tales usually wove lessons and advice on accepted notions of achieving success into their themes, plots, and characters, as well. The rise of a key character often formed an important element in the stories. On the other hand, the business settings served only as a backdrop to driving plots of love and intrigue, but even brief mentions of a character's background in such stories often pointed to the changing attributes of middle-class male heroes regarding the place of college in forming their identities. All these stories offered idealized versions of perceived business reality. They were, in effect, morality tales laced with traditional American success themes—hard work, honesty, loyalty, and the like. But the settings and characters also reflected the profound changes with which businessmen and the new middle class generally coped. These tales provide a window on the way some authors and editors reflected on, articulated, and projected ideals and values fashioned for a new business age. The evolving treatment of college education provides a perfect example of how business fiction helped to adapt and reshape accepted cultural narratives of middle-class American identity and authority to fit emerging conceptions of success in a corporate world.

The typical hero of business fiction in the popular magazines around the turn of the century resembled the Horatio Alger hero, with some critical new corporate middle-class twists. While many such characters began as messenger boys and clerks and rose to run their own businesses, other characters appeared who worked their way up to serve in corporate positions as superintendents and managers, reflecting the changing business landscape. In the 1890s, for example, *Cosmopolitan* led the field in publishing business fiction and several of its stories featured the new corporate-style hero.[47] After 1900 the *Post* took business fiction even farther than *Cosmopolitan*. Each issue ran at least one, but quite often two, short tales of business in addition to the numerous articles offering business advice and information to the aspiring young man.[48] As late as 1910, when articles and stories noted the crisis of the clerk and the necessity of education, the ideal business hero often still rose without benefit of education.

Although these stories and characters preserved much of the self-made ideal (see chapter 1), they were in themselves a telling evolution, and collegiate references began to enter into the character sketches in business fiction at this time. Naturally, fiction in these magazines reflected the same discourse occurring elsewhere in the periodicals regarding the ways to fashion worthy successors to the self-made Captains of Industry. The first stories that explored this generational transition and the entrance of these sons into the business world often treated the college experience as something to be overcome—unquestionably good for rounding off the rough edges and making the future executive heir a gentleman leader, but also teaching effete and luxurious habits that only hard work at the bottom of the firm would break.[49] That these college-educated characters had entered so noticeably into fiction reflected the growing appeal of this new ideal.

Yet such fictional representations of this transformation also revealed a deep ambivalence toward the college-educated successors (often their sons) to the self-made man. They had to purge their college pretensions and prove their worth in a self-made fashion before their true worth (and the promise of their college education) could shine through. For instance, a comic piece of business fiction from the *Post*, "How Miss Wilcox Was Fired," captured the generational transition, negative stereotypes of college men, and the impending crisis of the uneducated clerk to rise within the system. A long-suffering clerk acts as the narrator of the tale, lamenting that the youngest son of one of the firm's partners had come home from college and quickly replaced the old clerk as head of the office. Old man Furber worships his young son and thinks he would run the business well as soon as the boy "worked the Latin and Greek out of his system." The older brother, George, and the devoted clerk, however, both thought that young Ed conducted business as "he went to his classes at college, as if he could miss a couple of days and make up for them later, when he happened to be in the humor." The action of the story, though, revolves around the hiring and firing of the beautiful but inept Miss Wilcox, over whom the brothers tussle as rivals for her affection. Eventually she falls for George, teaching the college graduate a lesson about business and responsibility in the process.[50] Young Ed represents the fulfillment of his self-made father's aspirations—a college-educated businessman, who, with the proper seasoning, becomes the ideal genteel businessman. But the college lifestyle, reflective on one level of the dangers of elite ideals, first has to be purged—the son must learn self-made lessons.[51]

If laziness was one typical knock on the college man, so were too-lofty expectations. The 1902 *Collier's* story "A Checked Love Affair" revolves around a young college graduate in love with his boss's daughter and his need to prove himself by rising, a task he accomplishes. Unlike many previous heroes, however, the lead character charges out of college into business, "filled with the laudable ambitions of showing Wall Street what a valuable thing a university education is to a business man, and of becoming president of the institution within five years."[52] This character (the unnamed narrator in the story) exhibits the stereotypical cockiness of the college-bred entering business, another trait about which businessmen constantly complained. The narrator admits, though, that after five years he remains only a teller, and that he had paid more attention to the figures at cotillions than those on ledgers—another typical complaint. Nevertheless, he too receives inspiration from the boss's daughter and her father who inform him that it must be a long engagement in order for the college boy to prove himself worthy of the salary necessary to support his proposed wife.[53] College men still possessed liabilities that only hard work at the bottom could purge, but the college boy in the *Collier's* story relished his business opportunity and went into the fray to teach Wall Street a lesson. And though at first suffering the requisite humiliation, he succeeded. As the first decade of the new century progressed, more and more short stories took up the theme of the college man entering business by paying one's dues and proving one's worth in a self-made fashion as major subthemes.[54]

Arthur Train's "The Inheritance" once again presented college as a playground of the rich, but in a new twist, developed the college-educated young sport as an ideal example of what he could accomplish if properly inspired through the promise of promotion and hard work. The author describes the college graduate character in the story, Bob Hammersly, as a "useless ornamental member of society."[55] His Harvard education provided little except to cultivate a "taste for wines, liquors, cigars, and a steady poker hand."[56] Known at his club as a gentleman, though, Hammersly finds himself the recipient of an interesting proposition. An older man at the club, who had no heirs, promises to leave his business and fortune to the young sport if Hammersly gives up alcohol and tobacco, and begins to work in the furnaces at the shop in the factory he may one day inherit—if he passes the test. Hammersly consents and eventually embraces a regimented, spartan life. The author plays up the young man's shop work, the hard toil, and satisfying labor. Due to the dearth of intellectual stimulation among his laboring co-workers, though, Hammersly takes up the reading habit that he had let slip since college, and his reading ranges over a wide array of topics. He earns the position of shop superintendent and from his reading on economics, labor, and sociology he opens a men's club for employees, which stimulates them intellectually and physically. In the end, the old man leaves nothing except a note stating that he had in fact willed young Hammersly a future. Of course, the young man is grateful.[57]

Hammersly perfectly exemplifies the leadership potential of the college man if trained in a self-made fashion to cultivate his special skills and manhood. Though his college education at first functions to color him as a stereotypical sport, he later displays the way his collegiate preparation forms a real intellectual foundation for growth and leadership; certainly it demarcates him from his working-class colleagues. Not only does he rise through the ranks and learn the business, he uses his intellect and education to make the business more progressive. He had worked with the laborers but was not of them, his college education and management-track training clearly setting him apart, but only after he had proven himself in self-made fashion.

Roughly after 1905, an increasing number of stories featured college-educated businessmen. The college experience received a different portrayal as well. Gone were references to immature behavior and immoral activity. More often the stories used college as a defining characteristic denoting intellect, ability, and potential, a potential almost always demonstrated again by working one's way up through the ranks. These stories broke down often into two sets. The college-educated business aspirant was either the son of a nouveau-riche, self-made man (or related to such wealth) or a college man (often middle class) hired into a corporation. Although on a first pass the second set of stories might seem more critical (and they are highly significant), one cannot dismiss the first set as inconsequential simply because the protagonists were wealthy. Taking the form of generational transition, such stories pointed to the heart of evolving ideas of what ideally composed the new corporate leader, the manager. What type of education and preparation would be best suited to mold future leaders? The answer that the magazines most often championed took on its most developed form in these two sets of business fiction stories. College education bestowed the requisite polish, modern training, and perhaps through athletic prowess manly character. In all these stories, however, working up through the ranks and stamping oneself in the self-made mold proved equally critical and marked these young businessmen not only as qualified but also as worthy and legitimate, proven so through the emulation of the self-made trajectory even if such a route was planned. Here again, magazine writers and editors took issues beginning to percolate through American society, amplified them, and disseminated ideal models for emulation.

College education and the proper training of future corporate leaders figured prominently in many stories. Normally, they took the form of "mentions," references that established a character's background. Omitting the Old Gorgon Graham series, there are twenty-four short stories in the *Post* containing significant mentions of a college man working up though the ranks, most of these mentions occurring after 1905. *Munsey's* and *Collier's* (which did not publish much business fiction) offered only six specific mentions, while *Cosmopolitan* boasted six, basically one a year between 1905 and 1910. (Keep in mind that such references are distinct from fiction that more pointedly mixed college and business.) One marvelous example of the subtle way significant collegiate references slipped into character formations, thereby establishing such idealized connections as normative for such heroes, occurred at the beginning of a prominent 1909 serial in the *Post*, "The White Mice," a tale of business intrigue and international adventure. The main character is Rodman Forrester, "a cele-brated Yale pitcher," who goes abroad on business for his father's company. "Roddy" graduates to this responsibility after just a brief (and seemingly requi-site for the college man) seasoning in the machine shops of one of his father's factories.[58]

In 1907 one serialized story, "The Cave Man," centers on business intrigue with two prominent characters possessing college educations. The first install-ment opens at an alumni day at Harvard with the main character, Wister, attending the function at his alma mater. The focus of this first story revolves around Wister's recruitment and training of his graduating cousin for a man-agement position in his auto manufacturing plant. Wister is delighted when Billy produces his senior thesis on the trust question for which he even received a grade of B rather than the traditional "gentleman's C."[59] Significantly, Wister sends Billy immediately upon graduation to the factory floor to be trained from the bottom up. The author interjects how the foremen relish the honor of training their future boss.[60] Billy (and Wister) epitomize the modern business hero. They head a progressive company, fight an evil trust spearheaded by a noncollege man, and use research and development to help forge an efficient "good" trust. Both are Harvard educated and obviously put their educations to good use, but whereas Wister's masculinity is signified not only by business sense but by athletic prowess (explored in chapter 5) Billy displays his worthi-ness by starting at the bottom to learn the ropes.[61]

Another group of short stories feature sons of self-made wealth who pro-ceed incognito to gain business experience at the bottom and rise on their own merits, in order to avoid any deference that might be given them due to their well-known names. In one 1909 serial "The Spread Eagle," Fitzhugh Williams abandons his studies at Oxford (though in good standing) immediately upon his twenty-first birthday in order to return to Cleveland and his father. After an idealized reunion with the old dad where they share cigars and a baseball out-ing, he informs his father that he wants to learn the family business his father built, but without any special favors, or as Fitzhugh put it, being credited with brains before he had earned them. He enters employment as a clerk under his mother's maiden name and, more importantly for the story, wins a girl on his own merits in the process.[62] The desire to rise without nepotism, of course, marks the hero as a modern self-made man despite his privileged past. His col-lege education seemed almost a prerequisite for legitimate leadership that a management-track, up-through-the-ranks training further seasoned.

While business fiction featuring the sons of self-made wealth constituted one representation of generational and business transition, another significant set of stories surfaced with an even more modern business hero. Business fiction increasingly mentioned college education or college athletics as components defining central characters, an important shift that reflected less the increasing numbers of college-educated businessmen than the idealization of that man as a new leader. More revealing were those short stories that dwelled or focused upon the collegiate backgrounds of central characters who were *not* sons of wealth and who epitomized the new corporate middle-class route to success.[63]

In the *Post*'s "The Triumph of Billy," the hero was a "Tech grad of '02" hired on by an Illinois electrical company—an industry that led the way in hiring college graduates as future managers. He fights both the prejudice of the self-made owner, whose daughter he loves, and the prejudices of class in the form of a rival in love from a prominent landed family. Billy emerges triumphant, winning the daughter and proving his worth (and that of all college men) to the self-made owner. Billy's rise through the company is somewhat ambiguous in the story, but the reader is left to assume he rose on his own merits from the lower ranks, since he is said to occupy a management position despite the fact that the owner preferred to promote noncollege men.[64]

In 1916 the "The Pampered Fledgling" featured a similar cast of characters negotiating the new channels of class and mobility. A girl from a prominent elite family, Eunice Weston, falls in love with Will Store, the son of the town drugstore owner—decidedly lower-middle class. Eunice's drunken older brother, signifying the corrupt older dictates of class, disapproves of the romance even though Will "had gone to technical college, earning most of his way through, and was now working for the telephone company in Pittsburgh."[65] In other words, Will personifies the new middle-class hero. Rising from solid but humble stock but not seeking to stay in the family business, he works his way through college and is hired on by a modern, progressive industry. The story details that Will has forty men working under him, indicating that he had risen quickly, probably on a management track but still demonstrating his merit by traditional self-made standards and his fitness to command men.[66]

College helped to define these new middle-class business heroes in these and similar stories as modern business professionals as well as worthy consorts to genteel young ladies, while also manly heirs in the self-made tradition.[67] A college education had ceased to indicate obvious elite character liabilities in need of purging. Identification as a college graduate had become a badge of status marking one for swift advancement, legitimizing the manager of men who, after a ceremonial self-made rise via a management track shuffling through the lower levels of a company, took his triumphal place as a modern leader of men. Indeed, in the two stories noted above, the characters' rise through the ranks was left implied, a telling shift from earlier years when a college man's swift ascent into management needed to be explained.

The characters that paraded through the business and general fiction of middle-class mass magazines around the turn of the century, and in the years following, provided vivid and revealing portrayals of the shifting idealized components of business success. Writers strove to adapt the self-made hero to the evolving corporate business setting, creating heroes that rose through the ranks of shop or office to positions of management. Business ideals dictated starting at the bottom, with everyone possessing the same opportunities. When college graduates began to enter the business fiction landscape, they too were required to begin at the bottom with no special favors. In fiction, college associations could function as cultural shorthand indicating the spoiled son of wealth. But fiction naturally mirrored transforming attitudes toward college education manifested elsewhere in the magazines and throughout society—the advent of manly college athletics and the increasing recognition of and desire for the mental and cultural benefits of college attendance. A growing number of characters in business fiction (or business-related characters in general fiction) appeared whose college identification hinted at positive character traits or potential leadership talent. These characters still had to struggle and prove themselves, but college had penetrated the equation of self-made business success. Soon, a college education helped explain and justify the distinctions of the rising business hero. The college-educated business hero seemed quite naturally to think of modern, progressive methods to improve production or address a labor issue. Rising through the ranks became more a ritual process, necessary for future managers to learn the business and remain true to the ideal of the self-made man. Some business-related stories, however, even left this process of self-made seasoning implied or unstated.

These new characters, this new hero in middle-class magazine fiction, might have reflected aspects of a shifting reality. But even in the second decade of the twentieth century, few firms systematically hired and trained college graduates. This new hero represented the way magazine fiction writers helped fashion a new ideal, a new "norm" for the middle-class American man long before it became a common reality. Such fiction helped to establish the parameters of the possible, and in this context one should remember the persistence of powerful racial assumptions imbedded in the new cultural narratives of middle-class masculine authority.

One story featured an immigrant college graduate working up to a position of authority and respect in business (see chapter 2). Montague Glass's "The Efficient Salamander," depicted the immigrant Jewish experience in America, and the middle-class reading public seemed fascinated by it. The "salamander" in the story was hired by two Jewish textile manufacturers out of a favor to his father, the owner of their building. Although the boy seemed more concerned with how a scientific manager should dress, he quickly diagnosed several efficiency problems. Ultimately in the story, though, his father disowned him over his love for one of the working girls, and he must then set to work to support her, which he does, eventually reconciling with the father. Of the few examples of fiction with immigrant characters, "The Efficient Salamander" was the only one to feature a true new immigrant.[68]

The college man rising through the ranks was a narrative developed for the readers of these periodicals, and it communicated a new route to secure superiority in a shifting world, all while preserving cherished notions of meritocratic advancement. This model of success culturally established a new ideal route that privileged the native-born white American and allowed them to claim, through college education, a professional and civilized education that naturally marked one for leadership, while the ideal of working up-through-the-ranks to management allowed them to claim to have earned it in self-made fashion. According to this masterful new narrative, native-born white executives deserved the respect and admiration of their laborers (if they conformed to this new model) both for their civilized authority (as college grads) and for their proven democratic rise.

Conclusion

In *Creating America*, Jan Cohn depicted Lorimer's "Letters from a Self-Made Merchant to His Son" as representative of a clash of cultures. The protagonist championed the old business culture of the self-made man in competition with the emerging corporate world with its college educated upstarts. It was a culture clash of sorts, but one that must be placed in a broader context of cultural adjustment amid massive economic change. Old Gorgon Graham and the self-made generation of businessmen he represented, in building up the great industrial and corporate organizations of America, had by their very success altered the rules of business. They faced the dilemma of how to find and train their literal and figurative heirs to lead these organizations.

The mass magazines were intimately intertwined with the emergence of this new middle class of corporate businessmen, who went by names from white-collar office workers to budding professional accountants to the manager and executive in office or factory. They and their families could increasingly turn to periodicals such as the *Post* for cues about how to make sense of their changing world, a world they had a hand in remaking. The new middle-class magazines guided and helped to shape shifting self-definitions.

A central element in this broader cultural adjustment was the creation of the twentieth-century organization man—the evolution of the heroes and ideal characterizations of the quintessential American businessman in a new era. The *Post* and other periodicals helped to forge a new set of ideals and icons, a synthesis of old and new that occurred alongside (and was bound up with) a re-ordering of conceptions of college, masculinity, and middle-class success. The college man and the businessman were separately redefined and, in the process, integrated to form a new ideal. All these changes were aimed at redefining the businessman and his ideal talents to fit an emerging corporate world, an environment the self-trained, self-made man seemed ill equipped to master.

We have examined the final and perhaps most critical element in the transformation of the businessman to fit the corporate age. Even with the changes masculinizing the colleges (through football, for example), there remained the strong tradition of the self-made ideal and the lingering doubts about the college man. Businessmen had long dismissed the college graduate as one who assumed a false superiority, an artificial and ornamental aristocracy ill-suited for the rigors of the business world. Additionally, there was the tradition of promoting up through the ranks and learning on the job in the office or factory. College could not substitute for such practical experience. This chapter, however, described the idealized merging of college and the business world. The celebration of the new self-made college student integrated the college man directly with the self-made tradition. Working one's way through college proved the undergrad's mettle. Even more significantly, this new model of the college graduate proving himself by moving up the ranks offered a blueprint for training the ideal corporate lieutenants. Whereas once work and practical experience had functioned as the only education a business leader required, allowing for inner qualities of character to shine through, college now became another marker of merit and distinction in the equation. Leading businessmen continued to trumpet that there would always be room for the talented self-made man to rise, but increasingly they described the qualities of leadership in terms that favored the college man, perhaps idealized versions of how first-generation captains of industry liked to think of themselves—rough but cultured or, at least broad-minded, self-made men. Of course, the college-educated business climber must first be seasoned through work at the bottom, ritually purged in self-made fashion from the feared excesses of college life.

The self-made hero survived but in an altered and hardly recognizable form in the idealized portrayal of the young corporate leader. The rise through the ranks was prescribed, part of the necessary training for college-educated managers, who alone could assuredly bring the mix of traditional and modern attributes necessary for executive leadership. Undeniably, too, this was a new model forged largely for the old-stock, native white American. Though some examples of immigrants going to college and potentially meeting the new mandates for business success occurred in the magazines, such examples were, again, rare. And no college-educated minorities entered the pages of these magazines. College men were christened within the self-made tradition, a significant and telling adaptation. Nevertheless, the self-made makeover of the college man and the celebration of his up-through-the-ranks rise in fact signaled the death knell of the traditional self-made man. What seemed to be preservation represented the last and perhaps most critical component facilitating a cultural transformation of idealized business masculinity and success in the emerging corporate age. Middle-class magazine contributors culturally constructed a new college experience and a new vision of the college-trained business professional that reconceived the traditional matrices of male power and authority. And they did so in ways that aligned with American notions of self-made meritocracy, while privileging native-born white middle-class men, something that in reality narrowed democratic avenues to power in the corporate world, a quite extraordinary cultural slight of hand.

The new cultural narrative of corporate success and authority now squarely included college, and that narrative as constructed and principally disseminated in these magazines laid out clear parameters of who could conceive of themselves rising along this new college-corporate trajectory. Certainly the possibility for others (immigrants, minorities and women) to conceive of themselves rising via a similar path remained intact. But with article after article and story after story containing remarkably similar visions of the proper college man and college-educated executive injected seamlessly into the cultural mainstream by these magazines, it is no wonder first that college attendance would begin to spike, but also that it would be viewed for quite some time as an opportunity primarily for the "right sort." Nevertheless, as this new narrative of authority in corporate America accelerated during the twentieth century, it should not be surprising that the new battleground for equality of opportunity would become access to higher education. Such battles were not simply the logical results of hiring policies or the growth of a postindustrial economy. First Americans' visions of college needed to be integrated into notions of middle-class identity and narratives of authority, a cultural transition the magazines spearheaded.

5

From Campus Hero
to Corporate Professional

Selling the Full Vision of the College Experience

Occupying the prime advertising space of an entire second page of a *Saturday Evening Post* in October 1909, a dramatic college scene beckoned the reader's attention. A Hart, Schaffner and Marx clothing ad depicted a handsome collegian, fist clenched in passion, as he led his comrades in cheers for the football team in action behind him on the grid-iron (figure 2).[1] Other magazine ads featured competing visions of idealized college men. "Adler's Collegian Clothes," for instance, portrayed the college man as both a sportsman and a scholar in their ads. Another of Adler's ads posed a young man reading intently (figure 3).[2] But these college images were not aimed solely at a college consumer; only about 5 percent of the college age population even attended college, less than 1 percent of the total population.[3] These ads aimed at, as another Adler ad clearly stated, "college men, business men, pro-fessional men," all "gentlemen" who demanded style.[4]

Only a few years before, these very same pages that encouraged "business men" and "professional men" to identify with college experiences had carried very different messages. The magazines had frequently featured articles on business success in which businessmen openly denounced college as a colossal waste of time and, worse, an experience that often ruined the future business

145

ROLLEGE men who wear our clothes are considered the best
dressed men in the bunch. The style, the all-wool fabrics, the
tailoring, are the reasons.

When you buy look for our mark in the clothes;
a small thing to look for, a big thing to find.

Hart Schaffner & Marx
Good Clothes Makers
Chicago Boston New York

David Adler & Sons Clothing Co.
Nobby Clothes Makers, MILWAUKEE

Figure 2. This Hart, Schaffner and Marx advertisement captures
the excitement of game day, with the robust college man leading
cheers as stalwart college men do battle on the gridiron. *Saturday
Evening Post*, 2 October 1909, p. 2.

Figure 3. Adler's offered a full line of
clothing marketing the ideal qualities
of the college man to all men. Note
the scholar and the sporting fellow
in the top panels. *Saturday Evening Post*,
14 April 1906, p. 15.

man. College bred only leisurely work habits and a pretentious disposition. It filled young men's minds with useless facts, only the knowledge of dead languages and ancient civilizations. Worse still, were the long-held associations between college education and the dubiously feminine enshrinement of piety and culture, connections that had earned the college man a reputation as a dandy, or an overcivilized "sissy." No collegiate imagery found its way into ad copy that conjured an idealized manhood before 1905. Yet seemingly overnight, collegiate ads aimed at men exploded—suddenly the college man as athlete and scholar appeared in depictions of an idealized American manhood.

In reality, of course, the transformation of the college man in American magazines had been occurring for almost a decade by 1905. But the burst of collegiate images in ads aimed at American men indeed signaled the dramatic fruition of a remarkable transformative process. The chapters thus far have focused on component elements of the full makeover of the college man for a new age. While we can catch glimpses of how the media often interwove elements (the curriculum, athletics, working student) to that end, this chapter seeks to highlight the best examples of how cultural spokesmen (businessmen, educators, fiction writers, and advertisers) writing in the middle-class magazines assembled the component pieces of the refashioned college experience and fused it securely to emerging notions of masculine business success. The ideal image of the college-educated businessman crafted in these periodicals helped establish the foundation for the popular acceptance of college in America, forming the parameters of expectations that would fire many imaginations that connected college to conceptions of masculinity, power, success, and authority in the dawning corporate age. The vision of a college-educated leadership formed a new narrative of power created to preserve authority for those deemed most appropriate for the task, reinforcing mainstream cultural assumptions as to who should exercise such authority.

Finally, however, we begin to probe a subtle but significant shift imbedded within these media representations of the manly college experience that ironically would alter the very perception and value of that experience. Consider, again, the character of Gorgon Graham. George Lorimer used the character and the series to offer an idealized blueprint for the preparation of future businessmen. The solution used college to merge prized attributes of Victorian manliness (culture and rugged, self-made qualities) with modern education and even expressions of passionate masculinity (football). It posited college as a very real place to potentially form an idealized masculinity in transition to a modern age, but still firmly built on Victorian ideals of character. But Graham was a character in a magazine, created by the editor of what would become the most popular mass periodical of the early twentieth century, a magazine that owed its existence to advertising. This unquestionably was a medium that played a key role in facilitating a modern consumer ethos.[5] Every facet of this and other magazines promoted self-indulgence (rather than the Victorian self-restraint) and guided readers toward idealized self-images. Even when seeming to sustain Victorian values, the very mode of their communication often facilitated an opposing ideology—promoting consumer fulfillment rather than self-denial. The appeal of college in shaping ideal manhood, naturally accommodated such cultural transitions. Part of the attraction of college hinged on the ability of the experience to sustain connections with honored Victorian traits of manhood— culture, refinement, character. And certainly, the college experience was poten- tially real, not a fantasy indulgence like a cowboy adventure story or a Tarzan novel. Nevertheless, in order to connect with readers, magazines inherently conjured ideal images, much in the same way that advertisements tapped into and created desires. This media itself, then, filters concepts through the lens of consumerism, inevitably distorting meanings. The magazine's embrace of col- lege, especially with regard to advertising images, ended up twisting the appeal of college into associations appropriate for a new age of consumption. Ulti- mately it not only distorted some of the original appeal of a college education (style over substance), as a consumer medium it invited all male readers to see themselves as the college man or the businessman wearing Hart, Schaffner and Marx or Adler suits. Advertisers could not characterize one line of clothing for immigrants and another for WASP college men. Inadvertently, then, magazines as a consumer medium would work to erode some of the very notions of exclu- sive WASP privilege that the narrative of college and corporate authority in these magazines had labored to create. Ironically, the seeds of democratic open- ness with regard to perceptions of college in no small way sprouted out of a con- sumer medium that had originally and powerfully conjured visions of college to constrict access for only the right sort of American man.

The Full Vision of the College Man
through Juxtaposition

One danger I risked in choosing to organize these chapters topically was that readers might not see what I saw when I opened these magazines, issue by issue. This would include not only the sheer volume of the discourse on college, but also the juxtaposition of articles, fiction, and advertising, which although deal- ing with different facets of college-going, served to mutually reinforce each other and transform the concept generally. While I demonstrate the interconnected messages and appeal of the various elements of the magazines regarding college, it still fails quite naturally to re-create the approximate experience of a would-be reader.

Concerns about the future pathways to manly opportunities for success and middle-class authority subtly but powerfully informed magazine discourse on the benefits of the college curriculum, the working student and the college man's opportunities in the business world. The same concerns informed at least the climate in which magazine writers discussed and characterized college athletics and the extracurricular. At times writers made such connections directly apparent. More often, though, such concerns swirled beneath the surface, or more precisely, quite often in the very next article or story. In this way the juxtaposition of articles or fiction in these magazines formed a prominent vehicle through which different aspects of the evolving college experience could and did serve to reinforce or qualify each other.

On the broadest level, pointing out how all elements of these different magazines engaged a topic relating to college and middle-class manhood ideals has been a chapter-by-chapter exercise in assessing such juxtaposition. Rising above all these magazines in order to survey them and to make sense of their discourse on college in their totality has been the purpose of this book. Some articles and fiction did indeed venture to touch upon all or most of the transforming notions of the college experience. But most often connections, or the subtle molding of a broader vision of college, and the formation of middle-class manhood such visions encompassed, occurred through the juxtaposition of articles, fiction, and ads touching on the various new ways of perceiving college, especially when related to the undercurrents of concern regarding paths to business success.

The most conspicuous (and intentional) examples of this juxtaposition involving collegiate topics were the *Post*'s College Man's issues, which at times could be pointedly devoted to one aspect of the college experience. The May 1900 number focused on the topic (and article) featured on the cover, former President Grover Cleveland discussing "Does a College Education Pay?" Other articles in the issue included Stanford's David Starr Jordan writing on "The College Man's Advantage in the Coming Century," Princeton's president Francis Patton's "Should a Business Man Have a College Education?" and the University of California's president asking "Is Scholarship a Promise of Success in Life?" A poem and two pieces of fiction touched on the lighter side of college life, but the overall focus was on the curriculum and its linkage to business and professional success. More often these issues, like the magazines in general, dealt with a broader spectrum of college life. One such issue not previously noted in this study ran in October 1902, offering a superb compact example of how the juxtaposition of article topics worked as a whole to forward a reformulated "total" vision of college life perfectly suited for the new demands of the middle-class man.[6]

The obvious overall theme that Lorimer as the *Post* editor wove into this college man's issue revolved around how college worked to prepare men for the world. But rather than focus on the curricular side, this particular number considered broader elements of the college experience. Though not the lead article, the humorist and playwright George Ade's "The Real Freshman," explored this new penchant for college-going in a lighthearted yet revealing way, charting the fictional matriculation of one William Greenfield, off to "old Atwater" (a fictitious Purdue, where Ade attended) class of "naughty-six." Ade exposed the true novelty of this new phenomenon, noting that whereas twenty years earlier, two families in his Midwest township sent sons to college and "braved public opinion in doing so," now twenty young men were off to college. The author attributed this to improving commodity prices and land values (farmers were beginning to enjoy their American "golden age"). Ade characterized young William's father from "Hicksburg" as not just a farmer but a self-made businessman who had invested in a grain elevator. In a classic "lament" about college education, Ade has William's father admit to increasing self-consciousness about his shortcomings during his interactions with the local judges, doctors, and lawyers. Taken together, William's father and progressive mother (described by Ade as a mainstay in the fight against rum and tobacco) fit the stereotype of Lorimer's ideal readers—a new middle class in the making.

William (and his parents, in effect) represented "the real freshmen" Lorimer so admired. "Not the chap who was predestined of a period fifty years ago to wear the orange and black of old Nassau [Princeton]," but rather, Ade wrote of William, the "child of nature, wondering out of the tall grass." He came from Hicksburg High with a smattering of algebra, "a suspicion of the dead languages, and a trace of the scientific method." Just as the citizens of the new towns in the Midwest longed for opera houses to announce their coming of age, so young William seemingly longed for college. He already knew the class yell and "felt as though he had been taken by the collar all of a sudden to a higher plane." In the end, Ade depicts William's rush into a fraternity and his transformation. "Within him throbs the glad knowledge that he embodies the tradition of a noble brotherhood," wrote Ade, "his letters abound with references to class rushes [fights] and team prospects and gridiron battles."[7]

In this one fictitious reflection, Ade captured the supposed aspirations invested in the college experience, and how the magazines reinforced them. He told readers a reassuring tale. Colleges had changed. They had democratized, yet they remained newly sacred places for the up-and-coming middle class, where youths from "Hicksburg" could become confident and refined clubmen, gentlemen scholars, and gridiron brawlers, all in the same place. Ade seemed to capture that curious swirling of elements that comprised the magazine's makeover of college, and thus indeed seemed to reflect their readers. Colleges should be special places, and William's feeling communicated such longings, yet simply by his very presence (and students like him) "old Atwater" retained a democratic air. And then there is the combination of rugged manly activities (rushes and gridiron battles) alongside references to now being part of a noble fraternal brotherhood.

While Ade's contribution in this *Post* issue indirectly reassured the *Post*'s parents about the soundness of sending sons to college and addressed mainly their aspirations and anxieties, the other articles of this issue tackled the subject of college as a fitting, manly place, squarely connected to business leadership. In "The Open-Air Education," Owen Wister pointedly addressed the connection between college athletics, manliness, and success. At one point Wister worked to directly counter a recent well-publicized denunciation of college as a place unfitting men for business. He advised a person to look "into the offices of [the] great banks and brokers of New York and Boston . . . [to find] college-bred men high among the seats of success; men of action and caution combined, clear thinkers and hard hitters." Several he could recall as prominent college athletes in rowing, football, or baseball as college athletics had indeed brought out their manly character traits. The other significant article, "From the President's Chair," presented the observations of the presidents of MIT, Sheffield Scientific at Yale, and Western Reserve University (the ubiquitous president Thwing), as they commented on "The Relation of . . . the University to the World," all related to college and business success. Henry S. Pritchett of MIT masterfully linked the importance of college to the coming Social-Darwinistic international struggle with Germany—a test of collective, national manhood and resolve. If the United States was to succeed in the "commercial and industrial battleground of the world," she had to channel her energy and support (like Germany) a system of education capped by the university that ministered "not just to the doctor and lawyer but also the banker and commercial traveler, and also the soldiers of the commercial army." Incidentally, Pritchett would famously continue his calls for the better organizing of American higher education, working his way into the good graces of Andrew Carnegie to become the first head of the Carnegie Foundation for the Advancement of Teaching, with a mandate to order the educational chaos to meet the international struggle he characterized.[8]

In "The College and the World-Life," Charles Thwing of Western Reserve University, like Pritchett, used the familiar martial references to curry favor with the *Post*'s male readers on the topic of college and practical success, but few matched Thwing's eloquence or his ability to inflate the ego's of *Post* readers. Recounting the progressive evolution of business conditions ("from partnerships to corporations, from single corporations to consolidations of corporations), Thwing characterized the new challenge before America's businessmen as discovering, applying, and relating the emerging "truths" of science and social science to advance civilization. He unequivocally addressed corporate businessmen as the new leaders of the age, with their own mandate of advancing mankind. And it was in this quest that college would bear a most important role. Colleges would discover truth, but Thwing focused on the challenge of applying and relating—the problems of management. "It demands the power to think," argued Thwing, "[and] the power to think is the supreme and superb intellectual creation of the college. . . . Such power the college, through the discipline of the classroom, through the quiet meditation of the student, through the struggle of the athletic field and the literary society and the debating club, is designed to give." Thwing united nearly all of the ideal new facets of the imagined college experience, sold (as it were) specifically as the ideal training for the future corporate leaders of American civilization then unfolding. College bestowed "character" and produced "noble personalities"—"fine without femininity, strong without severity, alert without nervousness, progressive without rashness, conservative without dullness," men of "vision . . . [and] vigor of will."[9]

Thwing was a prolific contributor to the *Post* and the other magazines on this very topic, but this particular piece merits extensive quoting. He featured key terms of traditional Victorian manhood—such as power and will, all connected to future corporate leadership as a sort of new nobility. And note the cautionary, "fine without femininity." At a time when the rising enrollments of women loomed as a troubling topic to college presidents already busy erasing the unmanly stereotypes attached to college, the reference perhaps exhibited his sensitivity to this issue and reflected the need to characterize college as ideally masculine. Thwing quite simply excelled at "selling" the total new vision of the college experience (athletics, scholarship, debating) as one fit for leaders of a new age. Writers like Thwing not only reshaped the image of college, part of their message (and success) involved stroking the egos and firing the imaginations of the "typical" readers of these magazines so that going to college (at least for their progeny) became vital to their self-perceptions.

Ade's "The Real Freshman," Wister's "Open-Air Education," and the contributions of the three college presidents, all aimed at familiarizing readers with the imagined new benefits of the college experience. Other lighthearted articles (one on "College Wit") and fiction (such as "Talks with a Kid Brother at College" noted later) rounded out the issue, but even the artwork accompanying these pieces helped to reinforce the new "total vision" of the college experience. A football scrimmage blazed across the top of the page of "The Open-Air Education." Ade's contribution also pictured football players and cheering undergrads. The drawings alongside "From the President's Chair" nurtured another facet of college's benefits, however, punctuating the presidents' messages. Separate images depicted an engineer (with draftsman's table), a researcher (with chemistry equipment), and a railroad manager (reading plans with a road-gang in the background). And, perhaps most intriguing, a beautiful, cheering female, pennant waving at a football game, graced the cover of the issue, yet no article or story within even mentioned coeducation.

Taken as a whole the articles and artwork flowed together in the issue to forward a grand vision of the college experience as crafted in these magazines—hitting upon all of the facets of the ideal college experience at one point or another. The visions conjured ranged from democratic and rugged to magical and sacred, sometimes (as with Ade) in the same article. And yet all such visions were aimed at molding men, and specifically leaders of corporate America, who would comprise a new nobility, but one seemingly democratically self-selected through the college experience.

The College Man as Future Business Leader— Prime Examples

The October 1902 *Post* College Man's numbers offered perhaps the finest example of how an entire issue could present a grand reconceptualization of college, middle-class manhood and business advancement. The *Post* was the most intentional with regard to college, but to some degree, all of the magazines in this study in their evolving discourse on college and "business" success (broadly conceived) in effect juxtaposed articles and fiction that as a whole worked to reshape the place of college in accepted notions of manhood.

Yale's president Arthur T. Hadley wrote for *Cosmopolitan's* Modern Education series in 1899. Unlike most writers in the series, who focused on the curriculum, Hadley incorporated a much broader conception of the value of a college education that included academic and the extracurricular together as part of an ideal preparation for worldly leaders in America. He championed liberal education as the ideal and time-honored training preparing one to rule in the business world. And in the article, Hadley aimed his comments directly at the businessman, when he warned that a specialized education could not mold the character necessary for real leadership. Through a technical education one only acquired the "superficial marks of the professional man," not the "character-development" provided by a liberal education. But Hadley believed this education included moral and physical preparation as well. After recounting that training for war comprised an important component of leadership training for the Persians, Greeks, and all great peoples throughout history, he argued that games or sports instilled the equivalent attributes of toughness and moral responsibility that the effects of war had provided in centuries past. He offered the classic example of English public schools including rugby as part of their successful liberal education of British leadership.[10] Playing upon the well-known positing of sports as the moral equivalent of war and the penchant for businessmen to utilize martial language and allusions, Hadley made quite clear the connection between cultivating martial virtues and a liberal college education that included the manly lessons of sports.[11]

When these magazines normally discussed college and "business" success, they focused on the changing curriculum. Two *Munsey's* articles, however, drew particular attention to the importance of the extracurricular in fostering future success. "The Football Heroes of Yesterday," exalted over a dozen stories, the central theme being how the great football players of old "made good" in the real world and extolling college football as an excellent preparation for success—a virtual advertisement for college and the sport—with rugged but virtuous college athletes furthering the cause of civilization through their leadership.[12] Direct connections between the value of the college extracurricular and business success were hardly limited to sports. A 1901 *Munsey's* article by Erman Ridgeway on college fraternities specifically noted the rising popularity of a college education due to the fact that many college men seemed to be assuming leading positions in business and professions. In describing how fraternities contributed to this formative process, the author fastened upon several layers of college education's new manly appeal. College not only trained the mind, "it fashions the whole man." He depicted college life in decidedly martial language, "full of fierce strife, keen anxiety and bitter disappointment." Scholarship, campus politics, and athletics were all highly competitive and molded "the whole man," tempered for life's battles, all while fraternities (as he amply described) furnished the supportive male camaraderie and fellowship to make one "the sort of fellow he ought to be." The college experience, he thought, thus supplied something, "a man . . . cannot get anywhere else."[13]

The greatest champion of this combination of all-around college hero was Senator Albert Beveridge, a favorite of Lorimer's, who also penned frequent articles in other periodicals (obviously a form of political self-promotion). This leading progressive Republican from Indiana had worked his way through De-Pauw University. His favorite topic revolved around the importance of college preparation for business and professional success. He could wax just as eloquent as Thwing on the benefits of a classically based liberal education. In "The Young Man and College Life," however, his chief topic centered on the broader benefits of college. In it he highlighted the manly virtues of the small college, filled with "poor boys who have to struggle and deny themselves," describing such ideal college men as possessing "hard muscles and nerves of steel tempered by days of labor in the open air." The world would care not, he argued, if one claimed the title of a "Yale Man." The world cares "that you should be a *real man* [italics in the original]." That he aimed the article squarely at the *Post*'s "businessman" reader, urging them to consider the importance of college education for their sons and heirs, is reflected in a reference highlighting West Point and Annapolis Cadets, who "toil and learn and deny themselves." "Are you going to have an easier time in your business [than officers in the military], he asked? No, he replied, the *Post* reader would "have a good deal harder time," and so should consider college the proper training ground for future businessmen to become "a trained, disciplined force." Finally he advocated athletics and the rough camaraderie of college life (specifically pranks and hazing) as vital elements of the experience. Sports in particular increased one's "effectiveness."[14]

The linkage of college education with athletics (particularly football) and with the rowdy extracurricular of campus life, was critical in the masculinization of college and its acceptance as a proper location for training future business leaders, something that the working student augmented. Magazines played the key role in assembling and disseminating the new image of American colleges as romanticized sites for sons to forge their manhood on the playing field and through campus "strife," while the young men simultaneously received genteel culture and training for the modern world. In the magazines the anxiety over future opportunities, the questions surrounding changing business identity, and the new, perceived value of college education all were intimately bound together with the celebration of the college scholar-athlete and the working student as a new ideal, civilized-primitive hero. The leading middle-class magazines in this study were filled with articles that highlighted these various new characterizations of the college man. This section has explored some key examples of contributors who took special pains to interweave all the elements of the college man as future leaders in American "business" broadly conceived. But articles that hit upon all of these elements together were not nearly as significant or powerful as the heroes emerging simultaneously in the short stories of these very same magazines.

Creating the College Educated Businessman in Magazine Fiction

One must keep in mind that the college man as corporate lieutenant did not emerge fully formed in magazine fiction. Concerns about the liabilities of college life formed an important undercurrent in stories and paralleled the worries offered up regularly in *Post* and other magazine editorials and articles on the college man in business. Editorialists, writers, and businessmen themselves ceaselessly criticized the college-bred youth for their arrogance and laziness in the pages of popular magazines. The college man often received the stereotype of a drinking and gambling sport—either the nouveau-riche brat or an elitist snob. Such characters regularly populated magazine fiction even when the story ultimately upheld a positive image of a college hero.[15] Early middle-class magazine fiction especially limited their utilization of college in a character's past to indicate old money or as training for one of the traditional professions, not business (see chapter 1).[16]

In fact the first magazine authors around the turn-of-the-century to couple college and business in a character's makeup linked a college past to stereotypically negative assessments of the college man. A *Cosmopolitan* story began with the principal character forced to drop out of college and go into business to prove himself, "a year of cut lectures, bed at sunrise, and waking at noon," branding him the typical college sport, overcivilized, effeminate, and weak.[17] Even more revealing were stories that dealt with the college man's direct entry into the business world. The long-running *Post* series, "Letters to Unsuccessful Men" and "The Prodigal," centered on the son of a self-made industrialist, who was expelled from college, the letters following his humorous adventures through a number of jobs until he finally worked in his father's shops and organized a strike. As with most of these stories, the college rascal turned out fine in the end, but first he had to be purged of collegiate liabilities through the hard knocks of the real business world.[18]

With the rising interest in college life and its reinterpretation in the magazines, and with businessmen warming to the idea of college education for their sons (future executives) as the years progressed, portrayals of fictional characters who ventured from college into business became gradually more positive. In the *Post*, for example, while in 1900 and 1901 two dozen articles (mostly in the College Man's numbers) specifically linked college and business success, fiction would become the main venue for portraying the kind of success articles could only approximate. Ten such fictional pieces ran in 1901; five or six a year showed up through 1904, and then came the growth of "mentions" in business fiction, basically four stories per year where the main character sported a college education (fifteen of them include the mention of football). *Collier's* published significantly fewer fictional business stories, but even there, three characters surfaced with a college and football pedigree; ten stories appeared in *Munsey's* (most after 1905), and one story per year ran in *Cosmopolitan* after 1905.

In 1902 and 1903, Jesse Lynch Williams penned the *Post* series, "Talks with a Kid Brother at College." The older brother, a college graduate already out in the world of business, pontificated to his younger sibling about his own college days and the competitive world awaiting the student upon his graduation.[19] While the installments on hazing and warnings about overindulging might have fed stereotypes of wasted college youth, they also depicted the fun and camaraderie of college much like George Fitch's Siwash tales would later.[20] Furthermore, Williams's fictional big brother lectured how the friendships formed, the character instilled, and the lessons learned out of class were critical benefits one took from college into the real world.[21]

In one 1903 installment, Williams had the big brother provide a clear statement on the overall significance of competitive sport and its connection to future business success. The younger brother received a stiff rebuke for failing to go out for the baseball team; his older and wiser brother went on to explain that the chief benefit of athletics, "is to teach you to quit being a quitter." To illustrate, he used the example of "Simple Simon," a fat freshman who had gone out for football at the time the elder brother had attended college. The laughter and taunts of fellow students subsided as Simon stuck it out year after year. After two years of "being kicked around by the varsity," Simon's fat had transformed into muscle so that he was a starter on the champion football team of America his senior year. The elder brother reminded his younger sibling that he in fact had seen Simple Simon at the club during break, the stout fellow with two gold footballs on his watch chain (an indication, perhaps, how some men wore their football pasts as badges of honor). Thus Simon not only embodied a manly regeneration that could occur at college, but also the rewards of effort and patient teamwork, all naturally capped by success in the real world. The elder brother continued his tutorial noting that to become a "man of force and self-reliance," one must be willing to accept "the bumps, thumps and discouragement."[22] In a

later installment, the brother was proud to learn that the kid brother had become the baseball manager (in the days before athletic directors and paid professional coaches, a highly responsible and manly job).[23] Although the messages
conveyed about the benefits of college were important, one of the most significant elements of these stories remained that the older brother (already in business) fully expected the younger one to follow. "Talks with a Kid Brother," like
"Letters from a Self-Made Merchant," offered college as a new route to forming the manhood of the businessman. They familiarized readers with this novel
possibility, while offering up caveats regarding the well-known extremes of college life, again serving as blueprints for this emerging ideal avenue to middle-
class identity.

Similarly, the fictional narrator of Fitch's Siwash stories of 1910 and 1911
usually recalled his exploits (from his football days, through raucous pranks,
wild parties, and even wilder adventures to support the school's athletic teams)
from a business office. One story, in particular, dealt with the peculiar travails
faced by college graduates (who themselves had been football players) in
finding suitable employment in the big city.[24] This story, "Sic Transit Gloria
All-America," followed two Siwash grads looking for wealth in New York and
determined to buy matching yachts within a year. Fitch humorously relates
through the pair some familiar lessons on humility for the college graduate in
the business world. It was a shock to the system after college. "Funny thing
about college. It isn't merely an education. It's a whole life in itself. . . . The
papers publish your picture in your football clothes. You dine with the professors, and prominent alumni come back and shake you by the hand. . . . When
commencement comes you move about the campus like some tall mountain
peak on legs . . . [then, in New York] it was three months before we got jobs.
They were microscopic jobs . . . [and] the office boy could have fired us and got
a way with it."[25] Eventually, and inevitably, though, these "old" college football
players proved their worth and moved up, earning offices and oversight of employees, stenographers at their command. One might recall, too, that Petey
Simmons, the master of "applied deviltry" at Siwash, naturally graduated from
college and stepped into a top management position, where he could continue
to utilize his vast organizational talents.[26] Through such stories, the path
through college and into business seemed well on the way to becoming a normative rite. Liberal culture and scientific rationality were important, but in fiction it was often the extracurricular experiences—the athletic competitions,
fraternity life, pranks, and parties—that offered the future businessman his
training in taking the heat and standing up for his fellows under pressure. Most
important, though, is the simple positing of college in such stories as typical, as

ordinary. Such cultural transformations function ephemerally but potently beneath the surface in magazine fiction.

While George Fitch and Jesse Williams both wrote in a humorous tone, much of the fiction that began to integrate a college past into a character's background was quite serious. And for most magazine authors the proper type of college man fit to succeed in business was the athlete and the football star. In 1901 the *Post* ran the first story to feature a college man in the business world. Home on summer break, young Carpenter in Henry K. Webster's "The Wedge," consented to help out a family friend determined to break a strike at his foundry and in need of workers. Having taken the engineering course at college, young Carpenter believed he could not back down from the demanding task, largely for the "honor of alma mater," as the owner-friend had made plain his doubt that the college boy could stand the labor.[27] Although he thought the foundry work difficult, Carpenter proved he could excel at it, passing this first test of rugged manhood. He had thus cancelled out the typical doubts dogging such college men (and many middle-class men) that they could not handle the rigorous labor of the working class.

From this first test he next rose to meet the challenge of managing men. Blocked at the foundry gate by the striking laborers, Carpenter rallied the immigrant strikebreakers, coaching them in the finer points of the Flying Wedge (an early offensive football formation). Declaring that he and his college teammates had mowed down bigger mobs than this, Carpenter organized the men into a scrimmage line. Then, with "twenty five molders from Cleveland with Becker Newton Carpenter, Jr, '02, at the head, locked into one body," they easily cleared a path through the striking workers. Webster described them in the standard language of the "scientific" football metaphor, working as one team, "a human locomotive." By the end of the strike, Carpenter had organized the immigrant workers into a marching club, a baseball team, and two football squads, with plans for a glee club when the strike ended. The strikebreakers even yelled out their version of college cheers at every stop on their way back to Cleveland.[28] This early story reinforced a romanticized and masculine image of college life, while celebrating, in no uncertain terms, the leadership potential of the college athlete in the business world. The story portrayed young Carpenter and, by extension, any college man as an ideal future manager and natural leader, who could rise up through the ranks (in this case metaphorically in short order) to prove more than a match for any group of laborers.[29]

Few stories combined college football and executive leadership like "The Wedge," but after 1900 and the awakening of interest in college education generally, brief background references to a collegiate football past for a business-related character recurred regularly, Yale being the most frequently mentioned.[30] Authors often used such references not only to highlight a character's masculinity but also to set up humorous contrast. In one, a young corporate man fretted whether to get married or to buy a car. Worrying over such choices, he bore a pale resemblance to the strapping boy who had "played Yale full-back."[31] Whether humorous or serious, though, when used for business-related characters, the athletic collegiate pedigree denoted natural authority, strength, and masculine vigor. It simultaneously reinforced the new manly appeal of college and a reworked vision of the businessman. In *Collier's* 1905 "The Goddess from the Car," for example, a Harvard alum and ex-fullback from one of their winning teams returned for the Yale game from managing a railroad in the West. Disappointed in the play of the squad and sorry for her husband, his wife inspired the boys at halftime to play as a team, which they triumphantly did.[32] Such references in stories simply bolstered the idea that naturally one could imagine a Harvard fullback commanding such a rigorous railroad enterprise taming the West.

These pointed references to a college past for businessmen perhaps betokened little more than an author's recognition of increasingly common phenomena—the rising college population, the popularity of football, and that more college men were heading into business. Rather than signifying possible liabilities or weaknesses of a business character, the collegiate football experience, by contrast, seemed to color these characters as instantly masculine, but also credible in their positions of authority. One serialized story of business adventure in the *Post*, however, further displayed the transformed meaning imbedded in fictional college references.

In John Corbin's "The Cave Man," college and the lead character's athletic past played prominent roles as he engaged in big business battles. The story centers on the figure of Wister, the young head of a leading car manufacturer. The driving plot of the serial revolves around the efforts of a manager of a rival company (and a rival to Wister in love) to force a consolidation on Wister, who naturally opposes such "trusts" as dishonest. Wister, though, is introduced as a humble warrior, embarrassed as old classmates chant his name and call for him—the old linemen who led the blocking for a famous runner and future Rough Rider—to lead a cheer, at a Harvard homecoming.[33] Wister resists the threats to join a trust and then forms his own "good" trust to defend himself and others.[34] The business battle is best symbolized with a polo match in which Wister faces a penalty-shot showdown against his business rival playing on the other team. Wister summons the will to put aside his pain and weariness just as he had against Yale years before when the team had depended upon him.[35]

The athletic past of Wister in this business story augments and clarifies his masculinity and fitness to lead.

When college entered into a fictional character's past as the new century progressed, the man most often was engaged in some sort of business activity, denoting a significant evolution.[36] Casting the college-educated businessman as a manly leader, however, involved more than inserting references to gridiron glory. Businessmen began seeing themselves as expert managers, a rising new professional class, and the magazines promoted this budding self-conception. If the curriculum seldom assumed center stage in magazine fiction (as it did in articles and editorials), the fact that college increasingly entered into the fictional backgrounds of business characters nevertheless owed a great deal to the perception of curricular change and its relevance to the shifting demands of the corporate world. A character with a technical or engineering education did tend to receive increased attention over time, which one might assume given the growing interest in scientific management. But even when stories featured the college graduate's ability to inject scientific efficiency into outdated business operation, the course of study was usually not specified.[37] In one such story, the innovative college lad who turned around his grandfather's importing business hailed from Yale, a school with a manly football reputation, but notoriously conservative in its curriculum.[38] Acquiring the refining qualities and breadth of liberal culture still received specific mention in some business-related fiction as well.[39] A collegiate background, then, could be used to emphasize one trait or refer to many things at once, and magazine authors, in fact, were using collegiate references as a sort of cultural shorthand. Through this new mass medium, collegiate references conveyed an amalgam of ideal qualities that had become associated both with the college man and the ideal emerging business leader.

Fiction on college effectively collapsed many aspects of college education—such as the refinements of liberal culture, breadth of learning, character formation, and scientific training—regardless of apparent contradictions within the curriculum. It often merged these intellectual traits with an indefinable something, a panache, a quality of leadership that was often signified through athletics or the extracurricular. Such ideal characterizations helped to account for the increased use of college references in fictional business characters and for the popularity of the college football tale. This civilized-primitive college man possessed all the qualities that American men were being told they should prize. There were some prominent stories that did indeed perfectly capture this amalgam—the ideal college man as business leader in "The Wedge," "The Matter with Carpenter" (chapter 2), and "The Cost" (chapter 4). But John Corbin's Wister in "The Cave Man" stands out as the purest embodiment of the ideal college man, much like Theodore Roosevelt, a progressive thinker and man's man. Wister's athletic prowess clarified his stalwart leadership ability. Corbin also described him as "academic," devoted to research and development, thereby uniting identifications of college with the liberal arts tradition and modern science.[40] Athletic, modest, charming, intelligent, Wister combined all of the ideal traits associated with college, both modern and traditional, and all wielded by a progressive-minded business executive.

The interconnected transformation in cultural perceptions of college and the ideal man these fictional characters represent is a remarkable story. But at a time when a relatively small portion of the American middle class even went to college, the creation of college-age characters or college-educated businessmen as heroes, in story after story, worked another more subtle yet profound transformation in American culture. These fiction writers not only refashioned and interrelated ideal notions of college, manhood, and success, they also helped to make attending college a normative expectation for the middle class, another element in how the magazines worked to weave these new and interrelated characterizations into the fabric of American cultural perceptions. The power of this new image of college, which magnified and distorted ideal qualities, also proved potent in advertising.

Selling College: The College Man in Magazine Advertising

Despite the intense interest in college education demonstrated by the new mass magazines, references to college life largely failed to surface in advertising copy around the turn of the century. No advertisers directly marketed to college men (or women). Even as *Collier's* offered in-depth coverage of the college athletic scenes and the *Post* devoted entire issues to college life, no advertisements utilized collegiate imagery or references celebrating the college man to sell products.[41] It would seem surprising, then, that advertisers did not jump on the bandwagon of interest. In reality, the college market was quite small, and more importantly the firm linkage of college with idealized middle-class notions of success and manhood simply had not been well established.[42]

Of necessity the magazines in this study had to appeal simultaneously to their readers' assumed tastes and ideals, as well as provide an agreeable climate for advertisers. And advertisers had to create messages that both resonated with readers and guided them toward specific purchases.[43] Richard Ohmann states that commodities that advertised successfully in these magazines either appealed to the urban lifestyle of the new middle-class readers, stressing products of efficiency and modern convenience (such as canned meats, quick breakfast foods, Kodak cameras, or safety razors), or they offered items such as pianos, furniture, and silverware (and high culture) typically associated with the upper-middle class.[44] The most typical and successful advertising in mass magazines during these years presented, on the one hand, products that appealed to the readers' sense of being modern in their style of living, while on the other hand, a parallel theme resonated with and fed readers' desires to achieve traditional signs of middle-class status through purchases that signaled culture and refinement. Similarly the social tableaux in advertising images (the background settings, such as furniture or the dress of people) consistently featured products (even modern and inexpensive ones) in decidedly upper-middle-class households that assumed a wish to emulate.[45] In these magazines, advertising functioned alongside editorials, articles, and fiction in an attempt to both align with and guide the emerging self-conceptions of being middle class in a changing world.[46] Like the magazines generally, ads invited readers to be modern at the same time reassuring them the products they purchased upheld and corresponded with traditional standards and ideals, all the while instructing them in a new language of meaning through commodities.[47]

Advertisers assumed that certain established ideals and longings already had resonance. Going to college had not yet been fully integrated into the accepted parameters of being middle class, especially for the business-minded man and his family who constituted the presumed readership of most mass magazines. The upper-middle class themselves had only recently begun sending their children to college, so that even when advertisers consistently illustrated advertisements with decidedly upper-middle-class settings and people, college was still not a widely assumed rite of passage necessarily meriting emulation. But all of this was changing.

Beginning around 1903, small ads marketed college pins, posters, and songs directly to the college-age readership and alumni.[48] These ads assumed a reader who was looking for such purchases. In other words, they did not seek to wield collegiate references to fashion a desirable image. A far more remarkable phenomenon involving college references in ads began in 1904, demonstrating the cumulative effect of the magazines' infatuation with college life. By that time magazines had been rehabilitating the vision of the college experience for about a decade (and in fact overall volume of coverage was just ending what I have termed a foundational peak period). Advertisements for clothing and other products initiated larger ads appealing directly to the college man and, more significantly, associating the image of the college man (and college-going in general) with youthful style, sophisticated refinement, and athletic manliness—a consumer amalgam of all that the magazines had represented as ideal in the college man and college life. Additionally, these ads often tied such collegiate references directly to the young businessman and business success. In other words, they reinforced the idealized connections between college and the business world, which other elements in these magazines had labored to establish.

One would expect the makers of watches and pens, products often given as gifts to young people starting out, to be the first to appropriate college imagery into their ad copy, and they did so on a minor scale. But it was the ready-to-wear clothing industry that first filled their ads with college references, exemplifying just how powerful and wide a currency collegiate images had attained. Usually their large ads, from a full page to at least a quarter of a page, occupied prime space in the magazines (back of the front cover, the last page, or surrounding the contents). But critically, this industry, more than any other, trafficked essentially in projecting an ideal image of American masculinity.

Ready-to-wear clothing manufacturers faced a problem around the turn of the century. They had to convince potential buyers that ready-to-wear clothes were of the highest quality, equal to that produced by tailors who outfitted the upper-middle class. A parallel project was to construct a desirable image associated with the clothes, one usually drawn from upper-middle-class lifestyle as ideal for emulation. The ads strove to convince customers that they were in fact gentlemen and deserved to dress the part.[49] Additionally, the ready-to-wear clothes had to offer something beyond affordable style, something that distinguished them from tailored clothes. Ready-to-wear clothiers had peopled their ads with well-dressed men beginning in the 1890s, but around 1904 the college man entered ad copy, and his presence pointed to how ready-to-wear advertisers endeavored to solve all of their problems.[50]

At first, ready-to-wear ads that specifically mentioned college in their texts played upon the most established associations equating college with American high society. A Daube, Cohn and Company advertisement from 1904 captured this practice well. The ad featured a young man in a suit, walking with a cane, while a young women in the background turned to peer after him. The text explained that "each garment [was] chockful of metropolitan style and elegance, reflecting the fashion of the boulevard and college campus." More explicitly, the Stein-Bloch Company pointed quite clearly to the audience targeted by the ready-to-wear manufacturers, those consumers that advertisers believed should want to emulate the style of the boulevard and college. "Tens of thousands of men working at professions and in offices—with limited incomes—have the same tastes, the same necessity, the same genuine idea of clothes as the smartly groomed society man or college man of wealth," the ad asserted, "to them these things are just as much business and social requisites."[51] While such specific elevation of the college man to the status of elite man of society faded, these early examples indicated the ways that ready-to-wear manufacturers first established the image of college men as models, which the working and salaried gentlemen who wore their clothes could emulate.

Ready-to-wear advertisers rapidly grew more sophisticated in how they utilized collegiate references in the ad copy. They dropped the explicit elevation of the collegian to an elite plane. Instead, the ads increasingly integrated college references in ways that associated their clothing with an idealized conception of the college man, and then invited the reader to identify with this ideal. Joe College possessed a natural sense of style, taste, and refinement. But he was also young and on a budget, and so sought affordability and quality. For example, a Hart, Schaffner and Marx ad from 1904 read, "some college men care most for athletics; some for studies; but they're all interested in good clothes," and this was why, the ad stated, most college men bought Hart, Schaffner and Marx, since they also were "interested in economy."[52] The Daube, Cohn and Company came out with a line called "Harvard Clothes" that promised "correct style and perfect fit" off the rack. One of their 1909 ads intoned, "a man may be better than his clothes but he has to prove it," offering "Harvard Clothes" as a new standard for the young man "who wishes to improve his wardrobe without increasing his expenditures" (figures 4 and 5).[53] Calling their lead line of clothes "Campus Togs," the firm of Chas. Kaufman and Brothers targeted "ambitious young men," and asserted that their clothes "surround the wearer with the atmosphere of breeding, culture and refinement so hard to describe but which depends so largely upon correct style."[54] The college man, while still used to symbolize refinement, was equated with all ambitious young men, inviting a blurred distinction.

A new line of clothes and a massive ad campaign launched by David Adler and Sons provide the best and longest lasting examples of how a company used college associations to index its product with an upper-middle-class lifestyle and with the college man's presumed sophistication, while simultaneously flattering the average male reader that they too should dress this way and partake of such associations. Adler's marketed their "Collegian" clothes as "the typical college clothes."[55] To reinforce the relationship with college style, they created a logo appearing in almost every ad thereafter consisting of the words "Collegian" inside a pennant-shaped design. Although Adler's billed their "Collegian" line as the "typical college man's clothes," from the beginning they sought to use appealing college associations to attract men from all walks of life. Their earliest campaigns stressed youthful style. "Young men who appreciate Good Style will admire," these "typical college clothes," as one ad proclaimed.[56] But the

FALL 1908

HARVARD CLOTHES

Accepted by the best-dressed young men in the country as the highest standard of appearance and quality.

Harvard Clothes mark a new era in the proper apparelling of young men. They possess exclusively *a snap, dignity and correctness* that is best described by the phrase "well-groomed."

Harvard Clothes can be secured anywhere in the United States at prices ranging from $15.00 for a *guaranteed all-wool suit*, to $35.00. They are designed particularly for the young man who wishes to improve his wardrobe, without increasing his expenditures.

Write today for our free fashion booklet explaining why it is to your advantage to wear the best clothes in America, and we will refer you to a Harvard dealer who will take pleasure in showing you the line.

Get our Free Style Book

Made only by

DAUBE, COHN & CO.
381 Fifth Avenue, CHICAGO

SPRING 1909

HARVARD CLOTHES

A man may be better than his clothes, but he has to prove it.

At the Harvard Shops the young man who wishes to improve his wardrobe without increasing his expenditures, will find *America's highest type of ready-to-wear clothing*.

This statement would have no significance did not the clothes themselves carry the evidence of its truth.

"*Harvard Clothes*" have established a new standard in young men's dress, from all standpoints of *quality, fit and "classy" appearance*.

Every careful dresser can make sure of obtaining the correct clothes for spring and summer wear by asking us for the name of a local dealer in "*Harvard Clothes*."

Write to-day for our free fashion book, which portrays authoritatively the correct styles for spring.

Get that Style Book

If you don't find Harvard Clothes, tell us

DAUBE, COHN & CO.
381 Fifth Ave., Chicago

Figures 4 and 5. Daube, Cohn and Company's Harvard Clothes line traded on the cachet of the Harvard name and its myriad associations with upper-class refinement and culture. Their illustrations in these two ads play upon both the refined image and the fun and camaraderie of college youth. *Collier's Weekly*, 3 October 1908, p. 28; and *Saturday Evening Post*, 10 April 1909, p. 46.

appeal, of course, was not exclusively to youthfulness. The "Collegian" line was for college men and "any man who cares particularly about perfect style, combined with points of refinement in the character of his apparel."[57] Phrases like "high art style" and terms like "refinement" technically only described the clothes, but the ads clearly connected such qualities to the clientele who wore the clothes, "college men, business men, professional men—to that element in fact which demands style."[58]

Although they featured youthful men, most of Adler's illustrations were not specifically collegiate. But they often did employ illustrations that conjured idealized college associations. A full-length page illustration (on the back of the front cover) in 1905 pictured exquisitely dressed young men cheering at some sort of event. One donned a freshman beanie, while another held a pennant that, of course, read "Collegian."[59] Two other illustrations portrayed academic scenes—a cap-and-gowned man studying and another of a young man reading in a library—playing upon the connections between college and manly cultured learning (see figure 6).[60] But, most scenes simply pictured well-dressed men, accompanied by beautiful and elegant women.[61] Consequently, even the ad art worked on one hand to augment the appealing impression of cultured, manly college youth, while on the other hand offering these attractive visions of a new self to the average (and noncollege) reader. One December 1905 Adler illustration of an older man and two younger men all in formal evening attire, might well depict the boys home from college.[62] This scene perfectly exemplified how Adler (and other companies) used college associations in concert with upper-middle-class social tableaux to promote the ideal refined image for their ready-to-wear clothes. While still positing the college man as a sophisticated model for emulation, this illustration and the Adler campaigns generally evidenced a subtle but important shift in how the reader was encouraged to think both of college and of himself.

Most ready-to-wear clothing ads eventually listed the college man and the professional man alongside the businessman as their target clientele, collapsing the conceptions into one. One illustration for their "Collegian" line even pictured a young man toting a briefcase rather than books.[63] A full page Hart, Schaffner and Marx ad highlighted their "Varsity" model for "college men and young business men."[64] One ad offering advice for the "young man starting out in his business life," included the comments of a collegian on the importance of appearance.[65] A full page Society Brand ad from 1910 offered an excellent description of the young man for whom they made clothing: "We have in mind that type of young manhood that fittingly portrays the Young American Gentleman—erect and of aristocratic bearing; the business young

Figure 6. This Adler's Collegian Clothes ad accentu-
ates the scholarly, cultured side of the college man, a
true gentleman to emulate. *Saturday Evening Post*, 17
October 1908, p. 33.

man, the professional young man, the college young man." Society Brand
Clothes gave "an air of refinement, of dignity, of class," that such men naturally deserved to celebrate.[66] Similarly, a Schloss Brothers ad pitched their
clothing lines to both college men and businessmen, claiming that their suits
"carry the stamp of Elegance, Distinction, and Refinement . . . the standard of
fashion for Gentlemen."[67] Refinement, dignity, class . . . such words pepper
these ads. And, while these terms described the clothing, the ads naturally
aimed also at conjuring an appealing masculine image to associate with their
clothing and with which the male reader would desire to identify. College men,

professional men, businessmen, they were *all* now gentlemen. They could be, and were presented as, the same man.

At the most basic level, of course, the ready-to-wear industry used collegiate references to help create an association between the product (modern, ready-to-wear clothing) and an appealing image of ideal, refined manhood that one could purchase at an affordable price. Through the magic portal of consumption, they offered the aspiring male readers of these mass magazines a way "to be classed with men of position . . . for not nearly as much as tailored clothes."[68] Nevertheless, the ads conveyed powerful messages regarding the status of the average businessman in society and how they should think of college in relation to themselves.

Through clothing ads in the first decade of the century, the salaried man or the young businessman was encouraged to think of himself as a gentleman, as needing to project a refined image in order to succeed, and to identify with the lifestyle of the upper-middle class. Such ads, in a way, democratized gentility without tarnishing its appeal. The ads simply encouraged businessmen—the new middle class—to conceive of themselves in such a world. Both college and the average businessman were being characterized in new ways: the idealized college man was depicted as cultured yet dignified; the young businessmen (the typical young American) could picture themselves moving in the same world as the college man. These powerful ad images and characterizations simultaneously bolstered the notion of colleges as a manly place of culture and refinement while prompting the businessman to identify himself as college caliber, as possessing similar qualities.

Despite the fact that ready-to-wear apparel ads used college to create an ideal masculine image to associate with their clothing, one prominent side of college life (athletics) remained notably absent in their ad copy. Illustrations and text that tied their patrons with youthful appearance had long been aspects of ad copy for ready-to-wear companies. Note the mantra from Society Brand clothes for "young men and men who stay young."[69] But very few ready-to-wear ad illustrations featured explicitly *college* athletic scenes (or any other athletic scenes) prior to 1909. Beginning in the 1909 season, however, an avalanche of college athletic illustrations suddenly appeared, accompanied by far more martial and masculine language.[70]

In the spring of 1909, Chas. Kaufman and Brothers's "Campus Togs" ads pictured young men cheering (a typical scene) but added into the background an action shot of the baseball game.[71] That same spring, Samuel W. Peck and Company inserted an illustration of the start of a sprint race, the men poised to lunge ahead, as well-dressed men looked on. The text of the Peck ad read, "there is something characteristic of vigorous young manhood about 'Sam Peck Clothes' that appeals very strongly to the young man, the business or professional man."[72] And, of course, in the fall advertisers filled their copy with actual scenes of the football action rather than simply attractive young figures cheering at the games. One full page Hart, Schaffner and Marx ad offered just such a scene—a handsome young man, fist clenched, leading cheers on the sidelines while the scrimmage raged in the background.[73]

The text of these ads grew more demonstrative in their depictions of the men who wore their clothes. Another Hart, Schaffner and Marx ad, in fact, perfectly captured the appeal of the college man in ad copy by defining the type of man who wore their clothes, "the athletic figure; the college type, broad shouldered, taper-waisted, full chested, with lots of anatomy in the legs."[74] Some clothiers argued that their suits actually accentuated such physical features or even imparted this look to those unfortunate enough not to conform to the ideal. But nearly all idolized this "college type."[75] Rosenwald and Weil declared their "Manly Clothes" were "cut for manly athletic lines," and with them one could "acquire an erect manly carriage."[76] "Campus Togs" embodied "what every aggressive, virile young man requires." [77] Samuel Peck's clothes provided "virile touches" to the "aggressive young fellow."[78] H. M. Lindenthal and Sons marketed their "Athlete" model; Hart, Schaffner and Marx continued to hawk their "Varsity" line.[79]

Seeking to link their clothing with desirable images of manhood, these ads played upon the ideal, athletic college man image and sustained associations between the young college man and cultured refinement, so that the images of virile masculinity and cultured manhood freely mixed in the pages of the *Post*, *Collier's* and other periodicals. Two Alfred Benjamin and Company ads perfectly illustrated the use of both ideals (manly/athletic and cultured) in one company's ad campaigns. The full-page illustration for a November 1909 ad depicted a large stadium with a football game in action on the field as a young man (a beautiful female on his arm) yells up to his friends—perhaps an alum returned for the game. A second ad from fall 1910 was set on a campus quad. Two professors walk in the background as the family bids farewell to their son. The Columbia University library served as a recognizable image of collegiate culture situated in the background (figures 7 and 8).[80] Hart, Schaffner and Marx also evoked both notions of college manhood in their ads. While a 1914 ad featured a standard football theme in its illustration (well-dressed men on a team sideline, football players in view), a 1910 ad pictured three men sharing a laugh on a college quad with the caption, "college styles . . . are models especially for young, athletic, stylish men."[81] And yet another ad featured a classic fraternity

Figure 7. This Alfred Benjamin and Company advertisement associates their clothes with the excitement and pageantry of a college game day, along with the manliness of the college athlete. *Saturday Evening Post*, 6 November 1909, back of front cover.

Figure 8. Complementing the rough, manly side of the college man, this Alfred Benjamin and Company ad trades on the learned and refined elements associated with the college man. *Saturday Evening Post*, 24 September 1910, p. 1.

scene—men gathered around a banjo player wearing a letter sweater, all singing a tune (figure 9).[82] "Campus Togs" still employed terms such as "breeding,
culture and refinement" to describe the men who wore their clothes in addition
to the newly added quality, "virile."[83] Finally, Samuel Peck and H. M. Lindenthal, though they touted their manly clothes and used athletic scenes, continued to name their suits the "University," "Oxford," and the "Princeton," thus
playing upon the cachet of refinement attached to these terms.[84] And they all
still wielded the term "gentleman" to define even the most aggressive and
manly of patrons (figure 10).[85]

    Certainly in evoking these collegiate associations advertisers hoped to ap-
peal to the college market. Most such ads appeared in the fall and spring. coinciding with school terms. But many college references appeared throughout the
fashion year (of course Adler's Collegian line always trumpeted the connections), and most ads explicitly using college imagery continued to promote their
clothing for the young professional and businessman. An Ederheimer, Stein
and Company ad from 1912 perfectly exemplified how advertisers used college
associations to embody ideal qualities applicable for other types of men. Theirs
were "the only 'real' college men's clothes," giving "the figure, the appearance
of physical strength and grace [that] will win respect and admiration." The ad
continued, though, that their clothes "give the professional young men prestige;
they make business friends; meet all the requirements of the social mixer."[86]

    Nearly all major apparel advertisers followed the same line of using both
ideal types, sometimes in the same ad or over a season. For example, the text of
Society Brand ads in October 1908 did not specifically mention college or the
businessman, but their ad art mixed both identities. Their October 3, 1908, illustration featured a young man in pinstripe suit, bow tie, and derby with a
book under his arm. Two weeks later what appears to be the same young man
now wears a business suit and reads a ticker tape (figures 11 and 12).[87] Hart,
Schaffner and Marx was probably the most persistent in establishing these associations in pushing their "Varsity" line. A 1911 ad proclaimed "Our Varsity,
the most generally favored suit model ever produced; college men and business
men like it."[88] Their ad illustrations now began to interact with the ad copy. An
October 1912 ad illustration featured young men in suits along with one in football gear, one with a letter sweater and another with a bull horn, while the text
touted the Varsity line for "young men in college as in business, where smart
style is an asset."[89] Hart, Schaffner and Marx, Adler's, Society, Lindenthal and
Sons, Kuppenheimers: all these companies ran ads that posited the college
man as an ideal type—refined, stylish, athletic. But they connected him to all
"vigorous young manhood," as a Samuel Peck ad noted.[90]

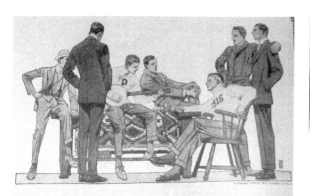

The right note in dress

A LITTLE later, the cheerful plunk of the banjo, and the "close work" of the "barbershop chord" will enliven the fraternity house. You may sing off the key if you choose; nobody cares much; but you'd better dress in tune.

Now's the time to get ready; you ought to have a copy of our Style Book as a guide; and tell your clothier what models you want.

Look at Model 54 at $25

Every dealer in our goods can show it; one of the best of the late styles for young men. Three button 30 inch coat; wide lapels, soft front; 6 button no-collar waistcoat; straight trousers with turnup and tunnel belt-loops. Model 54.

Plenty of others if you don't like that one; many new weaves and patterns; imported and domestic fabrics; tartan colors in plaids and stripes, chalk lines. At $25 and up you'll find some of the best values in clothes ever offered.

You will see in the window of the dealer who sells our clothes in your town a reproduction in colors of the above picture. The Fall Style Book is now ready. Send for a copy.

Hart Schaffner & Marx
Good Clothes Makers

Chicago   New York

BE SURE OF

[Collegian]

THIS LABEL

The Patch
Pocket
Collegian
$18 to $30

Adler's Collegian Clothes

are admired by all men who appreciate *quality* and value *style*. They're not "freakish" clothes—no ridiculous extremes. Such garments as we produce appeal to the critical classes—college men, business men, professional men, etc. We give our clothes *every desirable feature of fashion*, but we keep them refined looking—gentlemen's clothes in every sense of the word. Shown by all the best stores everywhere. Suits and overcoats $12.50 up to $35.00. Write for our illustrated book of fashion. It will post you on what to wear this Fall. *Mailed free.*

David Adler & Sons Clothing Co.
Nobby Clothes Makers   Milwaukee

Figure 9. This Hart, Schaffner and Marx advertisement highlights the manly bonding associated with the college years. *Saturday Evening Post*, 12 September 1914, p. 2.

Figure 10. Even Adler's marketed their gentlemanly college clothes by accentuating the vigorous and passionate side of the college man. Here the young collegian holds his hat, watching intently, as if he readies to run onto the field if needed. Note the text, "college men, business men, professional men." *Saturday Evening Post*, 3 October 1908, p. 42.

SOCIETY BRAND Clothes are different yet dignified. They embody the three essentials of good clothes, Quality, Workmanship and Good Form. Add just a touch of youthful and the result is Society Brand.

Made in Chicago by
Alfred Decker & Cohn
Sold through the better clothiers

Society Brand

SOCIETY BRAND Clothes are considered the height of perfection in modern dress for Young Men and Men who stay Young. Characteristic lines giving a dignified, gentlemanly appearance.

Figures 11 and 12. Alfred Decker and Cohn's Society Brand clothing line had long marketed its clothes to young men, often mentioning college and employing collegiate imagery. These two ads illustrate the constant blurring of the lines between images of the ideal man as college student and as businessman. *Collier's Weekly*, 3 October 1908, p. 5; and *Collier's Weekly*, 24 October 1908, p. 3.

Figure 13. Several advertisers utilized this scene, but Hart, Schaffner and Marx did it best. Such images integrated the notion of going to college into the fabric of middle-class life. *Saturday Evening Post*, 13 November 1909, p. 1.

Many ads wove college-going not only into the fabric of ideal male associations, but also into that of idealized middle-class life. Consider the numerous scenes in ads depicting the young man leaving for college as mother packs his clothes.[91] Or, as with a Hart, Schaffner and Marx ad from 1909, "home from college, wearing Hart, Schaffner and Marx," the illustration featured an idyllic vista of mom stirring a pot in the kitchen, the dog on the floor, her two handsome sons standing in the kitchen (figure 13).[92] A 1908 ad campaign of Kuh, Nathan and Fischer apparel company went the furthest in positing college as an aspect of middle-class life with their "Sincerity Talks" ads. The ads took an advice column form, assuming a familiar tone concerning "that college boy of yours" and "his Letters Home."[93] These ads discussed how fraternity life,

athletics, and "the structure of the class yell" assumed a major importance for
the presumed reader's son at college, but added (of course) that the boy likely
found that being well dressed mattered as well.[94] These ads stressed that their
models, such as "The Campus" and "Athletic," were not "sissified," but rather
"full-chested."[95] They posited college as a major aspect of a middle-class family's life, but they also circled back to the main point—fashioning an ideal masculine image around the college man.

Although the most numerous and powerful, apparel advertisements were
hardly the only ads to cultivate and disseminate the new place of college in
conceptions of masculinity and American life. By 1904 and then growing more
common, ads for shaving soap, men's garters and socks, watches, and tobacco
began to incorporate college settings and imagery, positing college as familiar
and ideal at the same time. Rowers and football players, waving pennants,
Gothic towers, dorm life, and fraternity bonding peppered advertising copy
year round. A Paris Garters ad featured three men lounging on a fence with
campus building (one a Gothic tower) lining the background.[96] A Howard
Watch ad illustration pictured a young rower with an *H* on his turtleneck with a
flock of rowers practicing in the background; another quarter-page ad featured
a dramatic football scene.[97] A full-page 1905 Murad cigarette ad in *Collier's* presented a football game with a cheering crowd scene (a Yale pennant even flut-
tered in the stands), and advised the reader to look around at the gridiron since,
"you can always judge a cigarette by its use among college men." Egyptian
Deities also employed a football scene in a 1915 ad with their regular caption,
"People of Culture, Refinement and Education" smoke Deities. Once again
collegiate images were used to evoke elite associations and also simultaneously,
through athletic references, solidify a virile masculine connection. An American Tobacco company ad (the makers of Bull Durham) effortlessly merged the
two aspects of the college man (cultured and manly) in an ad illustration from
1915 picturing a warm scene of college men gathered around a fraternity fire-
place. The ad seemed to speak to alums asking them to recall their days around
such a fire, singing songs with a pipeful of "manly" Lucky Strike.[98]

Refined yet manly, the messages in such ads only strengthened the evolving
vision of college men and college life cultivated elsewhere in the magazines.
They utilized the iconographic images and symbols of college life (the college
gates, quad scenes, dormitory rooms, football games), and the same language
found throughout magazine articles and fiction that touched on college life. In
so doing the ads again reinforced the reformation of the college man, another
element within the magazines that offered an appealing vision of collegiate
masculinity. And while most of the nonapparel ads targeted a college student

readership or their parents, they still worked to integrate college into the fabric of middle-class identity. Some pen ads, however, did refer to both college and business, one even noting that their pens would help the graduate hold that first position.[99] Although businessmen may not have been the prime targets of such ads, the messages employed in ads were still intended for the broadest appeal, to identify the college man with desirable qualities and associations applicable to all men. The college man seemed a natural choice for advertisers who sought an appealing masculine icon that simultaneously represented cultured refinement and the best of civilized manhood, while also signifying youthful vigor, potency, and the sheer physical power of the athlete. He was an icon all ambitious men were now invited to identify with, whether in college or not, since it was the qualities of ideal manhood that such ads celebrated. In this manner, the ads acted as the most powerful messages reinforcing the vision of an idealized college manhood, connecting college to visions of success and positing colleges as an appealing possibility with which all American men could identify.

Nevertheless, while advertising supported the overall re-envisioning of the college experience, it also accelerated another tendency inescapably present in the very nature of the magazine as a consumer medium. The ads collapsed the benefits of the college experience into an attractive style of life. They translated desirable attributes supposedly gained through college (honesty, courage, character, strength) into an amalgamated image to sell a commodity. College had first attracted editors, writers, and businessmen as an experience to transform boys into fit, manly men, ready for potential leadership. It was imagined as a substitute for war or the old self-made, business proving ground, all capped with intellectual training. It embodied the best of an imagined past and present. While this ideal, no doubt, inspired advertisers to incorporate college references into their messages, the hard transformative experience of college was subsumed, a silent subtext lost in the glow of youthful beauty and sophistication. College itself had become commodified.

Conclusion

Since the 1890s, the mass magazines had functioned as a cultural forum where new meanings and identities were hammered out and offered to the new corporate middle class. In response to a crisis of masculinity, especially for the generic American businessman, college itself had received a massive refashioning. In articles and fiction, college was recrafted as a place to acquire character (through sport or liberal culture) in keeping with traditionally honored ideals of self-made manhood. Yet writers and editors also posited college as a place to acquire the stamp of modernity, of scientific authority as a future corporate professional. At college, according to the magazines, one could also indulge in virile athletic tests of manhood, learning corporate teamwork as well as re-asserting one's potent masculinity through a variety of other extracurricular activities. All the while, the notion of college bestowing a cultural polish only increased. It still supposedly created gentlemen. Magazine fiction writers created perhaps the fullest and most vivid expressions of the new ideal business hero. Characters like Wister in "The Cave Man" or Carpenter in "The Wedge" displayed the toughness, resilience, courage, and broad intellect forged from their college experiences. They naturally rose to become leaders of men, admired by both the working class and peers alike. By routing the American Dream of masculine business success through college, magazine contributors invited an ailing manhood to imagine college as a place to satisfy the various and at times conflicting strains of ideal masculinity and business identity. And the articles and fiction presented in this chapter serve as the prime examples of how these middle-class magazines assembled the component facets of the ideal college man and his future as corporate leader.

Once college was anointed as a fit and proper place to train future leaders of the corporate world, advertisements added their reinforcement to these established themes. Whereas advertisers at first used college primarily to associate their products with upper-middle-class life, youth, or cultured refinement, later ads picked up on the college man as a dashing sport, an ideal physical type, or a handsome athletic man. Ads appealed especially to the young businessman, inviting even more young men to identify with college. These appealing images in articles, fiction, and advertising bombarded even the casual reader of these periodicals with their powerful messages, solidifying the place of college in the fabric of American manhood and sowing the seeds of popular acceptance that later would manifest itself in burgeoning enrollments during later decades.

This embrace of college also brought a seemingly inevitable tarnishing of the very experience exalted in the magazines. Articles and fiction could explain exactly how college could benefit the future executive or manager—or any man. They could make a liberal education seem the most perfect training of the intellect ever conceived for molding leadership as well as instilling that cultured panache. They could describe the rigors of the college experience that were assumed to transform the boy into the ideal man, yet how could an ad communicate this? Ads reduced subtle arguments to a few terms in a sentence (character, distinction, refinement), or an illustration. They collapsed the benefits of college to an appealing image and, more importantly, connected this appeal to commodities—a style of living more than a transforming experience.

The positing of college as a new route to ideal manhood in the magazines was predicated on the forging of real benefits—character, intellect, culture, scientific training, virile manhood. But the ads filtered this into convenient images, all subtlety lost.

Scholars have long commented on the shift from character to personality as one of the hallmarks of masculine cultural transformation, owing to the rise of the corporate workplace. And we have seen how the positing of college as part of the formula for masculine business success figured prominently in this transformation as well—first, as a way potentially to preserve the ideal of character in a new age and, then, how the medium that principally communicated this new option, in fact, facilitated its transformation. Advertising, in particular reduced the ideal of developing character in college to a component of a pleasing personality or appearance.

In the process of becoming an accepted aspect of American success and middle-class masculinity, a process chiefly spearheaded by the mass media, college had become in a sense commodified—part of an ideal style of life, an image one could choose like the correct suit model. The magazine image of college generally and the advertisements in particular encouraged the notion that one could acquire the appearance of refinement simply through attendance or even association, not unlike the person who purchased the five-foot shelf of Harvard Classics, attracted by the promise of a liberal education. Even if the books sat unread on the shelf, they allowed the illusion of cultured refinement to those who saw them.

That many Americans would eventually look at college more as a social opportunity than as an intellectual preparation is not news. Scholars have been too quick, however, to dismiss such students as barbarians at the gates. This overlooks the fact that college had not been that popular or attractive an endeavor. The desire (especially for American men) had to be created, fomented, cultivated, and disseminated. The process developed over time and was intimately related to how a consumer-oriented medium fashioned the image of a college experience aligned with the shifting imperatives of masculinity and broadly conceived business success.

The power of consumer forces worked another fascinating and unintended transformation. Although this chapter has not dealt pointedly with issues of race and color as in previous chapters, the visions of college and masculine corporate authority explored in this chapter unquestionably reinforced the notion that this college man would be, of course, native-born and white. Indeed the fiction and advertising copy formed some of the most potent visions of the generically WASP American college and corporate man for readers. Ironically, though, and especially evident in advertising, the same imagery that so power-fully supported the dominant ideal uniting native-born, white men with college and masculine authority for a corporate age, also could be viewed as generi-cally white, as inviting all white American men, even the "questionably white" immigrants, to see themselves in such new and powerful ways. What seems at first so exclusionary, as part of a cultural process that fashioned racial parame-ters to such imagined opportunities as college and corporate advancement, in reality could function in the opposite direction. Even if at that time such ads likely did serve more to bolster perceptions of college and notions of WASP ac-cess and privilege, what would stop a young Pole, Slav, or Italian from happen-ing upon an Adler's Collegian Clothes ad and seeing themselves at college? Such is the ironic magic of consumerism.

Conclusion

College and the Culture of Aspiration

In 1920 the *Saturday Evening Post* continued to ponder the essential question that had initially inspired the interest in college education more than twenty years before, when it asked "Do Opportunities Still Exist?" And at first glance, it seemed that the traditional self-made man still reigned supreme. In this specific article, the prolific *Post* writer Albert W. Atwood trumpeted the fact (in his opinion) that "the self-made man, the man who has risen from the ranks, is the type that permeates modern industry in this country." Corporations had not killed opportunity; they had just slightly altered the conditions in which men could rise. America's democratic ladder of opportunity remained stronger than ever. A closer scrutiny of the examples Atwood offered in his article, however, while not disproving the claims of democratic opportunity, certainly testified to the fact that these were not their fathers' self-made men. Atwood did note several clerks and shop hands that had ascended to high executive office, but college graduates and sons of owners formed a conspicuously large presence among the list of self-made examples. Six sons of Gustavus Swift sat on the board of Western Electric, although Atwood emphasized that each one had to earn his place. More significantly, though, the majority of business executives he noted had gone to college, and he again highlighted that these college graduates had worked their way through the organization. He even featured AT&T's method of training managers by shifting them through menial jobs in several departments, but he glossed over the fact that the company recruited most of these trainees directly off college campuses rather than from among their own pool of clerks and workers.[1]

Atwood's article exemplified how the mass media worked to recast the mythology of the self-made man for a new age, crafting new "self-made" trajectories to power. By the 1920s, the corporate canvassing of college campuses had begun in earnest. The *Post*, for one, had long commented on such practices, but after 1920 systematic recruitment of college graduates by corporations became widespread, as did special management-training programs designed for the college graduate. Atwood himself penned an in-depth look at the phenomenon in "Impatient Youth in the Business World." After first offering the typical criticisms often lodged against the college-bred in business—expecting too rapid a rise, Atwood placed some of the blame on the companies themselves, who employed recruiters in a fierce competition for graduates. He also noted and endorsed the trend among the major corporations (Bell Telephone was cited as the model) to erect special executive training programs distinctly for college graduates. The reason?—the growing opinion that the college man needed more challenges and stimulation than the noncollege man he worked alongside.[2] College men were like gifted children, who withered if not intellectually challenged.

Why did businessmen even care? What made the college man suddenly so precious? Another article, A. H. Deute's "When the College Senior Becomes a Business Freshman," articulated the prime rationale informing these changes. The college man's value came not from any immediate skills he brought as a new hire; he still had to learn from experience. It was what he could bring as an executive at the age of thirty-five, owing to his "broad education." His mental training made him at first an "efficient cog in the machine," but through his "imagination, sound judgment, [and] a capacity for clear thinking," he would one day work "up to a big position."[3] And as Atwood, Deute and many other writers and business contributors to the magazines observed in the 1920s, businesses were eager for college men to serve as the lieutenants and junior officers of an expanding corporate America. Such language should sound very familiar.

Such articles reported on a solidifying business reality, one that the mass magazines had helped to define and one that they would continue to augment and refine in the 1920s. But much of the magazine's enormous cultural impact in shaping Americans' collegiate expectations evades obvious detection if one relies solely on the magazines' attention to college-related subjects in the 1920s. One does not find the obvious infatuation with the college man or college life that earlier had gripped popular magazines. One still found the ideal college man in every element of the magazines, but college had ceased to be a hot new phenomenon, at least for magazine editors. Ironically, the preoccupation of the magazines with the college experience and the college man in business faded as the American middle class began their embrace of college education in earnest, their expectations informed in no small part by the "cultural work" of the mass magazines over the preceding decades. By the 1920s, going to college and the ideal of the college-educated business executive had become firmly implanted in American culture.

Scholars working in the history of higher education and American culture have long recognized and focused on the 1920s as the pivotal decade when Americans truly accepted higher education within their "culture of aspiration."[4] The twenties brought mushrooming enrollments, the advent of "big time" college athletics with the building of giant stadiums, and the fermentation of a youth culture dominated by college fraternities and sororities that set the style for the rest of American youth.[5] All of these occurrences sparked academic and national debates over admissions quotas and the purpose of the college curriculum as more Americans recognized that the American Dream was increasingly routed through the college gates. Scholars have traced the college's increasing centrality within the American culture of aspiration (along with many of the academic problems it spawned) to the longings and desires of America's broad middle class. What did they expect from college? The American middle class, according to David O. Levine, "stubbornly insisted on viewing the college as a social opportunity rather than an intellectual experience." Consider this quote from Rita S. Halle's *Which College*, a guidebook for aspiring parents that came out in 1928: "In this last decade, higher education has become such a fetich [*sic*] in America that all the youth of the country, rich or poor, from the cities and farms, fit or unfit, are seeking the roads that lead to the universities. To each, or to his parents, a college degree is a stamp of social superiority, its lack a social stigma. Each one believes that it is a magic key to happiness, success and riches."[6] The rising popularity of college, then, hinged on its seemingly sudden connection to notions of success.

Those exploring this fervent embrace of college by the Babbitts of the decade find ample evidence on American campuses that students (and, thus, their parents) expected college to yield corporate success. American colleges and universities founded new business schools and introduced new business courses to satisfy the demand among students.[7] Student newspapers around the country registered the aspirations of most students, when they openly promoted participation in the extracurricular of campus life as preparation for business success, applauded the elevation of business to professional status through college programs, and endorsed "everyman's dream [to become] an industrial exec-utive."[8] Moreover, the college peer culture that blossomed in the 1920s, which put a premium on conformity and adaptability, in many ways helped to set the pattern for corporate society, part of the rising ideal of personality and "other-directedness" over the ideal of Victorian character in American life. And the college man's penchant for fads, his attention to style, and his acknowledged place as a consumer trend setter, again served as a model that hastened the ac-ceptance of flexibility and appearance as critical elements of modern Ameri-can masculinity.[9]

What scholars have documented in the 1920s was, in fact, not a new cre-ation arising out of that decade but rather the fruition of shifting cultural ex-pectations with regard to college in American life that had begun much earlier. Since the expectations of the American middle class who stormed the campuses in the 1920s seemed so transparent, scholars rarely paused to ponder how those expectations themselves had formed, how the idea of going to college had be-come so intimately intertwined with corporate business success or male, middle-class identity.

Essentially this book has attempted to illuminate the origins of the place of college education in modern American life—to understand why Rita Halle could find a national market for her guidebook, *Which College?*, in the 1920s, when the most popular success guidebooks of 1900 deigned to mention college largely in order to dismiss it as a waste of time.[10] What had happened in the interim? At the same time that the success books of 1900 were dismissing col-lege, a new and more important venue for molding American perceptions was deep in the process of redefining the college experience to render it a fit prep-aration for middle-class men. American mass magazines spearheaded a cul-tural reconstruction of college and middle-class masculinity in tandem in the years surrounding 1900, as they emerged as a central national cultural forum, our nation's first truly national media. Americans did not choose to go to col-lege in the 1920s because the *Saturday Evening Post* said they should. But the hopes and visions that Americans invested in the college experience—the kind of lives they hoped for their children to achieve through a college education—suggested that the media messages of the previous three decades had not been lost on their audience. The key mechanism accounting for the transformation of college in American culture—how college became invested with meaning, may be found in the pages of mass magazines of those days. But asking such basic but unexplored questions as what cultural expectations informed the ris-ing popularity of college leads one to a deeper understanding of fundamental shifts in American society. This cultural reconstruction of college cuts to the very core of transforming notions of masculinity, male power, and authority in an emerging corporate America. And the American mass magazines formed the critical conduit of this cultural reformation.

Magazine editors and writers (including business contributors, academic reformers, and fiction authors) had originally fastened upon college education as an ideal preparation for a rising new generation of corporate middle-class leaders. College proved an ideally malleable experience. Various facets of college education or college life could be fashioned to meet a variety of evolving male longings and anxieties. With the college's links to the ideal of culture and a learned tradition, college attendance conferred the mark of gentility. Culture and the mental discipline of college also built key elements of character, that critical Victorian ideal encompassing so many virtuous traits necessary for success. Plus, most acknowledged (including most businessmen) that liberal education nurtured a broad vision, more vital than ever for the corporate manager who commanded much more than his self-made antecedent. It also was connected with the preparation of traditional professionals, bolstering the emerging middle-class notion that corporations increasingly would serve the public interest under the guidance of business professionals trained in college. At the same time, however, by virtue of the rise of science on campus, the college became a perfect education for the modern side of the developing professional ideal of middle-class businessmen—something the magazines celebrated and helped to fashion as well.

While the previously suspect college curriculum had been recast and its benefits intertwined with the ideal corporate lieutenant in periodicals, the magazines also encouraged a re-envisioning of college as a place to form an ideal manhood, as concepts of masculinity were in the process of transformation. In this transition, too, college proved an ideal place to accommodate often-conflicting concepts of manhood. Through college athletics, principally football, one could imagine the college experience forging the character, grit, and toughness of self-made, Victorian manhood, even as through the same activity one indulged in fantasies of passionate expression (an element of modern masculinity) rather than self-control. Similarly, athletics preserved the chance for individual glory even as it taught important lessons of cooperative effort and teamwork perfectly suited for the corporate world. And presentations of the campus extracurricular offered up in magazines posited college as a place to revel in rough male bonding and a carefree camaraderie, even as the messages in these representations reinforced the modern corporate value of fitting in with one's fellows. Magazine editors and writers contributed to a rethinking of the place of college in American men's lives that offered multiple ways of interpreting the college experience, and thus multiple ways of imagining and presenting one-self. They also firmly connected these visions to concepts of business success and the ideal corporate executive.

Far more completely than magazine articles, fiction and advertising articulated and rounded out the full vision of how the college experience could form the ideal middle-class man or model corporate executive. Fiction authors in the magazines utilized the full spectrum of manly collegiate identifications, especially when casting college-educated characters as heroes in magazine fiction. They offered numerous and vivid portrayals of college football heroes, who then worked their way up business organizations to positions of responsibility. In stories, the college-educated businessman changed from an object of derision to a leader of vision, a man who naturally rose to command. Tales of campus pranks and fraternal camaraderie promised experiences to last a lifetime, while other stories and references prompted readers to view the college campus as hallowed cultural ground, a special place (still encouraging that longing for genteel status). Magazine advertising strengthened the solidifying conceptions of the college experience. Ads reinforced the college man's association with ideal aspects of American manhood, and invited all men—particularly the generic middle-class "businessmen," to indulge in collegiate identifications—to be the virile athlete, the cultured and sophisticated collegian, and (of course) a paragon of style.

While such ads seemed to invite all men, however, in reality subtle but powerful forms of cultural exclusion coexisted with the seeming new openness and accessibility of a college education. In fact, constructing such exclusions formed a critical component of crafting the new college man and visions of middle-class corporate authority. This would not be a path for everyman or for women. Evolving notions of American masculinity were constructed around 1900 with certain longings and fears of native-born American men firmly in mind. Adapting to a shifting work environment was one demand necessitating reformulations, but the threat of new immigrants and "the new woman," exacerbated by the ideas of Social Darwinism (anxieties about a cultural and racial declension), also animated those writing for and contributing to the magazines.[11]

These were mass magazines for native-born white middle-class Americans, who saw themselves as generically WASP, or at least identified with that imagined historical tradition. No informative articles or editorials pointedly integrated examples of minorities or recent immigrants (or their sons and daughters) as college students or as college graduates working their way up. And while a handful of fictional college or college-educated characters who were minorities or immigrants did appear, they constituted a tiny percentage of the total surveyed for this study—exceptions that prove the rule. More revealing was the common story line of the native-born white college graduates "naturally" rising through the ranks to positions of authority over their working-class, laboring colleagues in magazine fiction, a central adaptation of the self-made ideal but where the college experience reinforced dominant racial assumptions in defining one as a superior leader. And, regarding the new woman, the magazine contributors performed a remarkably deft cultural slight of hand. Editors and writers fully embraced the notion of the college girl, and magazine fiction offered an array of college-educated women as love interests and wives. Inevitably, though, she conformed to her higher duties as wife or mother to support a male career. Precious few stories focused solely on women in college, or as college grads in the world with no mention of men. Just as often, a story involving college-educated men would neglect any mention of a college education (or any education) for a love interest or wife. The college-educated woman with very few exceptions was to be principally a worthy consort to the new college-educated male leaders of modern America. As cultural architects in the magazines crafted the college experience as a marvelous new opportunity and training for native-born white men, they quite naturally shaped the conception of who should see themselves rising through such a path to privilege and authority in modern America, powerful cultural assumptions that helped inform the parameters of appropriate opportunities in America.

Despite such subtle but potent exclusions, the magazine's integrated refashioning of the college experience, the college man, and the college-educated businessman did indeed work to popularize the new place of college in the American cultural narrative of success that informed the seemingly sudden explosion of interest in going to college during the 1920s and in the decades following. The cultural reconstruction of college orchestrated by the mass magazines vitally redefined not only the college experience but also facilitated transformations in masculinity and male authority. Only as constructed and disseminated in this forum could Americans view the college experience as one where a man could simultaneously be genteel yet tough and rowdy, cultured yet manly, polished yet professional—an ideal civilized-primitive leader, superior to any immigrant challenge and ready to captain a new America. Within the cultural forum of the magazines, writers and contributors used college to construct new narratives of manhood for the middle class in the dawning corporate age, and college proved an ideal location, an ideal experience, that allowed for multiple facets of an evolving masculinity to coexist seamlessly. No set of individuals provided unique models for emulation. No set of institutions, whether collegiate or in the world of business and the professions, set uniform standards to guide such creations of ideal manhood on such a national scale. The cultural forum of the mass magazines formed the perfect, the essential platform for the creation of college as cultural capital.

The overall vision of the college man and the college experience that the magazine coverage helped to fashion prior to 1920 was not yet a part of the cultural mainstream. Editors, writers, and admen did not reflect a new reality. Relatively small proportions of even middle-class men actually went to college. And for that matter American higher education was not homogenously native-born WASP. During the first decades of the new century numerous urban and Catholic institutions, like DePaul University for example, enrolled immigrant or non-WASP American youth as did the private liberal arts colleges serving African Americans.[12] The magazines in fact did something more significant than reflect a reality; they actively conjured an ideal, a new normative for the American middle class. They refashioned mainstream notions of "being" a white, middle-class American to include the revamped concept of college as an essential aspect of a reworked narrative of masculine authority.[13]

It is with fiction and advertising, however, that one can detect how the medium itself contributed to an alteration in the popular visions of college it had helped to create. These alterations also point directly to the way the media influenced popular collegiate expectations of the twenties that proved doggedly problematic. From the very outset in advertising and over time in fiction, references to college functioned as a kind of cultural shorthand that reduced ideals such as character, culture, and even toughness to an amalgamated image. Fiction and advertising seemed to gloss over how these ideal qualities formed, and instead focused on conveying an appealing image. The image became the message; the hard practice of forging ideal qualities became subsumed within the attractive results of the college experience. Advertising went the farthest, connecting an idealized college man to a certain style of life, commodifying college as a standard set of attributes one could acquire like a suit of clothing.

What is perhaps most ironic, advertising in providing some of the most potent visual images reinforcing the new ideal linking the WASP college man with visions of business, professional, and social masculine power could be read as indeed inviting all American men, but particularly "white" ethnic immigrants, to see themselves as that ideal man in the ads. In this way images that on one level strengthened associations between college and authority and were constructed originally to privilege native-born white American men, on another level could offer visions of a generic whiteness to questionably white immigrants. Such inviting ads alone cannot explain the rising enrollments of American ethnics in the interwar years or the advent of racial admission quotas at many elite institutions during those same years, aimed at keeping the racially questionable offspring of immigrants (particularly eastern European Jews) off the campuses.[14] But such ads undoubtedly formed part of a larger narrative of success and authority, newly integrating college matriculation, which proved highly attractive and which the magazines explored in this study played the vital role in creating and spreading—informing a broader culture of aspiration involving college.

The magazine, of course, is a consumer-oriented medium. To a certain degree editors and writers in these magazines, much like advertisers, sought to posit ideal images for emulation. And even those ideal concepts that seemed to uphold traditional Victorian values, when filtered through the media and advertising, underwent a transformation. In this way, the media worked to facilitate a cultural transformation from the Victorian era to the modern corporate and consumer age. The media makeover of college and the insertion of college into the fabric of American success and masculinity that this book has explored formed a significant and unheralded part of this overall transformation. And inevitably this worked to influence how Americans were encouraged to think of college, helping to inform the expectations they placed on the college experience—with both positive and negative ramifications.

If Americans in the 1920s viewed college primarily as an experience that furthered business and social opportunities and associated them with an attractive style of life, then the magazines had, in fact, helped to inform and channel their expectations. Guided by the magazines, American men's visions of college's benefits likely still rested upon cherished traditional values—genteel culture, rugged manhood. But the way in which magazines encouraged such visions, was linked by the 1920s more to cultivating personality than character—or the simple, consumer-oriented calculus that by attending college one could assume the image of the college man ideal. The older notions of forging character through college factored out of the equation, ironically, by the medium that had first popularized college as the best place to preserve these ideals in future leaders.

Nevertheless, it is too easy to dismiss the Babbitts of the 1920s, who stormed the colleges, as cultural Philistines. The ideal of acquiring culture remained, even if in a transformed state and even if more for the benefit of closing the deal than molding the man. Vestiges of the ideal remained in the middle-class culture of America. A reverence for learning was preserved. College could never be completely commodified. The essential, core idea of college as a potentially life-transforming experience that could shape inner qualities of character (while buffeted and reworked) continued to exist.

Similarly, it was unquestionably clear that the reconfiguration of the self-made myth narrative to include the college-trained man worked to bolster evolving middle-class notions of authority and to privilege the traditional WASP middle class. Few in the working class, especially immigrants, had the means to attend college and satisfy the developing requirements of rising up the ladder. And women, even female college graduates, were simply not written into the cultural narratives of power and authority. Nevertheless, the rhetoric of democracy survived within even these new cultural narratives of authority, so that college attendance as an avenue of opportunity remained operable for more than just the elite few. Yet, as culturally constructed, college became a credential that constricted democratic opportunity for a time. But what this study also equally helps to understand is how democratic ideals originally constructed within a new vision of college and its place in the trajectories of masculine success could work ultimately to inspire and rationalize demand for greater access to college.

Notes

Introduction

1. Bird S. Coler, "The Man Who Can't Go to College," *Saturday Evening Post*, 29 June 1901, p. 8.

2. See for instance Susan Faludi, *Stiffed: The Betrayal of the American Man* (New York: Harper Perennial, 2000).

3. Richard Weiss, *The American Myth of Success: From Horatio Alger to Norman Vincent Peale* (New York and London: Basic Books, 1969), 9.

4. Irvin G. Wyllie, *The Self-Made Man in America: The Myth of Rags to Riches* (New Brunswick, NJ: Rutgers University Press, 1954), 95–96.

5. U.S. Bureau of the Census (1961), *Historical Statistics of the United States*, 10 and 210–11, quoted in David K. Brown, *Degrees of Control: A Sociology of Educational Expansion and Occupational Credentialism* (New York: Columbia University Teachers College Press, 1995), 76.

6. Wyllie, *Self-Made Man in America*, 35 and 100–103. The quote is from Wyllie (35), but Wyllie drew from nineteenth-century advice literature such as Edwin T. Freedley, *A Practical Treatise on Business* (Philadelphia: Lippincott, Grambo and Co., 1854). Wyllie notes many examples of practical men of affairs dismissing the college man as useless. Judy Hilkey found the very same dismissals of the college man into the twentieth century. Judy Hilkey, *Character Is Capital: Success Manuals and Manhood in Gilded Age America* (Chapel Hill: University of North Carolina Press, 1997), 108–10.

7. Noted in Mark McKenzie, "Expectations of College Life Before 1940," *American Educational History Journal* 27 (2000): 88–92.

8. The progression by decade from 1870 is: 1870, 52,286 or 1.6%; 1880, 115,817 or 2.72%; 1890, 156,756 or 3.04%; 1900, 237,592 or 4.01%; 1910, 355,213 or 5.1%; 1920, 597,880 or 8.2%; and 1930, 1.1 million or 12.95%. *Digest of Education Statistics*, 1977–78, 85 and 94; and *Historical Statistics of the United States*, Series H, 751–56, compiled in W. Bruce Leslie, "Toward a History of the American Upper Middle Class, 1870–1940" (paper presented at the Cambridge University American History Seminar, 1994), 13.

9. F. W. Tausig and C. S. Joslyn, *American Business Leaders: A Study in Origins and Social Stratification* (New York: Macmillan, 1932), 55 and 184. Mabel Newcomer found in industry (in 1900) that 34 percent had some college, 24 percent college degrees, and 5 percent engineering degrees. By 1925 these percentages had increased to 49 percent for those with some college, 39 percent with college degrees, and 10 percent with engineering

191

degrees. Mabel Newcomer, *The Big Business Executive: The Factors That Made Him, 1900–1950* (New York: Columbia University Press, 1955), 73.

10. My definition of cultural capital comes from Pierre Bourdieu. Cultural capital encompasses forms of knowledge and cultural norms (skills and understandings) corresponding to the dominant culture. In contrast social capital consists of the connections and networks (family, friends, acquaintances) that form the group identifications of a person. Pierre Bourdieu, "The Forms of Capital," in *Handbook of Theory and Research of the Sociology of Education*, ed. J. G. Richardson (New York: Greenwood Press, 1986), 241–58.

11. David Noble, *America by Design: Science, Technology and the Rise of Corporate Capitalism* (New York: Knopf, 1977); Burton Bledstein, *The Culture of Professionalism: The Middle Class and the Development of Higher Education in America* (New York: W. W. Norton and Company, 1976); Roger L. Geiger, *To Advance Knowledge: The Growth of American Research Universities, 1900–1940* (New York: Oxford University Press, 1986); Clyde Barrow, *Universities and the Capitalist State: Corporate Liberalism and the Reconstruction of Higher Education, 1894–1928* (Madison: University of Wisconsin Press, 1990); Pamela Walker Laird, *Pull: Networking and Success since Benjamin Franklin* (Cambridge: Harvard University Press, 2006). One work that takes a functionalist stance but not in a traditional sense is Brown, *Degrees of Control.* Christopher Newfield, *Ivy and Industry: Business and the Making of the American University, 1880–1980* (Durham: Duke University Press, 2003).

12. Business historians touching on the increased hiring of college graduates include Alfred D. Chandler, *The Visible Hand: The Managerial Revolution in American Business* (Cambridge, MA: Harvard University Press, 1977); Quentin Schultze, "'An Honorable Place': The Quest for Professional Advertising Education," *Business History Review* 56 (Spring 1982): 16–32; and Olivier Zunz, *Making America Corporate, 1870–1920* (Chicago: University of Chicago Press, 1990).

13. For the onset of educational credentials in medicine and law due in part to the influx of immigrant practitioners, see particularly Paul Starr, *The Social Transformation of American Medicine* (New York: Basic Books, 1982); and William B. Johnson, *Schooled Lawyers: A Study in the Clash of Professional Cultures* (New York: New York University Press, 1978).

14. The following sources note the rise of a concept of professionalism in the early years of these corporate bureaucratic professionals, but also acknowledge that formal educational credentials took a long time to develop, well into the twentieth century. Harold Livesay, "The Profession of Management in the United States," in *The Professions in American History*, ed. Nathan O. Hatch (South Bend: University of Notre Dame Press, 1988), 199–220; Paul J. Miranti, *Accountancy Comes of Age: The Development of an American Profession, 1886–1940* (Chapel Hill: University of North Carolina Press, 1990); Monte A. Calvert, *The Mechanical Engineer in America, 1830–1910: Professional Cultures in Conflict* (Baltimore: Johns Hopkins University Press, 1967); and Pamela Walker Laird, *Advertising Progress: American Business and the Rise of Consumer Marketing* (Baltimore: Johns Hopkins University Press, 1998), chap. 9.

15. Newcomer, *Big Business Executive*, 73.

16. Some minimal educational credentials were becoming important after 1880, but not yet collegiate credentials. As early as 1880 at the Chicago, Burlington, and Quincy Railroad, the majority of mid-level managers had graduated from high school. Zunz, *Making America Corporate*, 49.

17. From 1880 to at least 1920, the high school rather than the college was the most

critical middle-class educational institution. Joel Perlmann, "Curriculum and Tracking in the Transformation of the American High School: Providence, R.I., 1880–1930," *Journal of Social History* 19 (Fall 1985), 29–55; Reed Ueda, *Avenues to Adulthood: Origins of the High School and Social Mobility in an American Suburb* (Cambridge: Cambridge University Press, 1987); and David F. Labaree, *The Making of an American High School: The Credentials Market and the Central High School of Philadelphia, 1839–1939* (New Haven: Yale University Press, 1988).

18. As one noted business historian, Harold Livesay, commented: "The profession of management is a social (cultural, if you prefer) phenomenon, not an economic one." Livesay, "The Profession of Management in the United States," 201.

19. Steven Sass, *The Pragmatic Imagination: A History of the Wharton School, 1881–1991* (Philadelphia: University of Pennsylvania Press, 1982); Michael W. Sedlak and Harold F. Williamson, *The Evolution of Management Education: A History of the Northwestern University J. L. Kellogg Graduate School of Management* (Urbana: University of Illinois Press, 1983); J. Cruikshank, *A Delicate Experiment: The Harvard Business School, 1908–1945* (Cambridge, MA: Harvard University Press, 1987).

20. Both Konrad Jarausch and Richard Angelo called for more scholarly attention to the appeal of the liberal arts. Jarausch, "Higher Education and Social Change: Some Comparative Perspectives," in *The Transformation of Higher Learning, 1860–1930*, ed. Konrad H. Jarausch (Chicago: University of Chicago Press, 1983), 32–34; and Richard Angelo, "The Social Transformation of American Higher Education," in *The Transformation of Higher Learning, 1860–1930*, 261–92.

21. Though he did not examine business, Samuel Haber criticized modernization theory for slighting the hard to quantify but palpable appeal of the educated, learned man as an aspect of professional authority. Samuel Haber, *The Quest for Authority and Honor in the American Professions, 1750–1900* (Chicago: University of Chicago Press, 1991): 202–4.

22. Laurence Veysey, *The Emergence of the American University* (Chicago: University of Chicago Press, 1965); Joseph Kett, *Rites of Passage: Adolescence in America, 1790 to the Present* (New York: Basic Books, 1977); David O. Levine, *The American College and the Culture of Aspiration, 1915–1940* (Ithaca, NY: Cornell University Press, 1986); Helen Lefkowitz Horowitz, *Campus Life: Undergraduate Culture from the End of the Eighteenth Century to the Present* (New York: Knopf, 1987); and W. Bruce Leslie, *Gentlemen and Scholars: College and Community in the "Age of the University," 1865–1917* (University Park: Pennsylvania State University Press, 1992). Kett notes the romantic activism of college life (the extracurricular), the gothic architecture, and manicured lawns as key motivations. Kett, *Rites of Passage*, 181.

23. On the growth of an American upper class see, E. Digby Baltzell, *Philadelphia Gentlemen: The Making of a National Upper Class* (Glencoe, IL: Free Press, 1958); Ronald Story, *Harvard and the Boston Upper Class: The Forging of an Aristocracy, 1800–1870* (Middletown, CT: Wesleyan University Press, 1980); Steven B. Levine, "The Rise of American Boarding Schools and the Development of a National Upper Class," *Social Problems* 28 (October 1980); Clifford Putney, *Muscular Christianity: Manhood and Sports in Protestant America* (Cambridge, MA: Harvard University Press, 2001), chap. 1; and Jerome Karabel, *The Chosen: The Hidden History of Admission and Exclusion at Harvard, Yale and Princeton* (New York: Houghton Mifflin, 2005), chap. 1.

24. Some exceptional works that deal with the rise of "culture" as a special and sacred endeavor include Lawrence Levine, *Highbrow/Lowbrow: The Emergence of Cultural*

Hierarchy in America (Cambridge, MA: Harvard University Press, 1988); and Alan Trachtenberg, *The Incorporation of America: Culture and Society in the Gilded Age* (New York: Hill and Wang, 1982), 140–81.

25. David K. Brown's *Degree's of Control* argued that corporate employers, unable to simply hire sons and acquaintances for management in their growing enterprises, increasingly turned to college graduates, whom they valued less for any technical expertise (Brown's statistics show that the vast majority took a liberal arts curriculum) than for their communication skills and supposed natural feeling of superiority (ironically one of the very things for which businessmen had consistently criticized college grads). Brown's study begins to connect the dots between college and the new middle-class world of corporate business, but due to the nature of his sociological analysis, he cannot follow through on the cultural issues he raises. In fact, the study downplays the very real attraction of the increasingly practical and scientific side of the college curriculum. Brown, *Degrees of Control*, 146–47. Two of the earliest scholars to approach the subject with regard to businessmen, Irvin G. Wyllie and Edward C. Kirkland, commented that some businessmen openly recruited college graduates for their supposed status as proper gentlemen. Wyllie, *Self-Made Man in America*, 111–13; and Edward C. Kirkland, *Dream and Thought in the American Business Community, 1860–1900* (Ithaca, NY: Cornell University Press, 1956), 71–80.

26. Living in cities and working in hierarchical, bureaucratic, and interdependent organizations, these white-collar workers and managers had less and less in common with the icon of nineteenth-century success, the small independent entrepreneur. Olivier Zunz mentions the emergence of a distinct new set of values and ideals such as the bureaucratic ethos in his introduction to *Making America Corporate*, 9–10. The best accounting of the overall transition in the world of business is Chandler, *Visible Hand*, 3–12. The statistical increases in white-collar workers during this period are astounding. For one overview see Jurgen Kocka, *White Collar Workers in America, 1890–1940: A Social-Political History in International Perspective* (London: Sage Publications, 1980). The nineteenth-century middle class has been chronicled by Paul Johnson, *A Shopkeeper's Millennium: Society and Revivals in Rochester, New York, 1815–1837* (New York: Hill and Wang, 1978); Mary Ryan, *Cradle of the Middle Class: The Family in Oneida County, New York, 1790–1865* (Cambridge: Cambridge University Press, 1981); and Stuart Blumin, *Emergence of the Middle Class* (New York: Cambridge University Press, 1989).

27. Most historians of masculinity note this change. On the Victorian ideal of the self-made man, see Wyllie, *Self-Made Man in America*, 21–40; E. Anthony Rotundo, "Learning about Manhood: Gender Ideals and the Middle-Class Family in Nineteenth-Century America," in *Manliness and Morality: Middle-Class Masculinity in Britain and America, 1880–1940*, ed. J. A. Mangan and James Walvin (New York: St. Martin's Press, 1987), 35–51. One particularly good examination of the shifts in the business world is Angel Kwolek-Folland, *Engendering Business: Men and Women in the Corporate Office, 1870–1930* (Baltimore: Johns Hopkins University Press, 1994).

28. Major works on the challenges to American men and the resulting shifts in conceptions of American masculinity, include Peter G. Filene, *Him/Her/Self: Sex Roles in Modern America*, 2nd ed. (Baltimore: Johns Hopkins University Press, 1986); Peter N. Stearns, *Be a Man! Males in Modern Society*, 2nd ed. (New York: Holmes and Meier Publishers, Inc., 1990); Joe L. Dubbert, *A Man's Place: Masculinity in Transition* (Englewood

Cliffs, NJ: Prentice-Hall, Inc., 1979); Elizabeth Pleck and Joseph Pleck, eds., *The American Man* (Englewood Cliffs, NJ: Prentice-Hall, Inc., 1979); J. A. Mangan and James Walvin, eds., *Manliness and Morality: Middle-Class Masculinity in Britain and America, 1880–1940*; Mark C. Carnes and Clyde Griffen, eds., *Meanings for Manhood: Constructions of Masculinity in Victorian America* (Chicago: University of Chicago Press, 1990); E. Anthony Rotundo, *American Manhood: Transformations in Masculinity from the Revolution to the Modern Era* (New York: Basic Books, 1993); and Michael Kimmel, *Manhood in America: A Cultural History* (New York: Free Press, 1997).

29. As many recent scholars of "whiteness" have explored, the American "self-made man" ideal arose during an earlier era of relative racial homogeneity (mostly northern and western European immigrant stock). New immigrants after 1890, though technically "white," increasingly found their racial status in question. One historian has noted that the history of nativism in this period is essentially the redefining of whiteness and notions of power. Matthew Frye Jacobson, *Whiteness of a Different Color: European Immigrants and the Alchemy of Race* (Cambridge, MA: Harvard University Press, 1998), 7–9. Also see Todd Vogel *ReWriting White: Race, Class, and Cultural Capital in Nineteenth-Century America* (New Brunswick, NJ: Rutgers University Press, 2004), chap. 3. David Roediger first explored this in *Wages of Whiteness: Race and the Making of the American Working Class* (New York: Verso, 1991).

30. The term is Rotundo's (*American Manhood*), but most scholars who examine the changes in male gender expectations see the same thing. John Pettegrew's recent work highlights the primitive and violent aspects of this shift due to the influence of Darwinism, what Pettegrew sees as de-evolutionary thinking. John Pettegrew, *Brutes in Suits: Male Sensibility in America, 1890–1920* (Baltimore: Johns Hopkins University Press, 2007).

31. Each of the authors mentioned in note 29 deal with these adaptations. Other works that have shaped my thinking are: Elliott J. Gorn, *The Manly Art: Bare-Knuckle Prize-Fighting in America* (Ithaca, NY: Cornell University Press, 1986), chaps. 6–7; T. J. Jackson Lears, *No Place of Grace: Anti-Modernism and the Transformation of American Culture, 1880–1920* (New York: Pantheon, 1981), 47–58; Christopher Lasch, *The Culture of Narcissism: American Life in an Age of Diminishing Expectations* (New York: W. W. Norton and Co., 1979), 100–124; Roberta J. Park, "Biological Thought, Athletics and the Formation of a 'Man of Character,' 1830–1900," in *Manliness and Morality*, 7–34; Robert J. Higgs, "Yale and the Heroic Ideal: Gotterdammerung and Palingenesis, 1865–1914," in *Manliness and Morality*, 160–75; Steven A. Reiss, "Sport and the Redefinition of American Middle-Class Masculinity," *International Journal of the History of Sport* 8 (May 1991): 5–27; John Lucas and Ronald Smith, *The Saga of American Sport* (Philadelphia: Lea and Febiger, 1978), chap. 13; Melvin Adelman, *Sporting Time: New York City and the Rise of Modern Athletics, 1820–1870* (Urbana: University of Illinois Press, 1986); Benjamin Rader, *American Sports: From the Age of Folk Games to the Age of Spectators* (Englewood Cliffs, NJ: Prentice-Hall, Inc., 1983), 75–86. Some of the excellent studies to examine the embrace of outdoor activity and the "strenuous life" include Kimmel, *Manhood in America*, 81–89, 134–35, and 181–88; Rotundo, *American Manhood*, chap. 10; Stearns, *Be a Man!*, 110–18; Gorn, *The Manly Art*, 192–202; Roderick Nash, "The American Cult of the Primitive," *American Quarterly* 18 (Fall 1966): 517–37.

32. Very good works covering the growth of American fraternal organizations include Mark C. Carnes, *Secret Rituals and Manhood in Victorian America* (New Haven: Yale

University Press, 1989); Mary Ann Clawson, *Constructing Brotherhood: Class, Gender and Fraternalism* (Princeton: Princeton University Press, 1989), 170–74.

33. Gorn provides one of the best looks at the embrace of the bachelor urban sporting culture by the middle-class man (once reviled as immoral). Gorn, *The Manly Art*, particularly chap. 6. More generally, see Lewis Erenberg, *Steppin' Out: New York Nightlife and the Transformation of American Culture, 1890–1930* (Westport, CT: Greenwood Press, 1981), chaps. 1 and 3, and 233–38; Trachtenberg, *The Incorporation of America*, chap. 4; Gunther Barth, *City People: The Rise of Modern City Culture in Nineteenth Century America* (New York: Oxford University Press, 1980), chaps. 5–6; and John F. Kasson, *Amusing the Million: Coney Island at the Turn of the Century* (New York: Hill and Wang, 1978).

34. Some of the excellent works touching on the new manly heroes include Rotundo, *American Manhood*, 227–46; Kimmel, *Manhood in America*, 141–54; Filene, *Be a Man!*, 86–94; Gail Bederman, *Manliness and Civilization: A Cultural History of Gender and Race in the United States, 1880–1917* (Chicago: University of Chicago Press, 1996), 217–39; Pettegrew, *Brutes in Suits*, chap. 3.

35. Stearns believes that the initial redefinition of the businessman as warrior and general stemmed from the big businessman's desire "to justify themselves to themselves" and to the wider world who had been taught that excessive wealth was wrong. Stearns, *Be a Man!*, 110–14. See especially, Kwolek-Folland, *Engendering Business*, chaps. 2 and 3.

36. One of the best works that fully explores this transformation in masculinity is Tom Pendergast, *Creating the Modern Man: American Magazines and Consumer Culture* (Columbia: University of Missouri Press, 2000).

37. No scholars have fully integrated a careful analysis of how college intertwined with evolving masculinity. Kim Townsend's *Manhood at Harvard* is an exception. Kim Townsend, *Manhood at Harvard: William James and Others* (Cambridge, MA: Harvard University Press, 1996).

38. Kett, *Rites of Passage*, 173–81; Rader, *American Sports*, 70–86; Lucas and Smith, *Saga of American Sport*, chaps. 12–15; Guy Lewis, "The Beginning of Organized Collegiate Sport," *American Quarterly* 22 (Summer 1970), 225–39; Lasch, "The Degradation of Sport," in *Culture of Narcissism*, 103–24; Michael Oriard, *Reading Football: How the Popular Press Created an American Spectacle* (Chapel Hill: University of North Carolina Press, 1993).

39. Bederman, *Manliness and Civilization*. Bederman does not mention college and does not explore how civilization might be linked to liberal culture. Similarly Joan Shelley Rubin connected the rise of a so-called middlebrow culture movement in the early twentieth century (Book-of-the-Month Club, etc.) with a continued wish to appear cultured, the survival in modern consumer form of the genteel, liberal culture tradition. Joan Shelley Rubin, *The Making of Middlebrow Culture* (Chapel Hill: University of North Carolina Press, 1992).

40. Edward W. Said, *Orientalism* (New York: Pantheon Books, 1978). My working notion of a discourse is derived from Michel Foucault, *Archaeology of Knowledge* (New York: Pantheon Books, 1972).

41. "Letters from a Self-Made Merchant to His Son," *Saturday Evening Post*, 3 August 1901, p. 11. It is no coincidence that Lorimer chose meat packing as the industry setting for this issue. When Lorimer dropped out of Yale, he left to work for Armour in Chicago. Helen Damon-Moore, *Magazines for the Millions: Gender and Commerce in the Ladies Home Journal and the Saturday Evening Post, 1880–1910* (New York: SUNY Press, 1994), 109.

42. "Old Gorgon Graham," *Saturday Evening Post*, 3 September 1904, p. 89.

43. "Letters," *Saturday Evening Post*, 17 August 1901, p. 11.

44. Graham admonished his son to work harder in "Letters," *Saturday Evening Post*, 22 February 1902, p. 11; and "Letters," *Saturday Evening Post*, 22 March 1902, p. 5. He preached against pride in "Letters," *Saturday Evening Post*, 26 October 1901, p. 5; Old Gorgon Graham recommended the Maine woods as more manly than purchasing "badly fitting clothes" during a European vacation. "Letters," *Saturday Evening Post*, 31 August 1901, p. 7. He urged his son to write and speak with directness like a business-man, rather than with the rhetorical flourishes of a college dandy in "Letters," *Saturday Evening Post*, 21 September 1901, p. 7; and in "Letters," *Saturday Evening Post*, 11 January 1902, p. 5. In the 26 October letter, he specifically criticized his son's complaining about a cantankerous Irish boss that the boy was forced to work under in the stock yards. The father mentioned socializing when a business associate noted receiving a letter from the firm that began "Dearest," the boy having mixed up his correspondence as a clerk. "Letters," *Saturday Evening Post*, 5 October 1901, p. 6.

45. These characters appeared in "Letters," *Saturday Evening Post*, 13 September 1902, pp. 5 and 17; "Old Gorgon Graham," *Saturday Evening Post*, 5 December 1903, pp. 2–3 and 55; and "Old Gorgon Graham," *Saturday Evening Post*, 12 March 1904, pp. 3–4.

46. "Letters," *Saturday Evening Post*, 3 August 1901, p. 11. Both series ("Letters" and "Old Gorgon Graham") proved highly popular. The character "Old Gorgon Graham" may even be found endorsing products in the advertisements of rival magazines. Ralston Purina Foods, *Cosmopolitan* 34 (March 1903): back cover.

47. "Letters," *Saturday Evening Post*, 22 March 1902, p. 5. Graham exhorted Piggy to more strenuous efforts by using the example of a small but fiery red-haired fullback they had both witnessed in action against Columbia, an early reference connecting college football and business, which would grow over time.

48. The first College Man's issue was October 28, 1899.

49. For instance, John Brisben Walker, "Modern College Education," *Cosmopolitan* 22 (April 1897): 681–88; and Arthur T. Hadley, "Modern College Education," *Cosmopolitan* 28 (November 1899): 104–13.

50. Erman J. Ridgeway, "College Fraternities," *Munsey's Magazine* 24 (February 1901): 729–42; and P. F. Piper, "College Fraternities," *Cosmopolitan* 22 (March 1897): 641–48.

51. Arthur Hobson Quinn, "The Last Five Yards," *Saturday Evening Post*, 28 October 1899, pp. 335–36.

52. Charles R. Flint, "How Business Success Will Be Won in the Twentieth Century," *Saturday Evening Post*, 17 November 1900, p. 8; and "Wanted: A Master," *Saturday Evening Post*, 28 February 1903, p. 15.

53. Francis L. Patton, "Should a Business Man Have a College Education?" *Saturday Evening Post*, 26 May 1900, p. 1094; and James B. Dill, "The College Man and the Corporate Position," *Munsey's Magazine* 24 (October 1900): 148–52.

54. Jesse Lynch Williams, "Talks with a Kid Brother at College—Horse Play," *Saturday Evening Post*, 16 May 1903, p. 3.

55. For example, Charles Macomb Flandrau, "The Diary of a Harvard Freshman," *Saturday Evening Post*, 19 January 1901, pp. 10–11; and advertisement for "Adler's Collegian Clothes," David Adler and Sons Clothing Company, *Saturday Evening Post*, 16 April 1907, p. 1.

56. See T. J. Jackson Lears's discussion of cultural hegemony and Antonio Gramsci, and the way Christopher Wilson applied Lears's thinking to popular fiction writers of the early twentieth century (many of whom wrote for mass magazines), whose fiction Wilson viewed as creating "commonsensicality." These writers used their discursive power to shape a new white-collar norm and notions of being a typical middle-class American. They defined this as the norm even when statistically it was not, according to Wilson, a direct example of the same type of cultural creation that was happening in the mass media during the same time. Christopher P. Wilson, *White Collar Fictions: Class and Social Representation in American Literature, 1885–1925* (Athens: University of Georgia Press, 1992), 20–21; T. J. Jackson Lears, "The Concept of Cultural Hegemony: Problems and Possibilities," *American Historical Review* 90 (1985): 567–93.

57. The assertion that national elites and institutions shaped certain cultural ideals is a much easier proposition for Europe than the United States. See Reba Soffer, *Discipline and Power: The University, History, and the Making of an English Elite* (Stanford: Stanford University Press, 1994); Pierre Bourdieu, *The State Nobility: Elite Schools in the Field of Power*, trans. Lauretta C. Clough (Stanford: Stanford University Press, 1996); and Paul R. Deslandes, *British Masculinity and the Undergraduate Experience, 1850–1920* (Bloomington: Indiana University Press, 2005).

58. Statistics taken from Matthew Schneirov, *The Dream of a New Social Order: Popular Magazines in America, 1893–1914* (New York: Columbia University Press, 1994), app. 1. In 1893 a price war began. Frank Munsey, the owner/editor of *Munsey's*, set the new standard by lowering his price to ten cents, with *McClure's* and *Cosmopolitan* soon following suit. The lower prices paid off. By April 1894, *Munsey's* circulation had risen from forty thousand to five hundred thousand. Richard Ohmann, *Selling Culture: Magazines, Markets and Class* (Lebanon, NH: University Press of New England for Wesleyan University Press, 1996), 25. The circulation numbers for the genteel monthlies are noted in John Tebbel and Mary Ellen Zuckerman, *The Magazine in America, 1741–1990* (New York: Oxford University Press, 1991), 59. Most genteel monthlies ranged in circulation from 40,000 to 150,000.

59. The Panic of 1893 made it possible to purchase printing materials more cheaply. This coincided with a technological breakthrough in photographic printing, the half-tone process, that allowed high quality inexpensive printing of photos, including photos of art pieces. Schneirov, *Dream of a New Social Order*, 75–76. Massive advertising sections, quite unlike anything in the quality monthlies, allowed magazines like *Munsey's* (the first to master the formula) to lower their price below cost with the advertising revenue providing healthy profits. An excellent overview of the symbiotic relationship between mass production, advertising, and mass magazines occurs in Ohmann, *Selling Culture*, 62–73, 96–97, and 251.

60. Schneirov, *Dream of a New Social Order*, 28–43. Schneirov is one of the few authors to examine the quality monthlies and point out the clear linkages as well as striking differences between the genteel publications and their mass magazine stepchildren. Also see Christopher P. Wilson, "The Rhetoric of Consumption: Mass-Market Magazines and the Demise of the Gentle Reader, 1880–1920," in *The Culture of Consumption: Critical Essays in American History, 1880–1980*, ed. Richard Wightman Fox and T. J. Jackson Lears, 39–64 (New York: Pantheon, 1983).

61. See Schneirov, *Dream of a New Social Order*, 103–17 for analyses of S. S. McClure, Frank Munsey, and John Brisben Walker. See also Damon-Moore, *Magazines for the Millions*, 109–21; and Jan Cohn *Creating America: George Horace Lorimer and the Saturday Evening Post* (Pittsburgh: University of Pittsburgh Press, 1989), 9-18, for analysis of George Horace Lorimer.

62. Schneirov, *Dream of a New Social Order*, 97. The last quote was from S. S. McClure, whose *McClure's* certainly qualified as another mass middle-class magazine.

63. Jan Cohn's work on the *Saturday Evening Post* and its editor George Horace Lorimer is informative on this account. For Lorimer "American" was a totem word, and it often was conflated to stand in for the modern businessman. And for Lorimer "businessman" itself was a generic and inclusive term that encompassed entrepreneurs, professionals, drummers, and clerks. Cohn, *Creating America*, 30–32.

64. Ohmann, *Selling Culture* 25.

65. While the editors and publishers rather than the advertisers charted the content of their magazines, they did recognize the emerging advertising needs of manufacturers and harnessed this, and even defended advertising. Neither Ohmann nor Schneirov argue that advertisers manipulated magazine content, however. Schneirov, *Dream of a New Social Order*, 87–91 and 255–56; and Ohmann, *Selling Culture*, 97. Pendergast recounted Lorimer's persistent desire not to allow advertisers to influence the content of the magazine. Pendergast, *Creating the Modern Man*, 61.

66. Ohmann, *Selling Culture*, 25.

67. Ibid., 220.

68. Ibid., 245.

69. Ibid., 233–34 and 246; and Schneirov, *Dream of a New Social Order*, 111 and 178–85.

70. Schneirov, *Dream of a New Social Order*, 110 and 158–60.

71. Schneirov, Ohmann, and Cohn noted this hybrid conception of ideal American values. The one difference, though, would be that Cohn gave more power to Lorimer as the central guiding force rather than to a process of cultural negotiation where the readership exerted some degree of influence or agency in shaping such values. Schneirov, *Dream of a New Social Order*, 175–78; Ohmann, *Selling Culture*, 225–30; Cohn, *Creating America*, 9–12 and 136.

72. Ohmann refused to view these advertising messages as overt manipulation by advertisers. Advertising's buoyant optimism (and magazines' conception of American life) reflected readers who were "at home with modernism because they were helping to create it." Ohmann, *Selling Culture*, 249.

73. The editors assumed a wish to be familiar with people, events, and places on "an upscale axis of respectability." Ohmann, *Selling Culture*, 245.

74. Ohmann described the high culture information and articles on elite activities as "cultural chatter" that enabled the middle class to strike the pose at least of mediated intimacy with that more elite world. They were in the loop if they so desired. Ohmann, *Selling Culture*, 230–39. Schneirov covers this as well. Schneirov, *Dream of a New Social Order*, 86–94.

75. Schneirov, *Dream of a New Social Order*, 255; Martin Sklar, *The Corporate Reconstruction of American Capitalism, 1890–1916: The Markets, the Law and Politics* (New York: Cambridge University Press, 1988), 6–12. The work of Stuart Hall, Dominick La Capra, and

Hayden White also fundamentally shaped the way I view magazine discourse. Hall writes that the media works "actively ruling in and ruling out certain realities . . . helping us not simply to know more about the 'world' but to 'make sense in it." Stuart Hall, "Culture, the Media and the 'Ideological Effect," in *Mass Communication and Society*, ed. James Curran, Michael Gurevitch, and Janet Woolacott (London: Edward Arnold in Association with the Open University Press, 1977). Dominick La Capra, *History and Criticism* (Ithaca: Cornell University Press, 1985); and Hayden White, *The Content of the Form: Narrative Discourse and Historical Perspective* (Baltimore: Johns Hopkins University Press, 1987).

76. When examining some advertising copy, this book at times references the *American Magazine*, which hovered around a respectable 300,000 readership from 1905 to 1915. Schneirov, *Dream of a New Social Order*, app. 1. In the 1920s, however, the magazine's numbers would go up, and it would run a consistent second to the *Post*.

77. Waldron K. Post, *Harvard Stories* (New York: Putnam's, 1893); John Seymour Wood, *Yale Yarns* (New York: Putnam, 1895); and J. L. Williams, *Princeton Stories* (New York: Charles Scribner's, 1895). See also John O. Lyons, *The College Novel in America* (Carbondale: Southern Illinois University Press, 1962).

78. The rise of the male reader and the "new cult of masculine writing" as a significant explosion in American literature and intellectual history has been explored by Christopher Wilson, *The Labor of Words: Literary Professionalism in the Progressive Era* (Athens: University of Georgia Press, 1985); and Pettegrew, *Brutes in Suits*, chap. 2.

79. Neither Frank Munsey nor Cyris Curtis (publisher of the *Post*) went to college. They built their publishing houses from scratch in Horatio Alger fashion. The same was true of P. F. Collier, although he spent a short time in a Roman Catholic seminary. John Brisben Walker, editor and publisher of *Cosmopolitan*, attended Gonzaga (Washington, DC), Georgetown, and West Point but did not graduate from any of these institutions, leaving West Point to become a military advisor in China before starting his career in journalism and publishing. William Randolph Hearst (publisher of *Cosmopolitan* after 1905) and Norman Hapgood (editor of *Collier's* during its prime to 1912) both attended Harvard—Hapgood graduating while Hearst was infamously expelled for a prank. George Horace Lorimer attended Yale for one year but left to work for family friend and meatpacker Philip D. Armour in Chicago (informing his Gorgan Graham character). Lorimer rose to oversee a department and then quit to form his own business. When this failed he finished college at Colby and entered newspaper work, where Cyris Curtis found him. Information on Munsey and Lorimer in Pendergast, *Creating the Modern Man*, 44–45 and 54. Background on Curtis and Walker in, respectively, Damon-Moore, *Magazines for the Millions*, 15–16, and Schneirov, *Dream of a New Social Order*, 105. Information on Collier, Hapgood, and Hearst in *Dictionary of American Biography*.

80. The educational background of these authors was pulled from both the *Dictionary of American Biography* and *Who Was Who in America* (Chicago: A. N. Marquis Company, 1940–66).

81. Tom Pendergast has revealed how magazines played a critical role in adapting Victorian to modern masculinity along similar lines outlined here, although he neglected to discuss the significance of college-going. See Pendergast, *Creating the Modern Man*.

82. The term "invented tradition" originated with Eric Hobsbawm, *The Invention of Tradition* (Cambridge University Press, 1983).

Chapter 1. The Crisis of the Clerks

1. Herbert H. Vreeland, "The Young Man's Opportunity in the New Business Order," *Saturday Evening Post*, 23 March 1901, pp. 2–3.

2. Bird S. Coler, "The Man Who Can't Go to College," *Saturday Evening Post*, 29 June 1901, p. 8.

3. Will Payne, "Those Contented Clerks: The Broad Line between Making Good and Making Money," *Saturday Evening Post*, 6 February 1909, pp. 6–7; and John Mappelbeck, "The Bank Clerk: His Life and His Job," *Saturday Evening Post*, 13 March 1909, pp. 12–13.

4. William Maher, "The Clerk Who Saves," *Saturday Evening Post*, 21 October 1899, p. 308; and "The Clerk Who Isn't Young," *Saturday Evening Post*, 21 May 1910, p. 24.

5. Some scholars have probed how businessmen, the new corporate middle class especially, reaffirmed their masculinity in a shifting business setting and how the new mass magazines participated in this reconstitution. Nevertheless, while such works imply the fusing of some self-made notions of manhood with modern masculinity's sanction of aggressiveness and personality, the value of cultured breadth in forming the ideal businessman received little attention, something I believe critical for understanding the eventual integration of college into the formula of middle-class manhood and corporate authority. Angel Kwolek-Folland, *Engendering Business: Men and Women in the Corporate Office, 1870–1930* (Baltimore: Johns Hopkins University Press, 1994); and Sharon Hartman Strom, *Beyond the Typewriter: Gender, Class and the Origins of Modern American Office Work, 1900–1930* (Urbana: University of Illinois Press, 1992). Jan Cohn, *Creating America: George Horace Lorimer and the Saturday Evening Post* (Pittsburgh; University of Pittsburgh Press, 1989); and Helen Damon-Moore, *Magazines for the Millions: Gender and Commerce in the Ladies Home Journal and the Saturday Evening Post, 1880–1910* (New York: SUNY Press, 1994).

6. "The New Outlook for Young Men," *Saturday Evening Post*, 15 July 1899, p. 46.

7. "The Rise of the Millionaire: John D. Rockefeller's Early Struggles," *Saturday Evening Post*, 29 January 1898, p. 16; and "Dreamers of the Business World," *Cosmopolitan* 29 (May 1900): 107–8. In the *Cosmopolitan* article, Rockefeller was praised as an organizer, reshaping a wasteful business sector.

8. Charles S. Gleed, "John Pierpont Morgan," *Cosmopolitan* 33 (May 1902): 33–35. This was the first in a new series, "Captains of Industry."

9. Irvin G. Wyllie, *The Self-Made Man in America: The Myth of Rags to Riches* (New Brunswick: Rutgers University Press, 1954), 39–40. See also, Richard Weiss, *The American Myth of Success: From Horatio Alger to Norman Vincent Peale* (New York and London: Basic Books, 1969).

10. For example, pushing scientific pursuits as a profession are Edward S. Holden, "On the Choice of a Profession," *Cosmopolitan* 24 (March 1898): 543–49; and N. S. Shaler, "Science as a Profession," *Saturday Evening Post*, 22 June 1901, p. 6. The ministry and law received treatment as well. Rev. Jenkin Lloyd Jones, "Making a Choice of a Profession—The Ministry," *Cosmopolitan* 34 (February 1903): 477–79; and Albert J. Beveridge, "The Young Lawyer and His Beginnings," *Saturday Evening Post*, 27 October 1900, pp. 1–2.

11. James L. Ford, "From Brakeman to President," *Munsey's Magazine* 24 (December 1900): 459–60. Examples in this series noted earlier are "Dreamers of the Business

World," 107–8; and Gleed, "John Pierpont Morgan," 33–35; Maher, "The Clerk Who Saves," 308; "What Constitutes a 'Self-Made' Man," *Saturday Evening Post*, 26 August 1899, p. 138; Robert C. Ogden, "Getting and Keeping a Business Position," *Saturday Evening Post*, 4 November 1899, pp. 345–46; "Why Young Men Fail: A Clear Explanation by Shrewd Business Men," *Saturday Evening Post*, 9 September 1899, p. 165.

12. Samuel E. Moffett, "Charles M. Schwab," *Cosmopolitan* 33 (July 1902): 284–86.

13. Frank A. Munsey, "Impressions by the Way," *Munsey's Magazine* 24 (November 1900): 308–9.

14. For *Cosmopolitan*, examples are "In the World of Arts and Letters," *Cosmopolitan* 23 (May 1897): 99–104; and "The Progress of Science," *Cosmopolitan* 23 (April 1897): 692–96. For *Munsey's*, "Artists and Their Work," *Munsey's Magazine* 12 (October 1894): 3–14; Ray Stannard Baker, "The Modern Skyscraper," *Munsey's Magazine* 22 (October 1899): 48–60; and Roswell P. Fowler and Chauncey M. Depew, "Modern Industrial Combinations," *Munsey's Magazine* 21 (July 1899): 586–91. For the *Post*, "Words of Brilliant Writers," *Saturday Evening Post*, 9 April 1898, p. 9; and Paul Latzke, "The Trust Builders," *Saturday Evening Post*, 15 November 1902, pp. 8–9.

15. Munsey characterized them as crude in "An Address," *Munsey's Magazine* 28 (February 1903): 662–66. Here, Munsey noted his support for unions to check capital, but he believed that in the end, trusts meant that the benefits of consumer efficiency would be spread for more people. See also Fowler and Depew, "Modern Industrial Combinations," 586–91; and Frederick Emory, "Our Commercial Expansion," *Munsey's Magazine* 22 (January 1900): 538–44.

16. Examples of the *Post*'s lamenting the loss of small businessmen and the rise of "Captains of Industry" who care only for dividends, along with his endorsement of Roosevelt's program to oversee the trusts, may be found respectively in "Where Are the Business Men?" *Saturday Evening Post*, 6 May 1905, p. 12; Will Payne, "Modern Business Practice," *Saturday Evening Post*, 21 July 1906, pp. 9–10 and 23; and "The Power of the Trusts," *Saturday Evening Post*, 1 February 1902, p. 14. *Cosmopolitan* in the 1890s had the Marxist slogan "From every man according to his ability: to everyone according to his needs" on their first page, and ran articles endorsing public control of monopolistic trusts, such as Richard T. Ely, "Public Control of Private Corporations," *Cosmopolitan* 30 (February 1901): 430–33. Additionally, both the *Post* and *Cosmopolitan* ran many short stories that were critical of callous Captains of Industry and monopolistic power.

17. James H. Collins, "Limiting Opportunity: The Salaried Man," *Saturday Evening Post*, 16 February 1907, pp. 3–5; and "Limiting Opportunity: The Man Who Works for a Trust," *Saturday Evening Post*, 30 March 1907, pp. 18–19.

18. Munsey, "Impressions by the Way"; and "Mr. Croker's Sermon to Young Men," *Saturday Evening Post*, 22 September 1900, p. 12.

19. Paul Latzke, "How Trusts Promote Men," *Saturday Evening Post*, 22 February 1902, pp. 4–5; Vreeland, "The Young Man's Opportunity in the New Business Order." In "The Making of a Railroad Man," the contributors from this industry debated which path (clerk or shop) up through the ranks best prepared the future executive, but each noted the need for technical or "scientific" training as they learned on the job. W. A. Gardner, "The Making of a Railroad Man: The Railroad Telegrapher," *Saturday Evening Post*, 21 July 1900, pp. 18–19; J. F. Wallace, "The Making of a Railroad Man: From the Viewpoint of the Engineering Department," *Saturday Evening Post*, 5 May 1900, p. 35;

E. P. Ripley, "The Making of a Railroad Man," *Saturday Evening Post*, 24 March 1900, p. 865.

20. On how Lorimer's *Post* devoted itself to promoting the businessman as the new hero of the age, replacing in prestige the older professions, see Cohn, *Creating America*, 11–12 and 36–37. On the way Lorimer held up the salesman as the new ideal business-man, one who facilitated efficient consumption but was neither a producer nor con-sumer, see Damon-Moore, *Magazines for the Millions*, 129–33. For a similar transfer of manly traits to the figure of the manager and salesman in business settings, see Kwolek-Folland, *Engendering Business*, 71–72.

21. Charles R. Flint, "How Business Success Will Be Won in the Twentieth Cen-tury," *Saturday Evening Post*, 17 November 1900, p. 8.

22. M. M. Kallman, "The Business Expert: Stories of a New Profession," *Saturday Evening Post*, 29 November 1902, pp. 8–9.

23. Edward Mott Woolley, "Cutting Out the Motions in Business," *Saturday Evening Post*, 9 September 1911, pp. 28–30; Edward Hungerford, "The General Manager," *Satur-day Evening Post*, 4 March 1911, pp. 41–43. Another example is "Scientific Management for All," *Saturday Evening Post*, 29 July 1911, p. 18. The term "Science of Business," ap-peared in an article pushing another form of the modern manager. See Forrest Crissey, "Special Counselors in Business System and Administration," *Saturday Evening Post*, 23 May 1903, pp. 16–17.

24. Cohn, *Creating America*, 85–86.

25. "The Professional Business Man," *Saturday Evening Post*, 6 February 1909, p. 16.

26. William J. Wilgus, "Making a Choice of a Profession," *Cosmopolitan* 35 (August 1903): 462–65.

27. Vreeland, "The Young Man's Opportunity," 2–3; and W. A. Gardner, "The Making of a Railroad Man: The Railroad Telegrapher," 18–19. Vreeland had a sub-heading in his article that stated it all: "A College Education Not a Help."

28. Russell Sage, "The Gospel of Saving," *Saturday Evening Post*, 9 December 1900, p. 11. Similarly, Albert B. Chandler, "To Young Men Beginning in Business," *Saturday Evening Post*, 11 January 1902, pp. 1–2.

29. Crissey, "Special Counselors in Business System and Administration," 16–17; and R. W. Conant, "Mind Training in Business," *Saturday Evening Post*, 25 October 1902, pp. 28–29.

30. Henry Alexander Harwood, "Wanted: $50,000 Men," *Saturday Evening Post*, 10 April 1909, pp. 16–17.

31. Advertisements for John D. Morris Company, *Saturday Evening Post*, 25 October 1902, p. 29; and the Success Company, *Saturday Evening Post*, 25 October 1902, p. 29. The Book-Keeper Company, for instance, hawked "Business Success" as early as 1899 in *Collier's*. Advertisement for the Book-Keeper Company, *Collier's Weekly*, 3 June 1899, p. 17.

32. Advertisement for *Harmsworth Self-Educator Magazine*, *Saturday Evening Post*, 23 February 1907, p. 28.

33. Advertisement for *Success Magazine*, *Saturday Evening Post*, 21 November 1903, p. 39. This ad noted that they offered a special section on career choice and featured an article by banker and railroad magnate John J. Hill on starting in a business career.

34. Advertisement for *System: The Magazine of Business*, *Saturday Evening Post*, 9 March 1907, pp. 16–17.

35. In other ads, *System* offered examples of business letters. Advertisement for *System: The Magazine of Business, Saturday Evening Post*, 21 September 1912, p. 37. Other examples of business publications were *Beach's Magazine of Business, Saturday Evening Post*, 8 May 1909, p. 62; and American School of Correspondence's Cyclopedia of Commerce, *Saturday Evening Post*, 29 January 1910, p. 32.

36. ICS, *American Magazine* 80 (December, 1915): 9; ICS, *Saturday Evening Post*, 21 March 1908, p. 29.

37. The quote came from advertisement for ICS, *Saturday Evening Post*, 19 December 1908, p. 31. Today we differentiate between trained professions such as banking, accounting, engineering, or business (marketing, finance, management), but these categories around the turn of the century were in their infancy. All were considered part of the business world, ways to specialize and move up in a new environment. Some examples include ads for the Home Correspondence School, *Saturday Evening Post*, 1 November 1902, p. 18; the Sheldon School, *Saturday Evening Post*, 14 September 1907, p. 25; American School of Correspondence, *Saturday Evening Post*, 31 March 1902, p. 908; and ICS, *Collier's Weekly*, 3 May 1902, p. 19. The latter ICS advertisement in *Collier's*, for instance, offered engineering training, foreign languages (for businessmen), and business skills such as bookkeeping and stenography.

38. The Railway Commercial Training School, *Saturday Evening Post*, 12 August 1905, p. 18; Gem City Business College, *Saturday Evening Post*, 1 July 1905, p. 18; the Tulloss School, *American Magazine* 81 (January 1916): 83; Bryant and Stratton's College, *Saturday Evening Post*, 13 October 1900, p. 17; Banks Business College, *Saturday Evening Post*, 10 June 1905, p. 21; and the National Mercantile Training School, *Saturday Evening Post*, 28 July 1900, p. 23. An excellent overview of the proprietary business college is Janice Weiss, "Educating for Clerical Work: The Nineteenth-Century Private Commercial School," *Journal of Social History* 14 (Spring 1981): 407–23.

39. Ad for Peirce School, *Saturday Evening Post*, 11 July 1903, p. 14. On the Peirce School see Jerome P. Bjelopera, *City of Clerks: Office and Sales Workers in Philadelphia, 1870–1920* (Urbana: University of Illinois Press, 2005), chap. 3.

40. Ad for Peirce School, *Saturday Evening Post*, 30 August 1902, p. 11.

41. Ad for the Commercial Correspondence School of Rochester, *Saturday Evening Post*, 27 August 1904, p. 20.

42. Ad for ICS, *Saturday Evening Post*, 21 March 1908, p. 29.

43. E. Anthony Rotundo, *American Manhood: Transformations in Masculinity from the Revolution to the Modern Era* (New York: Basic Books, 1993), 165–75.

44. Numerous scholars exploring masculinity in the late nineteenth century have commented on the rise of sports, the cult of strenuosity, the concern about "over-culture," and the specter of being labeled a "sissy," and they all have viewed this as part of male compensation for loss of autonomy in the workplace (as well as other threats). See John Higham, "The Reorientation of American Culture," in *American Civilization*, ed. Eugene Drozdowski (Glenview, IL: Scott, Foresman and Co., 1972), 265–67; Clyde Griffen, "Reconstructing Masculinity from the Evangelical Crisis to the Waning of Progressivism: A Speculative Synthesis," in *Meanings for Manhood: Constructions of Masculinity in Victorian America*, ed. Mark C. Carnes and Clyde Griffen (Chicago: University of Chicago Press, 1990), 183–204; Michael Kimmel, *Manhood in America: A Cultural History* (New York: The Free Press, 1996), 168–69.

45. "Academic," *Saturday Evening Post*, 1 September 1906, p. 14.

46. Wyllie, *Self-Made Man*, 103.

47. Quoting Elisha Benjamin Andrews, former president of Brown, in Coler, "The Man Who Can't Go to College," 8. The commonly held notion among businessmen that college had ruined many prospective businessmen may be found as far back as mid-century. Wyllie quoted warnings about the ill-effects of college from Edwin T. Freedley, *A Practical Treatise on Business* (Philadelphia: Lippincott, Grambo and Co., 1854); and from Horace Greeley, *Success in Business* (1867). Wyllie, *Self-Made Man*, 102–4.

48. Carnegie quoted in Wyllie, *Self-Made Man*, 101.

49. "Do Mental Gymnastics Make Strong Men?" *Saturday Evening Post*, 2 February 1901, p. 12.

50. "Should Your Boy Go to College?" *Munsey's Magazine* 13 (August 1895): 463.

51. Edward Bok, "The Young Man in Business," *Cosmopolitan* 16 (January 1894): 338.

52. Coler, "The Man Who Can't Go to College," 8.

53. "Should Your Boy Go to College?" 463.

54. Jurgen Kocka, *White Collar Workers in American, 1890–1940: A Social-Political History in International Perspective*, trans. Maura Kealey (London: Sage Publications, 1980), 86. Kocka's source was a 1903 article from the *Advocate*, a trade journal aimed at clerks.

55. Letter to the Editor from Ralph B. Peck, *Saturday Evening Post*, 17 April 1900, p. 927.

56. Roswell P. Fowler quoted in "Should Your Boy Go to College?" 462.

57. Unsigned illustration for James H. Collins, "The Art of Handling Men," *Saturday Evening Post*, 6 July 1907, pp. 10–11.

58. Jerome K. Jerome, "Summer Girls and Idle Fellows: Tea-Table Talk," *Saturday Evening Post*, 21 June 1902, pp. 3–4. This was part of an ongoing series that even boasted a cover illustration.

59. Examples of stories with such stereotypically lazy or corrupt college grads who are reformed out West, on the high seas, or in business (or are simply the villains) include Morgan Robertson, "The Nuisance," *Saturday Evening Post*, 16 September 1899, pp. 177–79; Lloyd Osbourne, "Frenchy's Last Job," *Cosmopolitan* 28 (November 1899): 55–72; Melville Chater, "Motorman Cupid," *Cosmopolitan* 28 (January 1900): 290–94; Emerson Hough, "The Hen at Heart's Desire," *Saturday Evening Post*, 21 May 1904, pp. 3–5; Will Payne, "Bensinger's Luck," *Saturday Evening Post*, 8 March 1913, pp. 3–5 and 68.

60. Edward Bok, "Young Man in Business," 338.

61. A *Cosmopolitan* article, "What Men Like in Men," mentioned specifically that men abhorred the sissy, someone who preferred the company of ladies to men and was "effeminate." Rafford Pyke, "What Men Like in Men," *Cosmopolitan* 33 (August 1902): 402–6.

62. Kocka, *White Collar Workers in America*, 86–87.

63. For *Munsey's*, "Literary Chat," "The Stage," and "The World of Music" were all recurring departments. *Munsey's* is the best known for its art reprints such as, "Artists and Their Work," *Munsey's Magazine* 12 (October 1894): 3–14.

64. "The Progress of Science," *Cosmopolitan* 23 (April 1897): 692–96; "Captains of Industry," *Cosmopolitan* 34 (December 1902): 177–79; Thomas L. James, "The Methods of Banking," *Cosmopolitan* 22 (March 1897): 475–87; "In the World of Arts and Letters," *Cosmopolitan* 23 (May 1897): 99–104; John Fiske, "John Milton," *Cosmopolitan* 34 (November

1902): 41–53; and Harry Thurston Peck, "Balzac and His Work," *Cosmopolitan* 27 (July 1899): 238–45.

65. "The Opera and Drama," *Collier's Weekly*, 15 April 1899, p. 16; "New Plays and Players," *Collier's Weekly*, 13 September 1902, p. 6; and "A Glimpse at Recent Fiction," *Collier's Weekly*, 8 April 1905, pp. 23–24.

66. G. G. Williams, "Getting On: A Young Man's Business Reading," *Saturday Evening Post*, 19 September 1903, p. 72.

67. Frank A. Vanderlip, "The Business Man's Reading," *Saturday Evening Post*, 25 January 1902, p. 5. The inaugural piece of Forrest Crissey's series "Men of Action" noted with satisfaction how the self-made businessman profiled in the article possessed a "large, comprehensive and costly" library, while he graced his walls with some of the world's best art. Forrest Crissey, "Men of Action," *Saturday Evening Post*, 30 September 1899, pp. 222–23.

68. Arlo Bates, "The Home College Course: Literature and Its Uses," *Saturday Evening Post*, 27 March 1902, pp. 12–13.

69. William H. Maher, "The Clerk Who Reads," *Saturday Evening Post*, 20 January 1900, p. 643; and William Matthews, "How Shall a Young Man Educate Himself?" *Saturday Evening Post*, 7 March 1903, p. 15. See Thomas Augst, *The Clerk's Tale: Young Men and Moral Life in Nineteenth-Century America* (Chicago: University of Chicago Press, 2003), for an excellent work detailing the inner life of the clerk and his efforts to define himself through reading and writing.

70. Thomas B. Bryan, "The Money Matters of the Young Business Man," *Saturday Evening Post*, 28 April 1900, pp. 1010–11.

71. James H. Canfield, "The Average Young Man and His Library," *Cosmopolitan* 30 (April 1901): 609–12.

72. Coler, "The Man Who Can't Go to College," 8.

73. Edward Boltwood, "The Heminway Crescent," *Munsey's Magazine* 27 (June 1902): 415–20.

74. Ad for American Newspaper Association, *Saturday Evening Post*, 16 May 1903, p. 21. In 1904, the Century Company presented a library of fifteen masterpieces of literature, similar to the 1910 "Everyman's Library," which was edited by a professor and touched on every branch of literature. Ads for the Century Company, *Collier's Weekly*, 2 April 1904, p. 3; and E. P. Dutton and Company, *Saturday Evening Post*, 15 October 1910, p. 41.

75. Ridpath's was marketed over the years by two (and perhaps more) different publishers. Advertisements for Ridpath's *History of the World* are Merrill and Baker Publishers, *Collier's Weekly*, 24 October 1903, p. 21; Western Newspaper Association, *Saturday Evening Post*, 26 September 1908, p. 43.

76. Advertisement for the University Society, *Saturday Evening Post*, 10 October 1903, p. 23.

77. One example of a book broker that advertised the classics, histories, and other literature is David P. Clarkson, the Book Broker, *Saturday Evening Post*, 13 March 1909, p. 43.

78. Payne, "Those Contented Clerks."

79. "Getting a Business Education," *Saturday Evening Post*, 23 July 1910, p. 18.

80. Mappelbeck, "The Bank Clerk," 12–13.

81. "The Clerk Who Isn't Young."

82. An excellent study of the impact of managerial hierarchies and the adoption of new office technologies is JoAnne Yates, *Control through Communication: The Rise of System in American Management* (Baltimore: Johns Hopkins University Press, 1989).

83. James H. Collins, "The Rise of the Bookkeeper," *Saturday Evening Post*, 5 July 1913, pp. 18–19. Perhaps responding to the shifting dynamic of business success, a *Post* editorial later in July 1913 rejoiced that seemingly fewer young men were flocking to white-collar positions and were opting for good, clean laboring positions with "some pay and prospects," since the bookkeeper of the day seemed "on the verge of nervous prostration." "Clean-Collar Jobs," *Saturday Evening Post*, 19 July 1913, p. 20.

84. Payne, "Those Contented Clerks," 7.

85. "Getting a Business Education," 18.

86. These headline quotes came respectively from advertisements for International Correspondence Schools, *Collier's Weekly*, 21 May 1904, p. 27; and ICS, *Collier's Weekly*, 31 October 1903, p. 28.

87. Advertisement for ICS, *Saturday Evening Post*, 29 July 1911, p. 38.

88. Advertisement for American School of Correspondence, *Saturday Evening Post*, 18 September 1909, p. 37.

89. Advertisement for ICS, *Saturday Evening Post*, 29 July 1911, p. 38.

90. Vaughn Kester, "The Mills of the Little Tin Gods," *Cosmopolitan* 25 (May 1898): 101–11.

91. "Getting a Start at Sixty," *Saturday Evening Post*, 5 August 1911, pp. 3–6 and 34. Another short story relating to the crisis of the clerks is Harris Merton Lyon, "The City of Lonesome Men," *Collier's Weekly*, 20 January 1912, pp. 14–15 and 25.

92. Poultney Bigelow, "Can a University Help Me to Earn a Living," *Collier's Weekly*, 18 October 1902, p. 8.

93. This study was noted in Kocka, *White Collar Workers in America*, 112.

94. Lorimer, "The Old Man's Son," *Saturday Evening Post*, 27 October 1900, p. 14.

95. Henry B. Fuller, "Why Is the Anglo-Saxon Disliked?" *Saturday Evening Post*, 6 January 1900, p. 590.

96. David Roediger, *The Wages of Whiteness: Race and the Making of the American Working Class* (New York: Verso, 1991); Dana D. Nelson, *National Manhood: Capitalist Citizenship and the Imagined Fraternity of White Men* (Durham and London: Duke University Press, 1998). Recent scholarship has guided my assumptions on the contested nature of whiteness for the new immigrants around the turn of the century. See Matthew Frye Jacobson, *Whiteness of a Different Color: European Immigrants and the Alchemy of Race* (Cambridge, MA: Harvard University Press, 1998); and Roediger, *Working toward Whiteness: How America's Immigrants Became White; the Strange Journey from Ellis Island to the Suburbs* (New York: Basic Books, 2005). Jacobson and Roediger both argue as well that we must take the notion of race seriously for this time period. Americans (immigrants included) saw themselves as of a different "race," and this included an assumption of inherited cultural traits.

97. For *Cosmopolitan* see Goldwin Smith, "The World Menace of Japan," *Cosmopolitan* 43 (October 1907): 604–7; Charles Kroth Moser, "The Wife of Tong Hom," *Cosmopolitan* 43 (August 1907): 397–406; and Charles Somerville, "The Yellow Pariahs," *Cosmopolitan* 47 (September 1909): 467–75. For *Collier's* see Chester H. Rowell, "Orientophobia: A Western Editor's Views of the White Frontier," *Collier's Weekly*, 6 February 1909, pp. 13

and 29; and Peter Clark Macfarlane, "Japan in California," *Collier's Weekly*, 7 June 1913, pp. 5–6, 20–23.

98. Edward Boltwood, "The Old Neighborhood," *Munsey's Magazine* 36 (December 1906): 357–62.

99. Harvey J. O. Higgins, "The Gianellis: From the Field Notes of a Settlement House Worker," *Collier's Weekly*, 6 April 1912, pp. 12 and 42. On the racial differences of Italian immigrants, see also "The Black Hand Scourge," *Cosmopolitan* 47 (June 1909): 31–41; Frank Marshall White, "Against the Black Hand," *Collier's Weekly*, 3 September 1910, p. 19; and Edith Wyatt, "Chicago's Melting Pot," *Collier's Weekly*, 27 August 1910, pp. 21–22.

100. The quote is from the second installment, Honore Willsie, "What Is an American? Part II, the Conquest of the Workingman," *Collier's Weekly*, 16 November 1912, p. 20.

101. Willsie, "What Is an American? The Suicide of the Anglo-American," *Collier's Weekly*, 9 November 1912, pp. 13–14; and Willsie, "What Is an American? Part II," p. 21; Willsie, "What Is an American? Part IV, the Making of the American Child," *Collier's Weekly*, 7 December 1912, pp. 16 and 30. Despite even his crassest statements, the author surprisingly admitted that no scientist could prove these negative traits purely hereditary, which offered the hope of assimilation.

102. During and after World War I, *Post* editor George Horace Lorimer, entering the real height of his editorial and cultural power, became a virulent xenophobe. For the 1890–1915 time period, however, while it still assumed cultural traits to be hereditary and used what we might consider harsh racial characterizations, the *Post* was easily the most accepting and tolerant magazine toward all immigrant groups, including Asians. On Lorimer's later xenophobia, see Cohn, *Creating America*, 146–56. Examples of the *Post's* openness are, "The Attraction of Prosperity," "Work of Conscience," and "New Citizens from Japan and Italy," *Saturday Evening Post*, 2 February 1901, p. 24; and Albert J. Beveridge, "Americans of Today and Tomorrow," *Saturday Evening Post*, 5 September 1903, pp. 4–5.

103. "One Way Out: A Middle Class New Englander Emigrates to America," *Saturday Evening Post*, 8 October 1910, pp. 7–9.

104. Ibid., 40–42, and 45–46.

Chapter 2. The College Curriculum and Business

1. "Should Your Boy Go to College?" *Munsey's Magazine* 13 (August 1895): 461. The article pointedly addressed the question of business success, asking, "is a college course the best training for a boy designed for a business career?"

2. Francis L. Patton, "Should a Business Man Have a College Education?" *Saturday Evening Post*, 26 May 1900, p. 1094; Charles F. Thwing, "Should Railroad Men Be College Men?" *Saturday Evening Post*, 11 January 1902, pp. 11–12. Articles that directly raised the issue of college education for the businessman and thus advocated such a path include those of Benjamin Ida Wheeler, "Is Scholarship a Promise of Success in Life," *Saturday Evening Post*, 26 May 1900, p. 1095; James B. Dill, "The College Man and the Corporate Position," *Munsey's Magazine* 24 (October, 1900): 148–52; Thwing, "Making a Choice of Profession—Insurance," *Cosmopolitan* 34 (March 1903): 575–78; and Senator

Albert J. Beveridge, "The Young Man and College Life," *Saturday Evening Post*, 10 June 1905, pp. 1–2.

3. William J. Wilgus, "Making a Choice of a Profession," *Cosmopolitan* 35 (August 1903): 462–63; Poultney Bigelow, "Can a University Help Me to Earn a Living?" *Collier's Weekly*, 18 October 1902, p. 8; "Wanted: A Master," *Saturday Evening Post*, 28 February 1903, p. 15.

4. Grover Cleveland, "Does a College Education Pay," *Saturday Evening Post*, 26 May 1900, p. 1089.

5. Bigelow, "Can a University Help Me to Earn a Living," 8. Other articles that highlighted the increasing opportunities for college men as leaders for the new age were Francis B. Crocker, "The Young Man and the New Force," *Saturday Evening Post*, 22 June 1901, pp. 1–2; and "Dividends Paid on College Parchments," *Saturday Evening Post*, 24 November 1901, p. 6.

6. In one such "lament" from a 1903 *Cosmopolitan* article, the general manager of the Erie Railroad regretted not having gone to college because he found that no branch of modern business did *not* require scientific knowledge. Daniel Willard, "Making a Choice of a Profession: Civil Engineering," *Cosmopolitan* 35 (October 1903): 659. An excellent dissection of the various meanings attached to terms like mental training and its new association with scientific investigation rather than the classical curriculum's mental discipline occurs in Julie Reuben, *The Making of the Modern University: Intellectual Transformation and the Marginalization of Morality* (Chicago: University of Chicago Press, 1996), 61–72.

7. As *Munsey's* put it in 1895, most "of those who have gained success without a college course look back upon their early days with a sense of having missed something that would have helped them all through life." "Should Your Boy Go to College?" 461. This article captured a classic lament from one of the self-made men consulted for the article, who stated frankly, "I cannot help wishing sometimes that in my youth I had had a better opportunity for developing my natural abilities." Ibid., 462. And an early *Post* writer noted that successful businessmen often regretted not acquiring a liberal education, and thus sent their sons and spent great sums of money later in life in the hopes of buying the social status a broad education bestowed. E. S. Martin, "Education and Dollars," *Saturday Evening Post*, 1 July 1899, p. 10.

8. Bigelow, "Can a University Help Me to Earn a Living?" 8. One U.S. Bureau of Education report quoted an observer from the University of Berlin in 1905, who noted that American businessmen seemed to desire more than technical training for their college trained employees. They seemed to want a training that enabled a person in business "to participate in intellectual activities previously monopolized by the aristocratic classes." In other words they longed for genteel respectability. Irvin G. Wyllie, *The Self-Made Man in America: The Myth of Rags to Riches* (New Brunswick, NJ: Rutgers University Press, 1954), 113–14.

9. *Digest of Education Statistics*, 1977–78, 85 and 94; and *Historical Statistics of the United States*, Series H, 751–56, compiled in W. Bruce Leslie, "Toward a History of the American Upper Middle Class, 1870–1940," (paper presented at the Cambridge University American History Seminar, 1994), 13.

10. David K. Brown, *Degrees of Control: A Sociology of Educational Expansion and Occupational Credentialism* (New York: Teachers College Press, 1995).

11. Scholars working on the cultural construction of masculinity during this period acknowledge a period of deep anxiety and shifting definitions of how gender was constructed. See Anthony Rotundo, *American Manhood: Transformations in Masculinity from the Revolution to the Modern Era* (New York: Basic Books, 1993); and Gail Bederman, *Manliness and Civilization: A Cultural History of Gender and Race in the United States, 1880–1917* (Chicago: University of Chicago Press, 1995), 11–23. See also my introduction and chap. 4 for more detail.

12. Those who most conspicuously argue for the direct power of hegemonic capitalism are David Noble, *America by Design: Science, Technology and the Rise of Corporate Capitalism* (New York: Knopf, 1977); Clyde Barrow, *Universities and the Capitalist State: Corporate Liberalism and the Reconstruction of Higher Education, 1894–1928* (Madison: University of Wisconsin Press, 1990); Joel Spring, *Images of American Life: A History of Ideological Management in Schools, Movies and Television* (New York: SUNY Press, 1992); and Christopher Newfield, *Ivy and Industry: Business and the Making of the American University* (Durham: Duke University Press, 2003).

13. Matthew Schneirov, *The Dream of a New Social Order: Popular Magazines in America, 1893–1914* (New York: Columbia University Press, 1994), 80–94 and 110–11, especially.

14. John Brisben Walker, "Modern College Education," *Cosmopolitan* 22 (April 1897): 685.

15. Ibid., 681.

16. Timothy Dwight, "Modern Education," *Cosmopolitan* 23 (August 1897): 438–39; Charles F. Thwing, "Modern Education," *Cosmopolitan* 24 (April 1898): 665.

17. Thwing, "Modern Education," 665.

18. Arthur T. Hadley, "Modern Education," *Cosmopolitan* 28 (November 1899): 104–5.

19. Hadley argued that "liberal education in the proper meaning of the word is the education which rightly belongs to the free man . . . [and] fits a member of the ruling class . . . for the duties and enjoyments of his position." "Higher education of this sort," Hadley believed, "must train gentlemen." Hadley, "Modern Education," 104–5.

20. Adam Singleton, "What Is a Gentleman?—A Lady?" *Cosmopolitan* 29 (August 1900): 398–400; Rafford Pyke, "What Men Like in Men," *Cosmopolitan* 33 (August 1902): 402–6.

21. Schneirov, *Dream of a New Social Order*, 92–95. For an example of *Cosmopolitan's* effort to supply uplifting cultural edification see "In the World of Arts and Letters," *Cosmopolitan* 23 (May 1897): 99–104.

22. During the nineteenth century, acquiring the proper literary and artistic tastes became an increasingly important aspect of achieving the inner character traits idealized by most Americans. Laurence Veysey, *The Emergence of the American University* (Chicago: University of Chicago Press, 1965), 180–251. Many liberal culture partisans, especially at Harvard and Yale, would also cast the benefits of such a liberal education in far more masculine terms during the last decades of the century. Kim Townsend, *Manhood at Harvard: William James and Others* (New York: W. W. Norton and Company, 1996), 80–131; and Robert J. Higgs, "Yale and the Heroic Ideal, Gotterdammerung and Palingenesis, 1865–1914," in *Manliness and Morality: Middle Class Masculinity in Britain and America, 1800–1940*, ed. J. A. Mangan and James Walvin (New York: St. Martin's Press, 1987), 160–75.

23. "Should Your Boy Go to College?" 461. The author of the article simply calls the mayor "Colonel Strong." Technically, William L. Strong was elected mayor of Manhattan in 1894. Subsequently the mayor's office was elected on a citywide basis rather than by borough.

24. "Culture and Success," *Saturday Evening Post*, 12 October 1901, p. 12.

25. Patton, "Should a Business Man Have a College Education?" 1094.

26. Wheeler, "Is Scholarship a Promise of Success in Life?" 1095.

27. "Should Your Boy Go to College?" 461–62.

28. Albert J. Beveridge, "The Young Man and College Life," *Saturday Evening Post*, 10 June 1905, pp. 1–2; and "What Makes the Wheels Go Round," *Saturday Evening Post*, 20 September 1902, p. 12.

29. Most agreed that the college graduate's "well-trained mind" proved advantageous. Thwing, "Should Railroad Men Be College Men?" 11.

30. Ibid., 12.

31. Russell H. Crittenden, "The Practical Course for Young Men," *Saturday Evening Post*, 27 October 1900, p. 6.

32. Patton, "Should a Business Man Have a College Education?" 1094. The Arnold quote is "Culture is to know the best that has been said or thought in the world."

33. Charles F. Thwing, "The Chief Worth of a College Education," *Saturday Evening Post*, 30 January 1909, p. 5.

34. Ibid.

35. "Should Your Boy Go to College?" 463.

36. From 1900 through the end of the decade, the *Post* printed numerous articles and editorials calling for a shorter college course to enable the young man to get his start in life sooner. William Matthews, "The Age for Entering College," *Saturday Evening Post*, 22 December 1900, p. 10; "Saving Valuable Years," *Saturday Evening Post*, 1 August 1903, p. 14; and "Three Years or Five at College?" *Saturday Evening Post*, 7 April 1906, p. 14.

37. Bird S. Coler, "The Man Who Can't Go to College," *Saturday Evening Post*, 29 June 1901, p. 8. See also David Gray, "Do Mental Gymnastics Make Strong Men?" *Saturday Evening Post*, 2 February 1901, p. 12.

38. "Cut Out Educational Frills," *Saturday Evening Post*, 6 June 1903, p. 14; Lorimer made this point again in "Why Greek and Latin," *Saturday Evening Post*, 13 January 1906, p. 12. The *Post* contained various editorial sections. Unless these commentaries received specific attribution, which they often did, they are assumed to come from Lorimer.

39. "The Dead A.B.," *Saturday Evening Post*, 17 March 1906, p. 12.

40. "The Boy at College," *Saturday Evening Post*, 7 September 1907, p. 14.

41. D. K. Pearsons, "Freshwater Colleges," *Saturday Evening Post*, 26 May 1900, p. 1110; John Corbin, "High Life and Higher Education," *Saturday Evening Post*, 14 November 1903, pp. 10–11 and 20; "Our Freshwater Colleges," *Saturday Evening Post*, 13 May 1905, p. 12; and, "Gentlemen in Hard Luck," *Saturday Evening Post*, 20 March 1909, p. 18.

42. "Education Becoming Democratic," *Saturday Evening Post*, 11 February 1911, p. 22; and "Democracy and Education," *Saturday Evening Post*, 11 March 1911, p. 24.

43. Still the best discussion of the rise of the "utility" or practical ideal in American higher education is Veysey, *Emergence of the American University*, 57–120.

44. H. G. Prout, "Railroading as a Profession," *Munsey's Magazine* 22 (March 1900): 876–77.

45. "The Golden Age of the Engineer," *Saturday Evening Post*, 27 October 1900, p. 14.

46. "Dividends Paid on College Parchments," *Saturday Evening Post*, 24 November 1900, p. 6.

47. Crocker, "The Young Man and the New Force; Electrical Engineering," 1–2; Arthur S. Wright, "The Value of Technical Training," *Saturday Evening Post*, 22 June 1901, p. 7; and William A. Scott, "The School of Commerce," *Saturday Evening Post*, 22 June 1901, p. 2. Similar articles in this number were N. S. Shaler, "Science as a Profession," *Saturday Evening Post*, 22 June 1901, p. 6; and W. H. Schuerman, "College-Trained Engineer," *Saturday Evening Post*, 22 June 1901, p. 6.

48. "The New Era in Commercial Education," *Saturday Evening Post*, 11 November 1899, p. 378.

49. Crocker, "The Young Man and the New Force," pp. 1–2.

50. Roger Babson, "A New Profession for the Young Man," *Saturday Evening Post*, 27 May 1911, pp. 37–38. One *Post* editorial from 1905 called for a university of business to "train men to finance as a profession" in order that they could be directors of organizations with purely "detached" professional interests. "Business as a Profession," *Saturday Evening Post*, 29 July 1905, p. 12.

51. Ibid.

52. Daniel Coit Gilman, "Modern Education," *Cosmopolitan* 23 (May 1897): 36.

53. Henry Morton, "Modern Education," *Cosmopolitan* 23 (June 1897): 186.

54. Elisha Benjamin Andrews, "Two New Educational Ideals," *Cosmopolitan* 23 (September 1897): 573, 574.

55. "The Cosmopolitan University," *Cosmopolitan* 24 (January 1898): 335–40.

56. Walker had pronounced that the university targeted a new group, and the only statistics compiled on enrollments fit the profile of the new middle class perfectly. A sampling of roughly 2,500 applicants found the vast majority to be either businessmen (795) or clerks (471), with mechanics (298) and teachers (256) the next highest. Unfortunately, nothing is recorded regarding their choice of courses. Walker, "The Cosmopolitan University," *Cosmopolitan* 24 (November 1897): 101–2. The upper-middle class of the old literary monthlies would not have needed voice culture and manners instruction. The new middle-class men, who were struggling to rise yet also wished for the stamp of legitimacy, longed for such culture and also the broad liberal knowledge that magazines and books told them marked a gentleman.

57. Some conspicuous examples from *Cosmopolitan* include "Some Examples of Recent Art," *Cosmopolitan* 24 (April 1898): 669–72; Harry Thurston Peck, "Balzac and His Work," *Cosmopolitan* 27 (July 1899): 238–45; George E. Waring, Jr., "Great Business Operations: The Utilization of City Garbage," *Cosmopolitan* 24 (February 1898): 405–12; and John H. Bridge, "The Story of the World's Largest Corporation," *Cosmopolitan* 35 (October 1903): 657–59.

58. A general historical overview of Cosmopolitan University is found in Susan Waugh McDonald, "From Kipling to Kitsch, Two Popular Editors of the Gilded Age: Mass Culture, Magazines and Correspondence Universities," *Journal of Popular Culture* 15 (Fall 1981): 50–61.

59. For example, David Starr Jordan, "A Consideration of Herbert Spencer's Essay on Education," *Cosmopolitan* 29 (July 1900): 266–76.

60. For instance, "A Great College Year," *Saturday Evening Post*, 27 October 1900, p. 15; and "Better Looking Students," *Saturday Evening Post*, 27 October 1900, p. 15.

61. "The New Kind of Graduates," *Saturday Evening Post*, 18 July 1903, p. 14.

62. "The Broadening of the Colleges," *Saturday Evening Post*, 27 October 1900, p. 15; and "The Modern College Man," *Saturday Evening Post*, 27 October 1900, p. 15.

63. David Starr Jordan, "The College Man's Advantage in the Coming Century," *Saturday Evening Post*, 26 May 1900, p. 1090.

64. Russell H. Crittenden, "The Practical College Course for Young Men," *Saturday Evening Post*, 27 October 1900, p. 6.

65. John Corbin, "Which College for the Boy?" *Saturday Evening Post*, 7 September 1907, pp. 8–9. The characterization of Cornell as "democratic" may seem a stretch, but we are dealing with perception. Many praised even Yale and Princeton for their democracy in that once a student was in, he could rise on his merits (usually through athletics) and be admitted into the "right" clubs.

66. The University of Michigan was described as a democratic Yale, where the sons of farmers, mechanics, shopkeepers, and clerks intermixed, and where the curriculum combined the liberal aspects of Yale and the German-research aspects of Harvard. John Corbin, "Which College for the Boy?" *Saturday Evening Post*, 19 October 1907, pp. 9–11. Wisconsin is covered in Corbin, "Which College for the Boy?" *Saturday Evening Post*, 22 June 1907, pp. 3–5. The University of Chicago was described by Corbin in "Which College for the Boy?" *Saturday Evening Post*, 20 July 1907, pp. 14–15 and 18.

67. Corbin, "Which College for the Boy?" *Saturday Evening Post*, 17 August 1907, p. 6. He noted that even in Princeton's graduate schools, "science has not quite exorcised the humanities." Corbin, p. 7.

68. For Princeton, Corbin described the nature of that campus's democracy as "organized" as opposed to the unorganized and natural democracy of the West. Corbin, "Which College," 17 August 1907, p. 7.

69. "Practical Education as Applied," *Saturday Evening Post*, 18 April 1908, p. 18. For instance, he praised the outcome of true liberal education—character—in an editorial eulogy of esteemed Harvard professor Nathaniel Shaler (a committed teacher of men rather than a lonely scholar). "The Making of a Man," *Saturday Evening Post*, 26 May 1906, p. 14; and "Culture and Success," *Saturday Evening Post*, 12 October 1901, p. 12.

70. "A Liberal Education," *Saturday Evening Post*, 3 December 1904, p. 18.

71. "Too Much Common Sense," *Saturday Evening Post*, 11 August 1906, p. 16.

72. "Silk Purses and Sows Ears," *Saturday Evening Post*, 4 November 1905, p. 14.

73. For example, "The Educational Stepladder," *Saturday Evening Post*, 11 August 1906, p. 16; "Education That Pays," *Saturday Evening Post*, 28 July 1906, p. 16. "Education Becoming Democratic," *Saturday Evening Post*, 11 February 1911, p. 22, rejoiced in the rise of the great state universities that had put classical literature in its proper place—only one aspect of the humanities, not the end.

74. Veysey, *Emergence of the American University*, 342–46.

75. See "The Dignity of Advertising," *Munsey's Magazine* 13 (June 1895), 319; and "Educational Advertising," *Saturday Evening Post*, 20 May 1905, p. 14. Gruber Garvey and Matthew Schneirov also comment on this for other magazines, as well. Ellen Gruber Garvey, *Adman in the Parlor: Magazines and the Gendering of Consumer Culture, 1880s to 1910s*

(New York: Oxford University Press, 1996), 11–15; and Schneirov, *Dream of a New Social Order*, 87–91.

76. Richard Ohmann, *Selling Culture: Magazines, Markets, and Class at the Turn of the Century* (New York: Verso, 1996), 89–117.

77. For example, ICS, *Saturday Evening Post*, 21 March 1908, p. 29. In half- and full-page ads, the text screamed "The trained man wins" or asked, "you don't want to remain in the time-clock and dinner pail class all your life?" International Correspondence School [ICS], *Saturday Evening Post*, 21 March 1908, p. 29; and American School of Correspondence, *Saturday Evening Post*, 20 March 1909, p. 39.

78. As early as 1902, the Home Correspondence School advertised legitimate college courses in the ancient and modern languages, literature, mathematics, and the sciences, all offered under the "direct personal charge" of professors from Cornell, Harvard, and Yale. Another school ran the slogan "college in your cottage." Home Correspondence School, *Saturday Evening Post*, 13 December 1902, p. 17; and National Correspondence Schools, *Collier's Weekly*, 25 May 1901, p. 28. Home Correspondence School, *Saturday Evening Post*, 28 July 1900, p. 22, also mentioned instructors from Brown and Harvard, and the fact that their courses could lead to an A.B.

79. Intercontinental Correspondence University, *Saturday Evening Post*, 22 October 1902, p. 21; and Intercontinental Correspondence University, *Saturday Evening Post*, 25 February 1905, p. 31. The 1905 ad listed twenty courses, and all except Consular Service and World Politics dealt with commerce. The American School of Correspondence actually did offer a B.S. in engineering through the Armour Institute, but in 1909 announced that due to "the call of business" and the need for men trained in the "bigger phases" of their work, they opened new courses in commerce, accounting, and business administration. American School of Correspondence, *Saturday Evening Post*, 18 September 1909, p. 37.

80. Peirce School, *Saturday Evening Post*, 31 July 1909, p. 29.

81. Colleges and universities made forays onto the advertising pages of these magazines as well, though the ads were not numerous or very large (with the exception of Valparaiso University and Pittsburgh), and almost always emphasized professional or business course work—ultimately supporting my arguments. See, Valparaiso University, *Saturday Evening Post*, 31 July 1909, p. 29; University of Pittsburgh, *Saturday Evening Post*, 13 August 1910, p. 47; Harvard University, *Saturday Evening Post*, 13 April 1907, p. 24; and University of Michigan, *Saturday Evening Post*, 13 April 1907, p. 24.

82. As early as 1903, the American Newspaper Association offered their "Library of the World's Best Literature" for the busy "man of affairs." Similarly, in their ads for a Shakespeare Library, the University Society appealed explicitly to aspiring young men who desired culture, but depicted their product as "a necessary part of a liberal education." American Newspaper Association, *Saturday Evening Post*, 16 May 1903, p. 21; and University Society, *Saturday Evening Post*, 17 October 1903, p. 21.

83. Eliot was contracted to compile three to four volumes per month and enlisted the help of faculty members. Hugh Hawkins, *Between Harvard and America: The Educational Leadership of Charles Eliot* (New York: Oxford University Press, 1972), 292, 294.

84. Joan Shelly Rubin, *The Making of Middlebrow Culture* (Chapel Hill: University of North Carolina Press, 1992), 27–29.

85. P. F. Collier and Son Publishers, advertisement for Harvard Classics, *Collier's Weekly*, 12 June 1909, back cover.

86. Hawkins, *Between Harvard and America*, 200–202; and Veysey, *Emergence of the American University*, 90–98.

87. Hawkins, *Between Harvard and America*, 200–203. The quote is from an Eliot speech noted by Hawkins (203).

88. Ibid., 204; and Veysey, *Emergence of the American University*, 90.

89. "Reading for Americans," *Collier's Weekly*, 5 June 1909, p. 9. This was the first announcement of the project.

90. P. F. Collier and Son, Inc., *Saturday Evening Post*, 24 August 1912, p. 45. Hawkins pointed out that the Harvard Classics was not a collection of the Great Books as someone like John Maynard Hutchins or Mortimer Adler would have defined them. Eliot saw it rather as a record of human thought and achievement, including the modern sciences. Moreover, Eliot envisioned the Five Foot Shelf much as the smorgasbord of Harvard electives. One could choose to focus on certain areas and acquire guides for more information to suit one's taste. Hawkins, *Between Harvard and America*, 294–95.

91. The Review of Reviews Company, for example, quickly attempted to outflank the Harvard Classics. The Review of Review's "Masterpiece Library" had narrowed the books "a cultured person must read down to a three foot shelf." Hawkins, *Between Harvard and America*, 294.

92. The quotes appear respectively in, The Mentor Association, *American Magazine* 81 (March 1916): 109; and The Mentor Association, *American Magazine* 81 (January 1916): 69.

93. The Mentor Association, *American Magazine* 81 (February 1916): 100.

94. The Mentor Association, *American Magazine* 82 (November 1916): 121.

95. H. K. Webster, "The Matter with Carpenter," *Saturday Evening Post*, 26 March 1904, pp. 6–7 and 28.

96. Richard Walton Tully, "Love and Advertising," *Cosmopolitan* 40 (April 1906): 670–78.

97. Ibid. Two prominent *Post* serials fleshed out characters who fully exemplified the new college-educated leader in the business world—liberal education's role in grooming gentleman leaders. Hampden Scarborough in David Graham Phillip's "The Cost" (1903) and Wister in John Corbin's 1907 serial "The Cave Man" will be featured in chaps. 4 and 5.

98. For instance, "The Triumph of Billy" (1906), featured Billy Helmerston, a tech grad of '02, employed by an electrical company. The story revolved around Helmerston's love for the daughter of the owner of the company and the problems of class that accompanied the attraction. Herbert Quick, "The Triumph of Billy," *Saturday Evening Post*, 8 December 1906, pp. 5–7.

99. A good general example is a comic tale by George Fitch from 1911, "Sic Transit Gloria All-America," discussed in chap. 5. George Fitch, "Sic Transit Gloria All-America," *Saturday Evening Post*, 15 April 1911, pp. 15–17.

100. Elizabeth Meriwether Gilmer, "The Summer Beau Company, Ltd.," *Cosmopolitan* 43 (August 1907): 381–87.

101. Andrews, "Two New Educational Ideals," 568.

102. Booker T. Washington, "Problems in Education," *Cosmopolitan* 33 (September 1902): 506–14; and J. M. Oskison, "A Carlisle Commencement," *Collier's Weekly*, 4 June 1910, pp. 21–22 and 26.

103. Hayden Carruth, "Old-Man-With-His-Head-On," *Cosmopolitan* 40 (March 1906): 591–94.

104. Adachi Kinnosuke, "The Jinrikisha Man: A Tale of Student Life in Imperial Japan," *Saturday Evening Post*, 18 November 1899, pp. 405–6. The Chinese, Scandinavian, Irish, and German college students can be found, respectively, in Isobel Strong, "Under the Banyan," *Munsey's Magazine* 24 (October 1900): 108–11; George Fitch, "Initiating Ole," *Saturday Evening Post*, 18 September 1909, pp. 5–7 and 34; "One Way Out: A Middle Class New Englander Emigrates to America," *Saturday Evening Post*, 8 October 1910, pp. 7–10; and Fritz Krog, "Father and Son," *Munsey's Magazine* 41 (May 1909): 244–46.

105. Montague Glass, "The Efficient Salamander," *Saturday Evening Post*, 26 August 1911, pp. 13–15.

106. Jordan is quoted in "The Question of Women Students," *Saturday Evening Post*, 28 October 1899, p. 330. Stanford's female enrollment had jumped to 41 percent of the entire university, but Jordan attributes the lack of male enrollment to a "slump in athletics."

107. Excellent studies of women's rising enrollments exist, but none closely examines the discourse on going to college in the mainstream media. Helen Lefkowitz Horowitz, *Alma Mater: Design and Experience in the Women's Colleges from Their Nineteenth-Century Beginnings to the 1930s* (New York: Knopf, 1984); Barbara Miller Solomon, *In the Company of Educated Women: A History of Women and Higher Education in America* (New Haven: Yale University Press, 1985); and Lynn D. Gordon, *Gender and Higher Education in the Progressive Era* (New Haven: Yale University Press, 1990).

108. Mrs. Burton Harrison, "The Education of a Woman of Fashion," *Saturday Evening Post*, 26 May 1900, p. 1104; and G. Stanley Hall, "The Question of Co-Education," *Munsey's Magazine* 34 (December 1905): 588–92.

109. "The New President of Mt. Holyoke," *Saturday Evening Post*, 26 May 1900, p. 1098; and "Colleges and Women," *Collier's Weekly*, 27 November 1909, p. 9. The *Post* editorial celebrated her academic prowess and drive, especially in that she sought and received "special student" status in order to study at all-male Brown.

110. "Women's Colleges," *Saturday Evening Post*, 28 October 1899, p. 334; Alice Katherine Fallows, "The Girl Freshman," *Munsey's Magazine* 25 (September 1901): 818–28; P. F. Piper, "College Fraternities," *Cosmopolitan* 22 (March 1897): 645; and Forrest Crissey, "How Modern College Students Work Their Way Through," *Saturday Evening Post*, 6 June 1903, pp. 10–11.

111. Harold Bolce, "The Crusade Invisible," *Cosmopolitan* 48 (February 1910): 310–20; and Bolce, "Away from Ancient Alters," *Cosmopolitan* 48 (March 1910): 519–28.

112. Bolce, "The Crusade Invisible," 313.

113. Ibid., 310.

114. Bolce comments on their service in "Away from Ancient Alters," 525. The *Post* editorial "Send the Girl to College" and the Butler article both made the same arguments regarding the better match of college-educated mates lessening marriage woes.

115. Martha Keeler, "Magic Wands and Stepping Stones: A Talk to the Girl Graduate at the Entrance to the Land of Self-Support," *Collier's Weekly*, 7 June 1913, pp. 26–27;

Charles Belmont Davis, "Court Circles at Wisconsin," *Collier's Weekly*, 23 July 1910, pp. 14–16; and "The Girl Freshman."

116. In her examination of fiction about women in college covering some of this same time period, Shirley Marchalonis similarly found that depictions of women in college tended to be descriptive and somewhat conservative. Authors usually wanted to reassure readers that a college education, while a precious thing for cultivating the person, was nothing to be feared and indeed formed ideal women conforming to prevailing norms. Shirley Marchalonis, *College Girls: A Century in Fiction* (New Brunswick: Rutgers University Press, 1995).

117. Geraldine Fitz Gerald, "Whose Fruit Is Dreams," *Munsey's Magazine* 41 (May 1909): 168–70; and Arthur B. Reeve, "The Case of Helen Bond," *Cosmopolitan* 50 (December 1910): 113–24.

118. George Hibbard, "The New Frankenstein," *Munsey's Magazine* 35 (September 1906): 755–61.

119. Robert Herrick, "Mother Sims," *Saturday Evening Post*, 17 November 1900, pp. 10–11; Edwin L. Sabin, "The Memoirs of a Co-Ed: A Little Learning Is a Dangerous Thing," *Saturday Evening Post*, 4 January 1908, pp. 1–2 and 30–32; and Francis Lynde, "The Lion and the Lamb," *Munsey's Magazine* 39 (June 1908): 336–49. For another story where the college girl's cultural study is stressed and romance plays the dominant role, see also Josephine Dodge Daskam, "Her Fiancé—A Story of Smith College," *Saturday Evening Post*, 27 October 1900, pp. 3–4.

120. Harrison Rhodes, "When Culture Comes in at the Door," *Saturday Evening Post*, 2 April 1904, pp. 13–15.

121. Martha Wheeler, "The Tri-State Meet," *Munsey's Magazine* 39 (August 1908): 683–84; and Dorothy Canfield, "A Quiet Path to the Pierian Spring," *Munsey's Magazine* 38 (March 1908): 784–86. The third story mentioned is Martha Wheeler, "Shouldering the Burden," *Munsey's Magazine* 38 (January 1908): 516–18. This story revolves around sympathetic classmates who attempt to shield a weak-performing student from the knowledge she has flunked all her courses, so that she can leave school to help an ailing father with a modicum of dignity.

Chapter 3. Athletes and Frats, Romance and Rowdies

1. Nathaniel Butler, "Shall I Go to College?" *Saturday Evening Post*, 28 October 1899, p. 329; Maurice Thompson, "The War against the Classics," *Saturday Evening Post*, 28 October 1899, p. 329; "Presidents as Fraternity Men," *Saturday Evening Post*, 28 October 1899, p. 323; Jesse Lynch Williams, "The Great College-Circus Fight," *Saturday Evening Post*, 28 October 1899, pp. 324–26; Harmon S. Grant, "The College Man's Game," *Saturday Evening Post*, 28 October 1899, p. 337; and Arthur Hobson Quinn, "The Last Five Yards," *Saturday Evening Post*, 28 October 1899, pp. 335–36.

2. Cover illustration, *Saturday Evening Post*, 28 October 1899.

3. Major works on the challenges to American men and the resulting shifts in conceptions of American masculinity include Peter G. Filene, *Him/Her/Self: Sex Roles in Modern America*, 2nd ed. (Baltimore: Johns Hopkins University Press, 1986); Peter N. Stearns, *Be a Man! Males in Modern Society*, 2nd ed. (New York: Holmes and Meier Publishers, Inc., 1990); Joe L. Dubbert, *A Man's Place: Masculinity in Transition* (Englewood

Cliffs, NJ: Prentice-Hall, Inc., 1979); Elizabeth Pleck and Joseph Pleck, eds., *The American Man* (Englewood Cliffs, NJ: Prentice-Hall, Inc., 1979); J. A. Mangan and James Walvin, eds., *Manliness and Morality: Middle-Class Masculinity in Britain and America, 1880–1940* (New York: St. Martin's Press, 1987); Mark C. Carnes and Clyde Griffen, eds., *Meanings for Manhood: Constructions of Masculinity in Victorian America* (Chicago: University of Chicago Press, 1990); E. Anthony Rotundo, *American Manhood: Transformations in Masculinity from the Revolution to the Modern Era* (New York: Basic Books, 1993); and Michael Kimmel, *Manhood in America: A Cultural History* (New York: Free Press, 1997).

4. Rotundo, *American Manhood*, 232–46.

5. Ibid., chaps. 10 and 11; Elliott J. Gorn, *The Manly Art: Bare-Knuckle Prize-Fighting in America* (Ithaca, NY: Cornell University Press, 1986), chaps. 6–7; Christopher Lasch, *The Culture of Narcissism: American Life in an Age of Diminishing Expectations* (New York: W. W. Norton and Co., 1979), 100–124; Roberta J. Park, "Biological Thought, Athletics and the Formation of a 'Man of Character,' 1830–1900," in Mangan and Walvin, *Manliness and Morality*, 7–34; Robert J. Higgs, "Yale and the Heroic Ideal: Gotterdammerung and Palingenesis, 1865–1914," in *Manliness and Morality*, 160–75; Steven A. Reiss, "Sport and the Redefinition of American Middle-Class Masculinity," *International Journal of the History of Sport* 8 (May 1991): 5–27; John Lucas and Ronald Smith, *The Saga of American Sport* (Philadelphia: Lea and Febiger, 1978), chap. 13; Melvin Adelman, *Sporting Time: New York City and the Rise of Modern Athletics, 1820–1870* (Urbana: University of Illinois Press, 1986); Benjamin Rader, *American Sports: From the Age of Folk Games to the Age of Spectators* (Englewood Cliffs, NJ: Prentice-Hall, Inc., 1983), 75–86.

6. Works covering the growth of American fraternal organizations include Mark C. Carnes, *Secret Rituals and Manhood in Victorian America* (New Haven: Yale University Press, 1989); Mary Ann Clawson, *Constructing Brotherhood: Class, Gender and Fraternalism* (Princeton, NJ: Princeton University Press, 1989); Kimmel, *Manhood in America*, 170–74. On the quest for outdoor regeneration, see John Pettegrew, *Brutes in Suits: Male Sensibility in America, 1890–1920* (Baltimore: Johns Hopkins University Press, 2007). On the embrace of the bachelor urban sporting culture by the middle-class man (once reviled as immoral), see Gorn, *Manly Art*, chap. 6.

7. Some of the excellent works touching on the new manly heroes that have influenced this study include Rotundo, *American Manhood*, 227–46; Kimmel, *Manhood in America*, 141–54; Gail Bederman, *Manliness and Civilization: A Cultural History of Gender and Race in the United States, 1880–1917* (Chicago: University of Chicago Press, 1995), 217–39; and Pettegrew, *Brutes in Suits*, chap. 3.

8. Masculinity scholars have built on the path-breaking work of such intellectual/cultural historians as Warren I. Susman, *Culture as History: The Transformation of American Society in the Twentieth Century* (New York: Pantheon, 1984); and Jackson Lears, *No Place of Grace: Antimodernism and the Transformation of American Culture, 1880–1920* (New York: Pantheon Books, 1981). For a full exploration of this transformation in masculinity, see Tom Pendergast, *Creating the Modern Man: American Magazines and Consumer Culture, 1900–1950* (Columbia: University of Missouri Press, 2000).

9. Many note how the muscular Christianity movement and the passion for competitive sports affected higher education. Joseph F. Kett, *Rites of Passage: Adolescence in America, 1790 to the Present* (New York: Basic Books, 1977), 173–81; Rader, *American Sports*,

70–86; Lucas and Smith, *The Saga of American Sport*, chaps. 12–15; Christopher Lasch, "The Degradation of Sport," in *Culture of Narcissism*, 103–24. See also Kim Townsend, *Manhood at Harvard: William James and Others* (New York: W. W. Norton and Co., 1996).

10. Bederman, *Manliness and Civilization*, 1–44.

11. Pettegrew, *Brutes in Suits*.

12. Dubbert, *Man's Place*, 166–68.

13. Ibid., 169. Rotundo related how the benefits of athletic competition were really not seen as a virtue until the late nineteenth century, when such side effects began to be celebrated for fostering martial virtues. Rotundo, *American Manhood*, 235–45. An excellent essay focusing on the glorification of martial virtues is Donald J. Mrozek, "The Habit of Victory: The American Military and the Cult of Manliness," in Mangan and Walvin, *Manliness and Morality*, 220–41.

14. For example, Mike Murphy, "How to Get Fit: Temperance, Out-of-Door Life and Reasonable Exercise, All the Business Man Needs," *Saturday Evening Post*, 25 May 1907, p. 20. Murphy, a former athletic trainer at Yale, was at Penn when he wrote the article. Other examples include, Dudley A. Sargent, "Home Gymnastics for the Business Man," *Saturday Evening Post*, 10 February 1900, pp. 724–25; Eugene Lamb Richards, "Athletics in the Future of the Nation," *Saturday Evening Post*, 21 April 1900, p. 982; William G. Anderson, "The Making of a Perfect Man," *Munsey's Magazine* 25 (April 1901): 94–104; J. William White, "Reasons for the Belief in the Value of Exercise and Athletics," *Saturday Evening Post*, 1 December 1900, pp. 15–17; and Sir Thomas Lipton, "The Sports That Make the Man," *Saturday Evening Post*, 11 May 1901, pp. 1–2. On the mass magazines' embrace of health and sport, see "New Secular Religion of Health" in Michael Schneirov, *The Dream of a New Social Order: Popular Magazines in America, 1893–1914* (New York: Columbia University Press, 1994), 127–60.

15. For example, Stanley J. Weyman, "Count Hannibal," *Munsey's Magazine* 25 (April 1901): 1–15; James S. Easby-Smith, "The Real Klondike," *Cosmopolitan* 24 (January 1898): 227–34; and Agnes and Egerton Castle, "Rose of the World," *Saturday Evening Post*, 12 November 1904, pp. 8–9 and 16–17. Matthew Schneirov and Richard Ohmann discussed the prominence of this type of fiction (and biography), as did Theodore Greene. While Greene saw such subjects as essentially antimodern heroes (autonomous fantasy heroes for middle-class men who could only dream of such prowess and adventure), Schneirov (on biographies) and Ohmann (on fiction) argued that such stories encouraged more the embrace of modern, aggressive traits—vigorous activity and action, or the celebration of middle-class rationality in action, rather than a reaction to powerlessness. Schneirov, *Dream of a New Social Order*, 185–94; Richard Ohmann, *Selling Culture: Magazines, Markets, and Class at the Turn of the Century* (New York: Verso, 1996), chap. 10; and Theodore P. Greene, *America's Heroes: The Changing Models of Success in American Magazines* (New York: Oxford University Press, 1970).

16. For advertisements on health see, Alois P. Swoboda, *Collier's Weekly*, 10 November 1900, p. 21; the Stone School of Scientific Physical Culture, *Collier's Weekly*, 17 May 1902, back cover; Pompeian Manufacturing Co., *Saturday Evening Post*, 23 February 1907, pp. 16–17. Examples of martial biographies include an advertisement for the Perkins Book Co., *Saturday Evening Post*, 1 November 1902, p. 17, which offered biographies of the "Heroes of History."

17. John Weston Allen, "Athletic Yale," *Munsey's Magazine* 12 (November 1894): 125–30. Yale had suffered only five defeats since 1875 in football. The article also looked briefly at the Yale crew, baseball, and track teams.

18. Juliet Wilbor Tompkins and Gilbert Tompkins, "The Winning Touchdown: A Football Song," *Munsey's Magazine* 15 (July 1896): 470–75. The pictures of the Ivy League captains were included in the regular section "In the Public Eye," *Munsey's Magazine* 20 (December 1898): 488.

19. The exact name of the piece changed, but one example was "Sport of the Amateur on Field and Water," *Collier's Weekly*, 8 April 1899, p. 25, which ran three pictures of the Harvard crew in training (one picture with a bare-chested man) and one picture of lettermen (sweaters sporting the capital H) with the Yard in the background.

20. Examples in the fall covering football include "Sports of the Amateur on Field and Water," *Collier's Weekly*, 21 October 1899, pp. 21–22; Walter Camp, "Harvard vs. Yale," *Collier's Weekly*, 2 December 1899, pp. 20–22; and Walter Camp, "Sports, Travel and Adventure," *Collier's Weekly*, 20 October 1900, pp. 22–24. Such coverage regularly continued in the years following, expanding to cover changes and controversies in the game. For example, "Harvard Conquers Yale in Football Battle," *Collier's Weekly*, 5 December 1908, p. 8; Walter Camp, "The All-America Football Team," *Collier's Weekly*, 19 December 1908, pp. 10–11; and Walter Camp, "Influence of the Tackle Play," *Collier's Weekly*, 15 October 1910, pp. 24–25.

21. Camp, "Harvard vs. Yale," *Collier's Weekly*, 2 December 1899, pp. 20–22.

22. Cover illustration, *Saturday Evening Post*, 7 June 1902; cover illustration, *Saturday Evening Post*, 27 October 1900; and cover illustration by J. J. Gould, *Saturday Evening Post*, 18 June 1904.

23. Bederman, *Manliness and Civilization*, 26–31.

24. Ibid., 88–120.

25. In characterizing the celebration of the college athlete, Roberta J. Park wrote that the college athlete "was the conspicuous exemplar of the man who knew how to discipline himself and dedicate his efforts to the pursuit of excellence." Park, "Biological Thought, Athletics and the Formation of the 'Man of Character,'" in Mangan and Walvin, *Manliness and Morality*, 22. The magazines took this vision, however, and trumpeted it far and wide.

26. Clifford Putney views the muscular Christianity movement as fulfilling a similar intellectual bridge uniting the cultivation of civilization (Christianity) and the proper harnessing of primitive competitive urges. College simply served that purpose in a more multifaceted (and potentially secular) way. Clifford Putney, *Muscular Christianity: Manhood and Sports in Protestant America* (Cambridge, MA: Harvard University Press, 2001), 6–8. Scholars of masculinity usually use the term "masculinity" to define the new, more passionate vision of masculine ideals that evolved during this time period, replacing the term manhood. While the ideals of manhood certainly were under transition, I did not find a rigid displacement of terminology, and have chosen to use the two terms more or less interchangeably.

27. Richards, "Athletics in the Future of the Nation," 982.

28. The quote is from White, "Reasons for Belief in the Value of Exercise and Athletics," 15–17.

29. W. G. Anderson, "The Making of a Perfect Man," 94–104.

30. Harmon S. Graves, "The College Man's Game," *Saturday Evening Post*, 28 October 1899, p. 337. Michael Oriard has stated that, "underlying virtually every narrative of football was the most fundamental issue of all: what it meant to be a 'man.'" Michael Oriard, *King Football: Sport and Spectacle in the Golden Age of Radio and Newsreels, Movies and Magazines, the Weekly and the Daily Press* (Chapel Hill: University of North Carolina Press, 2001), 226.

31. John Sayle Watterson, *College Football: History, Spectacle, Controversy* (Baltimore: Johns Hopkins University Press, 2000).

32. Michael Oriard, *Reading Football: How the Popular Press Created an American Spectacle* (Chapel Hill: University of North Carolina Press, 1993), 214–15. The embrace of football as part of a much wider discourse on masculinity included a newly enshrined "primitive," violent element, due to the interpretation and application of Darwinian ideas of evolution. See Pettegrew, *Brutes in Suits*.

33. Oriard, *Reading Football*, 36–51, 78–101, 142–44, and 211–16. Walter Camp, for instance, used scientific metaphors and celebrated the modern corporate values cultivated by football—the necessity of long training, efficiency, and cooperation, but he easily merged such language with descriptions that bolstered images of a rugged independent manhood (i.e., the hero of the game and his All-American team). A rival to Camp, Casper Whitney, championed football as a game instilling the qualities of upper-class leadership.

34. Graves, "The College Man's Game," 337.

35. Owen Wister, "The Open-Air Education," *Saturday Evening Post*, 25 October 1903, pp. 1–2. The author of *The Virginian* (hailed as the first "Western"), Wister was a frequent contributor to the *Post* and one of the greatest proponents of the strenuous life.

36. Eustace Clavering, "The Fortunes of Football," *Munsey's Magazine* 28 (October 1902): 66–73.

37. The *Munsey's* article on "The Perfect Man" quoted Aristotle's definition of a whole man—mind, body, and spirit. Anderson, "The Making of a Perfect Man," 94.

38. "A Sound Mind in a Sound Body," *Saturday Evening Post*, 30 April 1904, p. 12.

39. Oriard, *King Football*, 338, discusses (for the 1920s) how football fiction writers were able to explore controversial themes much easier than direct reporting coverage, owing to the nature of fiction.

40. John Tebbel, *George Horace Lorimer and the Saturday Evening Post* (Garden City: Doubleday, 1948), 286.

41. Quinn, "The Last Five Yards," 335.

42. Ibid.

43. Ibid., 335–36.

44. Ibid. Regular contributor to the *Post*, Jesse Lynch Williams, offered another all-around football hero who faced a moral dilemma testing his devotion to higher principles. Williams's "The Great College Circus Fight" also points to the rowdy elements that could color college life as more manly, as the college men brawled with a traveling circus. Williams, "The Great College Circus Fight," 324–25. Another story with a moral, democratic theme is Frank Norris, "Kirkland at Quarter," *Saturday Evening Post*, 12 October 1901, pp. 4–5. The magazine introduced Norris as the author of *The Octopus*. True to his muckraking leanings, Norris combined college football with social commentary. Kirkland was a great quarterback on a fair midwestern team. He was being recruited to

forsake his team for a better team in the East, tempted with visions of acceptance by the best clubs and the ability to really make a name for himself. After flirting with the offer, Kirkland comes to his senses and stays loyal to his team and principles.

45. Richard O'Connor, *Jack London: A Biography* (Boston: Little Brown, 1964), 76 and 152.

46. James Hopper, "The Idealist," *Saturday Evening Post*, 14 October 1905, pp. 6–8 and 22. See also, James Hopper, "The Strength of the Weak," *Saturday Evening Post*, 22 October 1904, pp. 4–5 and 22–23.

47. Hopper, "The Idealist," 22.

48. James Hopper, "The Redemption of Fullback Jones," *Saturday Evening Post*, 26 October 1912, pp. 12–14 and 57–58.

49. James Hopper, "The Freshman," *Saturday Evening Post*, 30 September 1911, p. 22.

50. For example, in Quinn's "The Last Five Yards," the author wrote of "two giant guards opening holes as they march slowly but surely down the field for an opening score." Quinn, "The Last Five Yards," 336. In "Kirkland at Quarter," Norris described the other team as "inferiors as individuals but by months of strenuous training welded together to form a single compact unit." Norris, "Kirkland at Quarter," 5. David Lamoreaux provided a detailed analysis of the Dink Stover stories in the context of corporate expansion and progressive angst that helped to inform my understanding of the college football story in middle-class magazines. Lamoreaux, "Stover at Yale and the Gridiron Metaphor," *Journal of Popular Culture* 11 (Fall 1977): 330–44.

51. Other writers integrating football into their characterizations of how college helped form the whole man are Arthur T. Hadley, "Modern Education," *Cosmopolitan* 28 (November 1899): 104–6; Charles F. Thwing, "First Principles for the College Man," *Saturday Evening Post*, 14 November 1903, pp. 26–28; "A Sound Mind and a Sound Body," 12; William Lyon Phelps, "The College Man Today," *Collier's Weekly* 21 June 1902, p. 9.

52. Owen Johnson, "The Varmint," *Saturday Evening Post*, 21 May 1910, pp. 21–22.

53. Ibid., 56.

54. Ibid., 55.

55. Hopper, "The Freshman," 60.

56. Ibid., 24.

57. Other sports surfaced as well to illustrate the lessons of manhood instilled at college. A prominent *Post* writer, Gouverneur Morris, even used lawn tennis in one of his stories to illustrate the ideal qualities of the college-educated, athletic hero. The hero attended Harvard and studied hard. He "doggedly" practiced lawn tennis, purposefully losing some matches in order to meticulously practice his groundstrokes. All this paid off, however, as he became Ivy League champion. Gouverneur Morris, "Which Was George?" *Saturday Evening Post*, 16 April 1909, pp. 5–7 and 44–46. Baseball also proved popular. A *Munsey's Magazine* story centered on a Midwest college baseball star who displayed his heroism after graduation by standing up for a wronged woman. David H. Talmadge, "The Luck of Monty Morrison," *Munsey's Magazine* 24 (February 1901): 791–94.

58. Pettegrew, *Brutes in Suits*, chap. 2.

59. Both Matthew Schneirov and Richard Ohmann explored how these new popular magazines celebrated modernity while still adhering to the cultivation of genteel culture like the quality monthlies of the nineteenth century. Schneirov even hypothesized that the fascination with the lives of the elite was part of a dream of abundance offered

the middle-class readership, encouraging the readers to aspire to emulate. Schneirov, *Dream of a New Social Order*, 76–86; and Ohmann, *Selling Culture*, 158–59.

60. Richard Titherington, "Picturesque Oxford," *Munsey's Magazine* 22 (November 1899): 201–9; Champe S. Andrews, "Where English Lawyers Are Made," *Cosmopolitan* 28 (March 1900): 555–63.

61. Titherington, "Picturesque Oxford," 201–2. The author actually praised Oxford as a "custodian of literature," a guardian of civilization against "the plutocracy of Commerce and Industry."

62. Douglas Story, "The Universities of Europe," *Munsey's Magazine* 26 (October 1901): 54–68.

63. Ethelbert D. Warfield, "The Expansion of Our Great Universities," *Munsey's Magazine* 25 (August 1901): 693–706.

64. One conspicuous example of this overlap (and one that additionally illustrates the mixing of genteel collegiate associations with manly attributes) was a story in *Munsey's* titled "Luxurious Bachelordom," which focused on how wealthy Eastern businessmen tastefully decorated their apartments. One of the photographs featured crossed fencing swords, scenes of a hunt, and Yale pennants on the wall. James L Ford, "Luxurious Bachelordom," *Munsey's Magazine* 20 (January 1899): 584–94.

65. Edward Boltwood, "College Rooms and Their Traditions," *Munsey's Magazine* 23 (July 1900): 447–57. The *Post* published a similar article with Herbert Copeland, "Furnishing the College Room," *Saturday Evening Post*, 27 October 1900, pp. 8 and 31.

66. Mrs. Burton Harrison, "Henley Week," *Cosmopolitan* 29 (July 1900): 241–52.

67. For instance, "The Election of a President of Yale," *Collier's Weekly*, 15 April 1899, p. 21; and "Graduating Classes of Yale, Columbia and Princeton," *Collier's Weekly*, 28 June 1902, p. 10.

68. P. F. Piper, "College Fraternities," *Cosmopolitan* 22 (March 1897): 641–48.

69. Erman J. Ridgeway, "College Fraternities," *Munsey's Magazine* 24 (February 1901): 729–42.

70. Honorable George F. Hoar, "The College Man of Yesterday," *Collier's Weekly*, 21 June 1902, p. 8.

71. Hopper, "The Idealist," 6. Nearly every football story always came down to one "big game," the scene of loyal fans described in detail.

72. Michael Oriard also commented on how the press popularized not only football, but built into their narrative descriptions of the spectacle of the big game—the people and the antics. Oriard, *Reading Football*, 92–100 and 112–20.

73. The first installments of both serials are Charles Macomb Flandrau, "Diary of a Harvard Freshman," *Saturday Evening Post*, 27 October 1900, pp. 10–11; and "Sophomores Abroad," *Saturday Evening Post*, 2 November 1901, pp. 3–4 and 16. "Sophomores Abroad" followed Tommy and his friend Berri on a trip to Europe.

74. The stories dealing with the problems noted in the text come respectively from Flandrau, "Diary of a Harvard Freshman," *Saturday Evening Post*, 27 October 1900, pp. 10–11; Flandrau, "Diary of a Harvard Freshman," *Saturday Evening Post*, 8 December 1900, pp 12–13; and Flandrau, "Diary of a Harvard Freshman," *Saturday Evening Post*, 10 November 1900, pp. 10–11.

75. Flandrau, "Diary of a Harvard Freshman," *Saturday Evening Post*, 27 October 1900, p. 11.

76. Flandrau, "Diary of a Harvard Freshman," *Saturday Evening Post*, 19 January 1901, p. 11.

77. As the popular magazine's fascination with college-going reached high tide in the first decade of the century, Harvard indeed received the lion's share of attention (and romantic word-images of "the yard" and glee clubs, etc.) from fiction writers creating an idealized image of American college life. See Charles Macomb Flandrau, "The Borrowed Sonnet," *Saturday Evening Post*, 26 May 1900, pp. 1091–93; and Arthur Train, "Randolph '64," *Saturday Evening Post*, 2 December 1905, pp. 1–4.

78. In Svetozar Tonjoroff, "For Services Rendered," *Saturday Evening Post*, 21 October 1911, pp. 16–17 and 57–58, the author touched on many standard themes, but highlighted the mystical chains that bound student to alma mater, as a famous alumnus finally returns, the story filled with romanticized reminiscences and word images of the "Hartford University."

79. Arthur Stringer, "The Professor of Greek: How He Found the Hellenes Again," *Saturday Evening Post*, 14 November 1903, p. 8.

80. Ibid., 8–9 and 32.

81. On Ralph Adams Cram and his medieval architectural influence in the United States, see Lears, *No Place of Grace*, 203–9.

82. Warfield, "The Expansion of Our Great Universities," 693.

83. Ibid., 694–703.

84. "Should Your Boy Go to College?" *Munsey's Magazine* 13 (August 1895): 461–65; and Bird S. Coler, "The Man Who Can't Go to College," *Saturday Evening Post*, 29 June 1901, p. 8. Both of these articles contained typical criticisms from self-styled, self-made men.

85. Grover Cleveland, "Old Fashioned Honesty and the Coming Man," *Saturday Evening Post*, 5 August 1905, pp. 1–2. The earlier article was Cleveland, "Does a College Education Pay?" *Saturday Evening Post*, 26 May 1900, pp. 1089–90.

86. John Corbin, "High Life and Higher Education," *Saturday Evening Post*, 14 November 1903, pp. 10–11 and 20; and "The Gentle Art of Snobbery," *Saturday Evening Post*, 20 March 1909, p. 18. Corbin later singled out Harvard and Yale as particularly undemocratic and snobbish. John Corbin, "Which College for the Boy? Harvard: A Germanized University," *Saturday Evening Post*, 21 September 1907, pp. 10–12 and 22.

87. Owen Johnson, "The Social Usurpation of Our Colleges—Part I," *Collier's Weekly*, 18 May 1912, pp. 10–11. Others in the series are, Part II on Harvard, 25 May 1912, pp. 12–14 and 36; Part III on Yale, 8 June 1912, pp. 12–13 and 23–25; Part IV on Princeton, 15 June 1912, pp. 17–18 and 24; and Part V on the fraternity system, 22 June 1912, pp. 17–18 and 24.

88. D. K. Pearsons, "Common Sense in College Endowments," *Saturday Evening Post*, 22 June 1901, pp. 18–19.

89. D. K. Pearsons, "Freshwater Colleges," *Saturday Evening Post*, 26 May 1900, p. 1110.

90. John Corbin, "Which College for the Boy? Princeton: The Collegiate University," *Saturday Evening Post*, 17 August 1907, pp. 6–7 and 23; Corbin, "Which College for the Boy? Michigan: Foremost of State Universities in the West," *Saturday Evening Post*, 19 October 1907, pp. 9–11 and 27; and Corbin, "Which College for the Boy? Wisconsin," *Saturday Evening Post*, 22 June 1907, pp. 3–5.

91. On athletics and self-supporting students fostering a democratic spirit see "Rich and Poor at Harvard," *Saturday Evening Post*, 2 September 1899, p. 9; and James L. Ford, "Our American Snobs," *Saturday Evening Post*, 15 March 1903, pp. 8–9.

92. Corbin, "Which College for the Boy? Harvard," 12.

93. Piper, "College Fraternities," 643–46. Similarly, the *Munsey's* author described the rush process and (to some degree) initiation ceremonies. Ridgeway, "College Fraternities," 734.

94. William Matthews, "The Age for Entering College," *Saturday Evening Post*, 22 December 1900, p. 9; and Copeland, "Furnishing a College Room," 8 and 31. The Copeland article advised, "let no one sneer at the idea of an attractive room being important to a college man."

95. W. S. Harwood, "Earning an Education," *Saturday Evening Post*, 29 July 1899, pp. 78–79.

96. Garrison Williams, "Through Harvard on Fifty Cents," *Saturday Evening Post*, 13 January 1900, pp. 607–9; James Melvin Lee, "How to Be Self-Supporting at College," *Saturday Evening Post*, 27 October 1900, pp. 26–27; Robert Shackleton, "How Boys Earn Money," *Saturday Evening Post*, 8 August 1903, pp. 16–17; and John Corbin, "Financing a College Education," *Saturday Evening Post*, 18 March 1911, pp. 10–11 and 60.

97. Corbin, "Which College for the Boy? Princeton," 6–7; Corbin, "Which College for the Boy? Michigan," 9–11; and Corbin, "Which College for the Boy? Wisconsin," 3–5.

98. Wallace Irwin, "The Shame of the Colleges: The Democratic Machine at Yale," *Saturday Evening Post*, 18 August 1906, pp. 8–9 and 20.

99. Irwin, "The Shame of the College: Princeton: Frenzied but Unashamed," *Saturday Evening Post*, 1 September 1906, pp. 3–4 and 23; and Irwin, "Shame of the Colleges: The University of Chicago: As Self-Made Antique," *Saturday Evening Post*, 25 September 1906, pp. 8–9.

100. Boltwood, "College Rooms and Their Traditions," 448, 450, 452, and 455. The photographs on each of these pages picture such "manly" accessories in the room as golf clubs, team photos, paintings of hunts or football scrums, crossed fencing swords, and beer steins. Michael Kimmel comments on the "colonization" of the home by men during this period in *Manhood in America*, 111.

101. Ridgeway, "College Fraternities," 729–34. Kimmel briefly notes how college fraternities fit into this trend in *Manhood in America*, 170–71.

102. One typical article critical of hazing is, David Starr Jordan, "College Discipline," *North American Review* 165 (October 1897): 403–8.

103. Julian Hawthorne, "The Crime of Hazing," *Munsey's Magazine* 32 (March 1905): 809–12. Nonetheless, books published to address public interest such as Henry D. Sheldon, *Student Life and Student Customs* (New York: D. Appleton and Company, 1901), and articles like "College Pranks: Old Grad Tales of Freshman Days," *Saturday Evening Post*, 7 June 1902, pp. 2–3, took a more informative and even entertaining tone.

104. Max O'Rell, "Early Influences: A Reminiscence of My School Days," *Cosmopolitan* 30 (November 1900): 57; and "College Pranks," 2–3. One *Post* editorial lauded fraternities for nurturing bonds of fraternal brotherhood that instilled valuable lessons. "The Good Side of Fraternities," *Saturday Evening Post*, 27 October 1900, p. 14.

105. "College Pranks," 2–3.

106. A good introduction to how hazing changed as American colleges and universities modernized is Winton U. Solberg, "Harmless Pranks or Brutal Practices? Hazing at the University of Illinois, 1868–1913," *Journal of the Illinois State Historical Society* 91 (Winter 1998): 233–59.

107. The quote comes from, Ridgeway, "College Fraternities," 729.

108. Stanley Waterloo, "The Crime of '73," *Saturday Evening Post*, 26 May 1900, pp. 112 and 114.

109. For instance, Charles Macomb Flandrau, "Diary of a Harvard Freshman," *Saturday Evening Post*, 2 March 1901, pp. 10–11; Jesse Lynch Williams, "At the Corner of Lovers' Lane: A Princeton Ghost Story," *Saturday Evening Post*, 27 October 1900; and Williams, "The Leg Pull—A Princeton Story," *Saturday Evening Post*, 12 October 1901, pp. 10–11 and 16.

110. Flandrau, "The Diary of a Harvard Freshman," *Saturday Evening Post*, 10 November 1900, pp. 10–11.

111. Jesse Lynch Williams, "Hazing," *Saturday Evening Post*, 23 February 1903, p. 12.

112. Other rowdy college tales include, Williams, "The Great College Circus Fight," 324–25; and Hamilton Williams, "Rusticated: An Irish College Story of the Roaring Sixties," *Saturday Evening Post*, 6 June 1903, pp. 4–6.

113. Marvin Litvin, *"I'm Going to Be Somebody": A Biography of George Fitch (Originator of the Word "Siwash")* (Woodston, KA: Western Books, 1991). Fitch also published similar college tales in other popular magazines, for instance: George Fitch, "Sam and I: A Love Story in Homeburg," *American Magazine* 80 (November 1915): 35–39 and 91.

114. George Fitch, "Initiating Ole," *Saturday Evening Post*, 18 September 1909, pp. 5–7 and 34; "Ole Skjarsen's First Touchdown: A Siwash College Story," *Saturday Evening Post*, 6 November 1909, pp. 15–17 and 44–45.

115. Fitch, "When Greek Meets Grouch: A Siwash Tale," *Saturday Evening Post*, 9 October 1909, pp. 5–7 and 26–27; "A Funeral That Flashed in the Pan: Sad Days at Old Siwash," *Saturday Evening Post*, 18 December 1909, pp. 5–7 and 24–25.

116. Fitch, "Formality at Siwash," *Saturday Evening Post*, 9 August 1913, pp. 8–9 and 41; "A Funeral That Flashed in the Pan," 5. The latter story mentions the profane parrot.

117. Fitch, "Petey Simmon's Confession," *Saturday Evening Post*, 19 July 1913, pp. 3–4 and 30. Other stories commented on drinking as well. For instance, one story mentioned the mock-turtles social club, "capacity 30,000 quarts," who "absent-mindedly" tipped over a streetcar. "When Greek Meets Grouch," 6.

118. Two examples with regard to fraternities are John Corbin, "His Majesty the Freshman," *Saturday Evening Post*, 14 January 1911, pp. 6–7 and 32; and Hawthorne, "The Crime of Hazing." Two with regard to football stemming from the brutal season of 1905, when several deaths occurred and many schools responded by banning football, are "Football Courage," *Saturday Evening Post*, 10 March 1906, p. 14; and Edward S. Jordan, "Buying Football Victories," *Collier's Weekly*, 11 November 1905, pp. 19–20 and 23. This was the first installment of a series in *Collier's* delving into serious problems in college athletics.

119. Fitch, "Colleges while You Wait: A Siwash Fragment Torn from the Career of Petey Simmons," *Saturday Evening Post*, 27 August 1910, pp. 5–7.

120. Fitch, "Ole Skjarsen's First Touchdown," 15–16.

121. "The Good Side of Fraternities," *Saturday Evening Post*, 27 October 1900, p. 14; Jesse Lynch Williams, "Safe Now in the Wide, Wide World," *Saturday Evening Post*, 5 July 1902, pp. 14–15; Ridgeway, "College Fraternities," 729–34.

122. Waldron K. Post, *Harvard Stories* (New York: Putnam's, 1893); John Seymour Wood, *Yale Yarns* (New York: Putnam, 1895).

123. Many of his stories made reference to the office or being in business, such as Petey Simmons going into management. Fitch raised the issue of the college being a poor business preparation and seemed to counter it with the Simmons example. Fitch, "Colleges while You Wait," 5.

124. Fitch, "The Funeral That Flashed in the Pan," 5.

125. Fitch eventually published two collections of these stories. Evidence that the images of college life that Fitch evoked entered into the fabric of American culture surfaced some thirty to forty years after the Siwash stories ran, as the term popped up in articles on the GI Bill. The Siwash reference occurred in Milton Mackage, "Crisis at the Colleges," *Saturday Evening Post*, 3 August 1946, pp. 9–10.

126. In 1905, the *Post* published Ade's poem "The College Widow," noting that it was written in 1900 and the inspiration for his successful play. It recounts the ecstasy felt by an undergraduate as he courts this fascinating and mature woman, only to be parted by graduation. He returns in six years to find her walking the campus still, with a doting sophomore in tow. "Ade's College Widow," *Saturday Evening Post*, 10 June 1905, p. 15.

127. Octave Thanet, "Miss Maria's Fiftieth: The Romance of a University Town," *Saturday Evening Post*, 30 April 1898, pp. 3–5. Edwin L. Sabin, "Puppy Love: The College Widow," *Saturday Evening Post*, 20 April 1907, pp. 8–9 and 31. Another story in this genre was Rupert Hughes, "The College Lorelei," *Saturday Evening Post*, 29 October 1910, pp. 14–17 and 52–54.

128. Advertisement for Rosenberg Brothers and Company, *Saturday Evening Post*, 13 March 1909, p 38. *Frank Leslie's Monthly* promoted subscription sales by advertising in the *Post* that they would send a "College Girl Calendar" free for subscribing. Advertisement for *Frank Leslie's Monthly*, *Saturday Evening Post*, 13 December 1902, p. 17. Other clothing ads offering sporting and coed scenes as posters (sometimes out of their style books, but noted as making good room decorations for dens) are advertisements for Samuel Peck and Company, *Saturday Evening Post*, 26 March 1910, p. 72; and Hart, Schaffner and Marx, *Saturday Evening Post*, 27 November 1909, p. 2.

129. I. K. Friedman, "How Miss Wilcox Was Fired," *Saturday Evening Post*, 12 August 1905, pp. 4–7 and 14; and Montague Glass, "The Efficient Salamander," *Saturday Evening Post*, 26 August 1911, pp. 13–16 and 40. Angel Kwolek-Folland explored the new sexual dynamics of women entering the office in *Engendering Business: Men and Women in the Corporate Office, 1870–1930* (Baltimore: Johns Hopkins University Press, 1994), 41–69.

130. Edwin L. Sabin, "The Memoirs of a Co-Ed," *Saturday Evening Post*, 4 January 1908, pp. 1–2 and 30–32.

131. Veysey, *The Emergence of the American University*, 272; and Colin B. Burke, "The Expansion of American Higher Education," in *The Transformation of the Higher Learning, 1860–1930: Expansion, Diversification, Social Opening and Professionalization in England, Germany, Russia and the United States*, ed. Konrad H. Jarausch (Chicago: University of Chicago Press, 1983), 114–15.

132. George Fitch, "Cupid—That Old College Chum: A Few Pink Nothings about Love on the Siwash Campus," *Saturday Evening Post*, 21 January 1911, pp. 10–12.

133. Kevin White examined the new types of male "heroes" in American literature of the 1920s that celebrated a more liberated and aggressive sexuality for the American man. While one does not see in this magazine literature a full-blown "male flapper" or "tramp bohemian," to use White's characterizations, I think that the ground-breaking college characters functioned as an essential precursor to these more liberated figures of the 1920s. Kevin White, *The First Sexual Revolution: The Emergence of Male Heterosexuality in Modern America* (New York: New York University Press, 1993), 36–56.

134. Walter Camp, "The All-America Football Team of 1911," *Collier's Weekly*, 9 December 1911, pp. 18–19 and 26. In Ralph D. Pain, "The Football Heroes of Yesterday," *Munsey's Magazine* 36 (December 1906): 340, Jonas Metoxen of Carlisle (an All-American prior to Thorpe) was hailed as a credit to "his race" for refusing to go professional on a "white men's team" and for living the "honest" life of a Wisconsin farmer since graduation. Oriard discusses the racist characterizations of the Carlisle teams in the American press in *Reading Football*, 229–47.

135. George Fitch, "Initiating Ole," *Saturday Evening Post*, 18 September 1909, pp. 5–7 and 34; and Wallace Irwin, "Letters from a Japanese Schoolboy: Feetball for Molly Coddles," *Collier's Weekly*, 17 October 1908, p. 14.

136. Isobel Strong, "Under the Banyan," *Munsey's Magazine* 24 (October 1900): 100–11.

137. Alice Katherine Fallows, "The Girl Freshman," *Munsey's Magazine* 25 (September 1909): 818–28; Crissey, "How Modern College Students Work Their Way," 11; Charles Belmont Davis, "Court Circles at Wisconsin," *Collier's Weekly*, 23 July 1910, pp. 14–15; and "Women's Colleges," *Saturday Evening Post*, 28 October 1899, p. 334.

138. Fallows, "The Girl Freshman"; and Piper, "College Fraternities," 645.

139. "Presidents as Fraternity Men," *Saturday Evening Post*, 28 October 1899, p. 323; and Frank S. Arnett, "College Days of the Presidents," *Munsey's Magazine* 26 (February 1902): 668–74. Some other examples in the *Post* were John J. Ingalls, "Garfield: The Man of the People," *Saturday Evening Post*, 26 August 1899, p. 129; A. Maurice Low, "The Strong Young Men of the Administration," *Saturday Evening Post*, 27 January 1900, pp. 652–54; and Robert Shackleton, "The New Senator from Indiana," *Saturday Evening Post*, 8 September 1900, pp. 8–10.

140. Arnett, "College Days of the Presidents," 668–69.

141. The reference to McKinley comes from "Presidents as Fraternity Men," 323; Roosevelt's inspirational note reference is found in Arnett, "College Days of the Presidents," 673.

142. Ingalls, "Garfield: Man of the People," 129.

143. Low, "Strong Young Men of the Administration," 652.

144. Shackleton, "The New Senator from Indiana," 8–9.

145. Two are Albert J. Beveridge, "The Young Lawyer and His Beginnings," *Saturday Evening Post*, 27 October 1900, pp. 1–2; and Beveridge, "The Young Man in the World," *Saturday Evening Post*, 30 September 1905, pp. 2–4.

146. Richard Lloyd Jones, "The Beginnings of Beveridge," *Collier's Weekly*, 15 October 1910, pp. 21–22.

147. Arnett, "College Days of the Presidents," 672. *Collier's* treated President Taft similarly, recalling his many college antics as one of the "short hairs" of the '78 class of Yale, but also highlighting his academic awards in math and prose alongside his prowess in wrestling, and noting too that he continued to refer to the school as "dear old Yale." Arthur H. Gleason, "Bill Taft of Yale," *Collier's Weekly*, 6 March 1909, pp. 19–20.

148. Townsend, *Manhood at Harvard*, in particular chap. 5. Also, Park, "Biological Thought, Athletics and the Formation of a 'Man of Character,'" 23, discusses how enthusiasm for football, praise of Theodore Roosevelt, and arguments for the strenuous life interacted and exploded in popular discourse during this period. Three excellent looks at Roosevelt and his impact may be found in Kimmel, *American Manhood*, 181–88; Pettegrew, *Brutes in Suites*; and Arnaldo Testi, "The Gender of Reform Politics: Theodore Roosevelt and the Culture of Masculinity," *Journal of American History* 81 (March 1995): 1509–33. On the necessity of regenerating particularly upper-class American men see Higham, "The Reorientation of American Culture in the 1890s," 25–48; Lears, *No Place of Grace*, chap. 1; Gorn, *The Manly Art*, chap. 6; Donald J. Mrozek, *Sport and American Mentality, 1881–1910* (Knoxville: University of Tennessee Press, 1983); and Richard Hofstadter, *Social Darwinism in American Thought, 1860–1915* (Boston: Beacon Press, 1955).

149. John Milton Cooper, Jr., *The Warrior and the Priest: Woodrow Wilson and Theodore Roosevelt* (Cambridge, MA: Harvard University Press, 1983), 86–88.

150. Curtis Guild, Jr., "Theodore Roosevelt at Harvard," *Harvard Graduate Magazine* 10 (December 1901): 182–83, quoted in Townsend, *Manhood at Harvard*, 257.

151. Louis Seibold, "Theodore Roosevelt," *Munsey's Magazine* 26 (November 1901): 182.

152. Ibid., 183.

153. Wister, "Theodore Roosevelt, Harvard '80," *Saturday Evening Post*, 12 October 1901, p. 3.

154. Ibid., 27. Townsend covers the Harvard connections of Wister and Roosevelt along with their shared vision of the strenuous life in *Manhood at Harvard*, 256–78.

155. Poultney Bigelow, "Theodore Roosevelt: President and Sportsman," *Collier's Weekly*, 31 May 1902, p. 10.

156. The Roosevelt issue was March 4, 1905. One main article was A. T. Packard, "Roosevelt's Ranching Days: The Outdoor Training of a President as a Man among Men," *Saturday Evening Post*, 4 March 1905, pp. 13–14.

157. Although we treat different aspects of Roosevelt's impact, Arnaldo Testi's main arguments and mine run parallel. He argued that Roosevelt masculinized social concerns (such as reform) and, thus, allowed such movements to be injected into mainstream American politics (without the effeminate and overcivilized stigma of being an elitist Mugwump). Testi, "The Gender of Reform Politics," 1524. If many considered Roosevelt an Eastern dandy, artificially seeking adventure, such characterizations did not surface in these magazines.

158. Flandrau, "Diary of a Harvard Freshman," *Saturday Evening Post*, 27 October 1900, pp. 10–11.

159. Ibid., 27 October 1900, p. 11; and 10 November 1900, pp. 10–11.

160. Ibid., 19 January 1901, pp. 10–11.

161. Ibid., 5 January 1901, pp. 8–9.

162. Ibid., 8 December 1900, pp. 12–13.

163. One example not already noted is Owen Johnson, "The Martyrdom of Hicky," *Saturday Evening Post*, 5 September 1908, pp. 5–7 and 33. Johnson characterized a perfect example of the new college, scholar-athlete hero. Doc Macrouder was a "genius of all trades." He ran the half-mile close to the two-minute mark, quarterbacked the football team, played organ in chapel and banjo for the glee club, and organized the school dramatic club.

164. Holworthy Hall, "Tutoring Henry," *Saturday Evening Post*, 27 July 1912, pp. 10–11 and 40–42.

165. Ibid., 10.

166. Ibid.

167. Ibid., 11.

168. Ibid.

169. Ibid., 11 and 40–42.

170. In "The Mollycoddle," the lead character undergoes a transformation of a different sort, but one that again involves college in forming the ideal civilized-primitive man. Mollycoddle was a term of relatively recent vintage in 1913, when the story was published, one of a group of words such as "sissy" that entered the American vocabulary. Stirred by a young lady's exhortations to be more manly, the "Molly" fought in a bar during a port of call defending another woman's honor, which proved manly enough for him to prove himself to the heroine. Harold MacGraith, "The Mollycoddle," *Saturday Evening Post*, 10 May 1913, pp. 5–7 and 39.

Chapter 4. Horatio Alger Goes to College

1. Wallace Irwin, "The Shame of the Colleges: Princeton: Frenzied but Unashamed," *Saturday Evening Post*, 1 September 1906, pp. 3–4. For the earlier exposé of Yale see Irwin, "The Shame of the Colleges: The Democratic Machine at Yale," *Saturday Evening Post*, 18 August 1906, pp. 8–9 and 20.

2. "In the Public Eye," *Munsey's Magazine* 26 (February 1902): 692–94. A strikingly similar article appeared in the *Post* in that same year featuring the sons of James J. Hill and how they trained in the "Great Northern Kindergarten" after their graduation from college, moving from one lowly job to the next and always rising through the ranks in each department, in this early form of management training. Forrest Crissey, "Sons of American Millionaires," *Saturday Evening Post*, 18 October 1902, pp. 8–9.

3. For example, "Letters from a Self-Made Merchant to His Son," *Saturday Evening Post*, 3 August 1901, p. 11.

4. Many scholars discuss this economic and social transformation. With regard to the economic and business shifts, the scholars who have informed this chapter include Alfred Chandler, *The Visible Hand: The Managerial Revolution in American Business* (Cambridge, MA: Harvard University Press, 1977); Thomas C. Cochran, *The American Business System, A Historical Approach, 1900–1955* (Cambridge, MA: Harvard University Press, 1957); and Martin J. Sklar, *The Corporate Reconstruction of American Capitalism, 1890–1916: The Market, the Law, and Politics* (New York: Cambridge University Press, 1988). On the influence of progressive ideas on American business, the scholars contributing to my thoughts include Sklar, *The Corporate Reconstruction of American Capitalism*; Gabriel Kolko,

The Triumph of Conservatism (New York: Free Press, 1963); Samuel P. Hays, *The Response to Industrialism, 1885–1914* (Chicago: University of Chicago Press, 1957; reprint 1973); James Weinstein, *The Corporate Ideal in the Liberal State, 1900–1918* (Boston: Beacon Press, 1968); and Robert Wiebe, *The Search for Order, 1877–1920* (New York: Hill and Wang, 1967).

5. Business and labor historians who have touched on the history of college graduates hired into corporations include Chandler, *The Visible Hand*; David Noble, *America by Design: Science, Technology, and the Rise of Corporate Capitalism* (New York: Alfred A. Knopf, 1977); Jurgen Kocka, *White Collar Workers in America, 1890–1940: A Social-Political History in International Perspective*, translated by Maura Kealey (London and Beverly Hills: Sage Publications, 1980), 122–23. Irvin Wyllie stated that he viewed the increased hiring of high school and college graduates as a result of the unwillingness and impracticality of waiting for the right man to rise through the ranks. While likely accurate, again such an observation does not illuminate the full compliment of changing values and attitudes that accompanied and informed such a decision. Irvin G. Wyllie, *The Self-Made Man in America: The Myth of Rags to Riches* (New Brunswick, NJ: Rutgers University Press, 1954).

6. Olivier Zunz, *Making America Corporate, 1870–1920* (Chicago: University of Chicago Press, 1990), 72–77; Angel Kwolek-Folland, *Engendering Business: Men and Women in the Corporate Office, 1870–1930* (Baltimore: Johns Hopkins University Press, 1994), 72–74 and 82–84. Zunz's study brushes over hiring college graduates as managers, though his vision of corporate self-creation helped inform my thinking. Kwolek-Folland emphasized the redefinition of management as manly based on rational superiority (brainwork over brawn) mainly in the insurance business.

7. Tom Pendergast, *Creating the Modern Man: American Magazines and Consumer Culture, 1900–1950* (Columbia: University of Missouri Press, 2000), 51–64.

8. Jan Cohn, *Creating America: George Horace Lorimer and the Saturday Evening Post* (Pittsburgh: University of Pittsburgh Press, 1989), 9–10; and Helen Damon-Moore, *Magazines for the Millions: Gender and Commerce in the Ladies' Home Journal and the Saturday Evening Post, 1880–1910* (Albany: State University of New York Press, 1994), 129–38.

9. Gail Bederman and Anthony Rotundo are the two historians who have particularly influenced my understanding of the shifting definitions of masculinity in this period. Both emphasize that gender ideals and constructs are not static but rather are malleable and constantly adjusting, though constructed not to appear so. Gail Bederman, *Manliness and Civilization: A Cultural History of Gender and Race in the United States, 1880–1917* (Chicago: University of Chicago Press, 1995); and E. Anthony Rotundo, *American Manhood: Transformations in Masculinity from the Revolution to the Modern Era* (New York: Basic Books, 1993).

10. Those who pointedly addressed how the magazines helped redefine the typical American businessman do mention college, but only in relation to a vague budding professional ideal. Damon-Moore, *Magazines for the Millions*, 138; Cohn, *Creating America*, 36–38; Richard Ohmann, *Selling Culture: Magazines, Markets, and Class at the Turn of the Century* (New York: Verso, 1996), 162–63; and Michael Schneirov, *The Dream of a New Social Order: Popular Magazines in America, 1893–1914* (New York: Columbia University Press, 1994), 110–11. Eyal Naveh, "The Transformation of 'Rags to Riches' Stories: Business Biographies of Success in the Progressive Era and the 1920s," *American Studies International* 29 (April 1991): 60–80; and Wyllie, *Self-Made Man in America*, both touch upon the increasing importance of college. Naveh recognized that business biographies by the 1920s

232 Notes to pages 122–126

used language that portrayed the successful businessman as possessing both self-made traits and those of an excellent executive such as cooperation and efficiency. Wyllie chronicled the ambivalence toward college education in the annals of success ideals, with some businessmen embracing the need for specialization and others dismissing it. Other works on the American success ethic are John G. Cawelti, *Apostles of the Self-Made Man* (Chicago: University of Chicago, 1955); and Theodore P. Greene, *America's Heroes: Changing Models of Success in American Magazines* (New York: Oxford University Press, 1970). Paula Fass, *The Damned and the Beautiful: American Youth in the 1920s* (New York: Oxford University Press, 1977), shows how colleges of the interwar years were training grounds for modern, other-directed corporate behavior and values. I think the transition simply started much earlier than she found.

11. Robert Shackleton, "The New Senator from Indiana," *Saturday Evening Post*, 8 September 1900, pp. 8–10. Beveridge's own book, *The Young Man and the World*, was marketed as a success manual just like those featuring Andrew Carnegie, but with working one's way through college as a central aspect of the story. D. Appleton and Company Publishers, advertisement of Albert J. Beveridge, *The Young Man and the World*, *Collier's*, 7 October 1905, p. 24.

12. James Melvin Lee, "How to Be Self-Supporting at College," *Saturday Evening Post*, 27 October 1900, pp. 26–27; and Garrison Williams, "Through Harvard on Fifty Cents," *Saturday Evening Post*, 13 January 1900, pp. 607–9.

13. William Lyon Phelps, "The College Man of Today," *Collier's*, 21 June 1902, pp. 8–9.

14. Forrest Crissey, "How Modern College Students Work Their Way," *Saturday Evening Post*, 6 June 1903, p. 10.

15. Ibid., 10–11.

16. Ibid. In another *Post* article of 1903, "How Boys Earn Money," the author opened with the story of a boy determined to work his way through Columbia. He lived in a barn, rose in the early morning to light furnaces, and ate canned tomatoes and bread. Robert Shackleton, "How Boys Earn Money," *Saturday Evening Post*, 8 August 1903, pp. 16–17.

17. Stephen Norwood devotes a chapter in his book to the student strike-breaker as part of the college man's response to the crisis of masculinity, a crisis that he notes connected with anxieties about proving the physical superiority of native-born white Americans over the new immigrant, striking workers. Stephen H. Norwood, *Strike-Breaking and Intimidation: Mercenaries and Masculinity in Twentieth-Century America* (Chapel Hill: University of North Carolina Press, 2002), chap. 1.

18. John Corbin, "Financing a College Education," *Saturday Evening Post*, 18 March 1911, pp. 10–11 and 60. Another article in the *Post* representative of the advice articles geared to help middle-class parents pay for college is Charles F. Thwing, "Going to College with No Money," *Saturday Evening Post*, 18 June 1904, p. 6.

19. "Getting on in the World," *Saturday Evening Post*, 19 January 1907, p. 22.

20. Ibid., 10 November 1916, p. 19.

21. Forrest Crissey, "Some Efficiency Secrets: An Apprentice Who Found a New Way," *Saturday Evening Post*, 28 September 1912, pp. 7 and 40.

22. Charles Macomb Flandrau, "Kicker Lang—A Harvard Story," *Saturday Evening Post*, 22 June 1901, pp. 4–5 and 20–22.

23. M. I. Brush, "My Rich Wife," *Saturday Evening Post*, 13 September 1913, pp. 8–10.

24. "Keeping Up Appearances," *Saturday Evening Post*, 11 November 1911, pp. 3–5 and 46. The *Post*'s business fiction writer, Will Payne, also worked allusions to the moral superiority of the self-supporting students into story lines. Will Payne, "The Mayfair Account," *Saturday Evening Post*, 4 May 1907, pp. 12–13 and 22–23. Similarly, the lead character in one *American Magazine* story from 1916, a self-made millionaire industrialist, delivered a commencement address at his alma mater in which he reflected upon what made men great. He fastened on the central feature of his own life, working his way through college while other students' fathers paid their way. Darraugh and Rosemary Aldrich, "The Highest Room," *American Magazine* 82 (July 1916): 38–41 and 78. Other stories that mention working through college are Svetozar Tonjoroff, "For Services Rendered," *Saturday Evening Post*, 21 October 1911, pp. 16–17 and 57–58; and Walter Prichard Eaton, "The Pampered Fledgling," *American Magazine* 82 (September 1916): 7–10 and 63. A more significant link between the working student and manly qualities can be found in James Oliver Curwood, "Jim Falkner, Pirate," *Saturday Evening Post*, 2 September 1911, pp. 6–8.

25. The main characters were introduced in the first two episodes. David Graham Phillips, "The Cost: A Tale of a Man and Two Women," *Saturday Evening Post*, 14 November 1903, pp. 1–3 and 18–19; and ibid., 21 November 1903, pp. 11–13. Dumont emerged as a corrupt businessman and a cheating husband in later installments. Phillips, "The Cost," 19 December 1903, pp. 10–11; and ibid., 26 December 1903, pp. 12–13 and 22–23.

26. Phillips, "The Cost," 21 November 1903, pp. 11–13.

27. Ibid. In the next installment he reforms a literary society to take the "faction and cast" out of its debates. See Phillips, "The Cost," 28 November 1903, p. 10.

28. Ibid., 5 December 1903, pp. 15–17 and 53.

29. Ibid., 12 December 1903, pp. 10–11 and 24.

30. Ibid., 5 December 1903, p. 16.

31. Adachi Kinnosuke, "The Jinrikisha Man: A Tale of Student Life in the Imperial University of Japan," *Saturday Evening Post*, 18 November 1899, p. 405; and Fritz Krog, "Father and Son," *Munsey's Magazine* 41 (May 1909): 244–46.

32. No business histories systematically examine the recruitment and training of college-educated managers or businessmen. Alfred Chandler and especially David Noble give it thoughtful though limited attention, however. Chandler, *Visible Hand*, 464–68; and Noble, *America by Design*, chap. 8. Statistics on college men in the business world are scarce, but Mabel Newcomber in her study of corporate boards found that 39 percent had some college training in 1900, compared to 51 percent in 1925, and 76 percent in 1950, a significant increase. More tellingly, though, the 1900 percentage was still ten times the number of college-trained men in the general population. Mabel Newcomber, "Professionalization of Leadership in the Big Business Corporation," in *The History of American Management: Selections from the Business History Review*, ed. James P. Baughman (Englewood Cliffs, NJ: Prentice-Hall, Inc., 1969), 245.

33. Graham's very first letter preached on the typical complaint that his college son was spending too much at Harvard, thus violating the ideal of frugality. He informed Pierrepont in this letter that he must start on the shop floor same as the son of the "cellar

boss." "Letters from a Self-Made Merchant to His Son," *Saturday Evening Post*, 3 August 1901, p. 11. In the second letter Old Gorgon Graham was alarmed that Pierrepont had taken to wearing sporty clothes and smoking. "Letters," *Saturday Evening Post*, 17 August 1901, p. 11. In later letters he argued against a potentially effeminizing trip to Europe after his son's graduation (favoring a trip to the Maine woods), writing personal letters on company time, and his son being too "chesty" and chafing under an Irish boss. "Letters from a Self-Made Merchant to His Son," *Saturday Evening Post*, 31 August 1901, p. 7; 21 September 1901, p. 7; and 26 October 1901, p. 5.

34. Pierrepont's start on the slaughterhouse floor is only alluded to by his father, who thought at times that he should have left his son there a little longer. "Letters from a Self-Made Merchant to His Son," *Saturday Evening Post*, 22 February 1902, p. 11. The letters that document Pierrepont's rise are, "Letters," 26 October 1901, pp. 5; and 11 January 1902, p. 5. In the continuation of this series as "Old Gorgon Graham," 21 May 1904, pp. 10–11; and 3 September 1904, pp. 8–9, he gives advice first on sales and then on how to run the company.

35. "Letters from a Self-Made Merchant to His Son," *Saturday Evening Post*, 26 October 1901, p. 5; and 5 October 1901, p. 6. "Old Gorgon Graham," *Saturday Evening Post*, 21 May 1904, pp. 10–11, advised against the use of French phrases in business correspondence.

36. "Letters from a Self-Made Merchant to His Son," 13 September 1902, pp. 5 and 17; and "Old Gorgon Graham," *Saturday Evening Post*, 12 March 1904, pp. 3–4. Another letter told of a rival meat packer's son, Percy, who took the four-years sporting course at Harvard. Percy took one million of his father's money and lost it speculating rather than tending to business. "Letters from a Self-Made Merchant to His Son," 3 August 1901, p. 11.

37. Charles A. Schieren, "Why Young Men Should Begin at the Bottom," *Saturday Evening Post*, 4 May 1901, pp. 4–5.

38. George Hebard Paine, "Engineering as a Profession," *Munsey's Magazine* 25 (August 1901): 750–54.

39. "Dividends Paid on College Parchments," *Saturday Evening Post*, 24 November 1900, p. 6.

40. Charles F. Thwing, "Should Railroad Men Be College Men?" *Saturday Evening Post*, 11 January 1902, pp. 11–12.

41. James H. Collins, "Limiting Opportunity: The Salaried Man," *Saturday Evening Post*, 16 February 1907, pp. 3–5.

42. "In the Public Eye," *Munsey's Magazine* 26 (February 1901): 692–94; and "Men and Women of the Hour," *Saturday Evening Post*, 2 August 1902, p. 14.

43. Forrest Crissey, "Presidents That Push," *Saturday Evening Post*, 30 May 1903, p. 13. See also, J. T. Harahan, "The Making of a Railroad Man," *Saturday Evening Post*, 6 January 1900, pp. 592–93.

44. Some typical examples include "The New Era in Commercial Education," *Saturday Evening Post*, 11 November 1899, p. 378; "Wanted: A Master," *Saturday Evening Post*, 28 February 1903, pp. 15–17; Poultney Bigelow, "Can a University Help Me to Earn a Living?" *Collier's Weekly*, 18 October 1902, p. 8; and William J. Wilgus, "Making a Choice of a Profession," *Cosmopolitan* 35 (August 1903): 462–65.

45. B. C. Forbes, "How I Pick $25,000 a Year Men," *American Magazine* 82 (September 1916): 18–19.

46. B. C. Forbes, "The Salaries That Are Paid in Various Lines," *American Magazine* 89 (January 1920): 24–25 and 124.

47. Sarah Orne Jewett, "The Gray Mills of Farley," *Cosmopolitan* 25 (April 1898): 183–96; and Brander Matthews, "A Young Man from the Country," *Cosmopolitan* 25 (September 1898): 527–40. Two other *Cosmopolitan* business-love stories that featured modern business characters, described in the first story as a superintendent and in the second as a manager, are Elmore Elliot Peake, "Out of the Shadow," *Cosmopolitan* 27 (October 1899): 642–48; and Frank H. Spearman, "A Black Rapids Love Story," *Cosmopolitan* 29 (June 1900): 201–6.

48. For instance, Alvah Milton Kerr, "The Man at the Lonely Station," *Saturday Evening Post*, 1 December 1900, pp. 6–7; and Willis Gibson, "The Agent at Missouri Station," *Saturday Evening Post*, 31 May 1902, pp. 6–8. Will Payne, "Two Men and a Chance," *Saturday Evening Post*, 5 August 1911, pp. 6–8; and "Getting a Start at Sixty," *Saturday Evening Post*, 5 August 1911, pp. 3–5 and 34. Another example is the October 15 issue of the *Post*, which boasted two articles of the retail business and one piece of humorous business fiction. James H. Collins, "The Retail Reconstruction: Building Business on Solid Information," *Saturday Evening Post*, 15 October 1910, pp. 8–9 and 65; Isaac F. Marcosson, "Making Merchants: How Big Stores Have Become Practical Business Universities," *Saturday Evening Post*, 15 October 1910, pp. 13–15 and 53–54; and Montague Glass, "Sympathy," *Saturday Evening Post*, 15 October 1910, pp. 3–5.

49. A few of the stories that incorporated characters where college marked them as ne'er-do-well sports and gamblers are A. T. Quiller-Couch, "Parson Jack's Fortune," *Collier's*, 19 April 1900, p. 14; Anne O'Hagan, "The Caddishness of Tressington," *Munsey's Magazine* 23 (August 1900): 601–7; Charles Battell Loomis, "Tales of Men of Many Trades: The Story of Hubbard Wilson, a Misfit," *Saturday Evening Post*, 24 March 1900, p. 865; and Will Payne, "Bensinger's Luck," *Saturday Evening Post*, 8 March 1913, pp. 3–5 and 68.

50. I. K. Friedman, "How Miss Wilcox Was Fired," *Saturday Evening Post*, 12 August 1905, pp. 4–7 and 14. In a *Cosmopolitan* story published in 1900, the principal character failed at college and began his business career working on a street railway line. Finding love prompted him to prove himself and rise in the firm, and only then could he shake off the leisurely collegiate habits of cutting lectures, going to bed at sunrise, and waking at noon. Melville Chater, "Motorman Cupid," *Cosmopolitan* 28 (January 1900): 290–94.

51. Unlike Ed, who hailed from the business middle class, the main character in the 1906 *Post* story "Muggles' Supreme Moment" stood for all negative genteel aspects of college life. In a quest to demonstrate his manliness to his old college mates, Muggles accepted an invitation to visit a lumber camp. Though he knew the correct way to sip tea and hold a sandwich, he failed in his supreme test to size up a tense situation with a cool demeanor and organize the working men under his leadership. But it also must be noted that Muggles's own college mates considered him effete, and one of them even ran the Canadian lumber mill, a sure sign of middle-class, college-educated manhood. F. Hopkinson Smith, "Muggles' Supreme Moment," *Saturday Evening Post*, 30 June 1906, pp. 5–6 and 30.

52. Paul Leicester Ford, "A Checkered Love Affair," *Collier's Weekly*, 7 June 1902, p. 13.

53. Ibid. Another good example is a short story in the *Post*, "The Crisis," centered on Percival Scawen whose uncle, worried about what to do with the "young rascal," arranged for Percival's hiring into a firm so that the boy could acquire "business habits and business instincts." Here again Percival's college sojourn was less preparation than an indulgence, but he soon proved his worth. George Hibbard, "The Crisis," *Saturday Evening Post*, 21 April 1900, pp. 963–65.

54. A short but instructive list of fiction in popular magazines that contained characters going into business after college include the following. In Isobel Strong, "Under the Banyan," *Munsey's Magazine* 23 (October 1900): 108–11, a Chinese Yale graduate decides to go into the family business in Hong Kong. In Katherine A. Whiting, "The Goddess from the Car," *Collier's Weekly*, 14 October 1905, pp. 19–21, the wife of a Harvard alumni and railroad owner delivers a rousing pep talk to the Harvard team before the Yale game. In Daisy Rhodes, "My Wife's Son: How Donald and I Became Friends," *Saturday Evening Post*, 30 April 1898, pp. 5–7, the college graduate and his stepfather set up a business together. Finally, in Eleanor Hoyt Brainerd, "Kidnapped by Bettina," *Saturday Evening Post*, 23 September 1905, pp. 1–3, the story begins with the young businessman hero, who having to run for the station recalls his glory days carrying the ball for Yale. And, Francis Lynde's, "The Lion and the Lamb," a long serial running in *Munsey's*, where the lead character inherits a failed coal mine after he graduates and works hard, along with his roommate and despite local intrigues, to make the mine a success. The first installment is Francis Lynde, "The Lion and the Lamb," *Munsey's Magazine* 39 (June 1908): 336–49.

55. Arthur Train, "The Inheritance," *Saturday Evening Post*, 11 June 1910, p. 9.

56. Ibid.

57. Ibid., 9–11.

58. Richard Harding Davis, "The White Mice," *Saturday Evening Post*, 13 March 1909, pp. 3–5 and 52–54.

59. John Corbin, "The Cave Man," *Saturday Evening Post*, 26 January 1907, pp. 3–5 and 31–32.

60. Corbin, "The Cave Man," 2 February 1907, pp. 15–17.

61. The trust proposal floated by Penrhyn and a polo match showdown with Penrhyn both occur in Corbin, "The Cave Man," 2 March 1907, pp. 9–11.

62. Gouverneur Morris, "The Spread Eagle," *Saturday Evening Post*, 4 September 1909, pp. 18–20 and 42. An additional story following a similar plot (assuming a false identity to learn the ropes from the bottom after college) is found in Will Irwin, "The Liar," *Saturday Evening Post*, 10 October 1914, pp. 14–16 and 46–48.

63. *Post* business writer H. K. Webster contributed perhaps the earliest example with his 1904 short story, "The Matter with Carpenter," featured in chap. 2. H. K. Webster, "The Matter with Carpenter," *Saturday Evening Post*, 26 March 1904, p. 6–7 and 28.

64. Herbert Quick, "The Triumph of Billy," *Saturday Evening Post*, 8 December 1906, pp. 5–7.

65. Walter Prichard Eaton, "The Pampered Fledgling," *American Magazine* 82 (September 1916): 7.

66. Ibid., 7–10 and 63.

67. For instance, in E. J. Rath, "The Lady and the Octopus: A Woman's Rights and a Man's Wrongs," *Saturday Evening Post*, 16 February 1907, pp. 5–7, the lead male character is fresh from college yet a superintendent of an electric company work crew.

68. Montague Glass, "The Efficient Salamander," *Saturday Evening Post*, 26 August 1911, pp. 13–16 and 40.

Chapter 5. From Campus Hero to Corporate Professional

1. Hart, Schaffner and Marx, *Saturday Evening Post*, 2 October 1909, p. 2.

2. David Adler and Sons, *Saturday Evening Post*, 14 April 1906, p. 15; and David Adler and Sons, *Saturday Evening Post*, 17 October 1908, p. 33.

3. *Digest of Educational Statistics*, 1977–78, pp. 85–94, and *Historical Statistics of the United States*, Series H 751–65, quoted in W. Bruce Leslie, "Toward a History of the American Upper Middle Class, 1870–1940" (paper given at the Cambridge University American History Seminar, 1994).

4. Advertisement for David Adler and Sons, *Saturday Evening Post*, 17 April 1909, p. 33.

5. Tom Pendergast explores how mass magazines facilitated the transition from Victorian to modern masculinity, including the way the model business attributes shifted to idealize more a pleasing appearance and personality than immutable character. Pendergast does not explore college connections, however, and this chapter reveals how the use of college images and references in ads introduced many of the essential components of modern masculinity long before the 1920s. Tom Pendergast, *Creating the Modern Man: American Magazines and Consumer Culture, 1900–1950* (Columbia: University of Missouri Press, 2000).

6. Grover Cleveland, "Does a College Education Pay?" *Saturday Evening Post*, 26 May 1900, p. 1089; David Starr Jordan, "The College Man's Advantage in the Coming Century," *Saturday Evening Post*, 26 May 1900, p. 1090; Francis L. Patton, "Should the Business Man Have a College Education?" *Saturday Evening Post*, 26 May 1900, p. 1094; and Benjamin Ida Wheeler, "Is Scholarship a Promise of Success in Life?" *Saturday Evening Post*, 26 May 1900, p. 1095.

7. George Ade, "The Real Freshman," *Saturday Evening Post*, 25 October 1902, pp. 3–4.

8. Owen Wister, "The Open-Air Education," *Saturday Evening Post*, 25 October 1902, pp. 1–2; and Henry S. Pritchett, "The Two Doors to Business Life," *Saturday Evening Post*, 25 October 1902, pp. 4–5.

9. Charles F. Thwing, "The College and the World-Life," *Saturday Evening Post*, 25 October 1902, p. 5.

10. Arthur T. Hadley, "Modern Education," *Cosmopolitan* 28 (November 1899): 104–6. References comparing college men to Ancient Greek heroes and other classical examples recurred repeatedly. Hadley resembled Thwing in that regard. Writers like Thwing and Hadley not only reshaped the image of college, they stroked the egos and sought to fire the imaginations of middle-class business readers. If businessmen were modern warrior-nobility, then college should be considered the natural training ground for such modern nobility, where the moral equivalent of war met the preparation of gentlemen. Another example is the University of Pennsylvania professor J. William White, "Reasons

for Belief in the Value of Exercise and Athletics," *Saturday Evening Post*, 1 December 1900, pp. 15–17.

11. Of course, part of the reason that American businessmen latched on to the rhetoric of warfare to describe their endeavors stemmed from the fact that they wished to obfuscate the reality that business was, in fact, less like the clash of heroes and more like the workings of a machine. Peter N. Stearns, *Be a Man! Males in Modern Society*, 2nd ed. (New York: Holmes and Meier Publishers, Inc., 1990), 110–18; Michael Kimmel, *Manhood in America: A Cultural History* (New York: Free Press, 1997), 110–11; and Donald J. Mrozek, "The Habit of Victory: The American Military and the Cult of Manliness," in *Manliness and Morality: Middle-Class Masculinity in Britain and America, 1880–1940*, ed. J. A. Mangan and James Walvin (New York: St. Martin's Press, 1987), 220–41.

12. Ralph D. Paine, "The Football Heroes of Yesterday," *Munsey's Magazine* 36 (December 1906): 335–40. Even small references served to further the connections between college, football, and characterizations of business success. The *Post's* editorial "He Never Saw Heffelfinger Play" ran in 1900 and it highlighted the post-collegiate career of "Pudge" Heffelfinger, one of the most popular Yale rushers of the 1890s. The editorial recounted a humorous anecdote then circulating of a New York lady at a Minneapolis dinner party talking of football, unwittingly conferring with Heffelfinger, and asking him if he had ever seen the famous man play at Yale. Lorimer used the story also to celebrate an ideal path to success, since Heffelfinger returned to Minneapolis after graduation to put his brains and character to work in his father's shoe manufacturing business. "He Never Saw Heffelfinger Play," *Saturday Evening Post*, 1 December 1900, p. 13.

13. Erman J. Ridgeway, "College Fraternities," *Munsey's Magazine* 24 (February 1901): 729–30. The "scientific opponent" reference once again evokes the lessons of Walter Camp, who by 1901 had been casting football as the ideal preparation for future managers due to its scientific rules for victory for nearly a decade. Michael Oriard, *Reading Football: How the Popular Press Created an American Spectacle* (Chapel Hill: University of North Carolina Press, 1993), 101–9 and 142–51.

14. Albert Beveridge, "The Young Man and College Life," *Saturday Evening Post*, 10 June 1905, pp. 1–2.

15. Recall such characters as the wastrel sport taught a lesson by the working student in "Kicker Lang," and the boy in "Tutoring Henry." Charles Macomb Flandrau, "Kicker Lang—A Harvard Story," *Saturday Evening Post*, 22 June 1901, pp. 4–5; and 29 June 1901, pp. 4–5 and 15; and Holworthy Hall, "Tutoring Henry," *Saturday Evening Post*, 27 July 1912, pp. 10–11 and 40–42.

16. For example, two stories in the *Cosmopolitan* (one a serial) contained college-educated characters (Harvard and Oxford). The Harvard lawyer also pursued music as a hobby, and the Oxford graduate, a missionary's son, became a scholar in, respectively, Arthur E. McFarlane, "The Canonic Curse," *Cosmopolitan* 33 (September 1902): 515–23; and Harold Frederic, "Gloria Mundi," *Cosmopolitan* 24 (April 1898): 610–27. As in the McFarlane story, college-educated characters were traditionally professionals or from elite families, not businessmen. For instance, Ellen Mackubin, "The Meaning of the Moment," *Saturday Evening Post*, 7 July 1900, p. 6, followed a trio of college friends, one of whom became a doctor, the other came from a wealthy New Orleans family. Morgan Robertson, "The Lobster," *Saturday Evening Post*, 25 August 1900, pp. 8–9, differentiated

between two friends who went into business and a third friend who went to college (depicted as an odd, academic type).

17. Melville Chater, "Motorman Cupid," *Cosmopolitan* 28 (January 1900): 290–94. See also Lloyd Osbourne, "Frenchy's Last Job," *Cosmopolitan* 28 (November 1899): 55–72. Jesse Lynch Williams, "The Advantages of a College Education," *Saturday Evening Post*, 26 May 1900, pp. 1100–101 and 1120; Richard Harding Davis, "The Grand Cross of the Crescent," *Saturday Evening Post*, 20 January 1912, pp. 3–5 and 30–32; and George Fitch, "Cupid vs. Geography," *American Magazine* 79 (May 1915): 11–15 and 78–80. For example, Octave Thanet, "The Argument for Doty," *Saturday Evening Post*, 10 February 1900, pp. 708–9. The nouveau-riche "mucker," Doty, spent most of his time at Harvard playing poker and died in a drunken boating accident.

18. "Letters to Unsuccessful Men," *Saturday Evening Post*, 10 November 1906, pp. 1–2 and 24. It should be noted, though, that here was yet another highly popular series that featured a son who must seemingly pass through the new rite of passage—college—full of pranks and misdeeds, before learning the harsh realities of the real world and succeeding in business. Another installment is "Jack Spurlock—Prodigal: In Which the Prodigal Gets a Job," *Saturday Evening Post*, 22 February 1908, pp. 10–11. See also in this vein George Hibbard, "The Crisis," *Saturday Evening Post*, 21 April 1900, pp. 963–65. Recall the college-educated son entering business in "How Miss Wilcox Was Fired," noted in the last chapter. I. K. Friedman, "How Miss Wilcox Was Fired," *Saturday Evening Post*, 12 August 1905, pp. 4–7 and 14.

19. Jesse Lynch Williams, "Safe Now in the Wide, Wide World," *Saturday Evening Post*, 5 July 1902, pp. 14–15, presaged the "Talks with a Kid Brother" series. It featured an older brother out of college writing to his graduating brother about the stiff challenges that awaited the lad in the business world. All of the "Talks" in the subsequent series took this same format. In Jesse Lynch Williams, "Talks with a Kid Brother at College," *Saturday Evening Post*, 4 July 1903, pp. 16–17, the older brother notes that he is in the business world, though the occupation was unspecified.

20. Installments that featured the rowdy side of college life include Williams, "Talks with a Kid Brother at College—Horse Play," *Saturday Evening Post*, 16 May 1903, p. 3; and Williams, "Hazing," *Saturday Evening Post*, 28 February 1903, p. 12. In Williams, "Talks with a Kid Brother at College," *Saturday Evening Post*, 27 June 1903, pp. 13–14, the college brother seemed to have gotten drunk and the older brother noted that it was alright to blow off steam every now and then.

21. Williams, "Talks with a Kid Brother at College," 4 July 1903, pp. 16–17. In this installment the older brother responded to the younger brother's senior-year epiphany that he seemed to have wasted the last three years. In Williams's first letter (which presaged the series), the older brother had likewise advised that part of the reason for going to college included having broader interests besides one's business or profession. Williams, "Safe Now in the Wide, Wide World," 15.

22. Williams, "Talks with a Kid Brother at College—Making the Team," *Saturday Evening Post*, 11 April 1903, p. 17.

23. Williams, "Talks with a Kid Brother at College—Horse Play," p. 3.

24. George Fitch, "Sic Transit Gloria All-America," *Saturday Evening Post*, 15 April 1911, pp. 15–17.

25. Ibid., 16. Additionally, the narrator and his friend end up hiring an ex-football hero as a laborer, though he soon goes to his college club in Manhattan and ends up landing a plum position.

26. Fitch, "Colleges while You Wait: A Siwash Fragment Torn from the Career of Petey Simmons," *Saturday Evening Post*, 27 August 1910, pp. 5–7.

27. Henry K. Webster, "The Wedge," *Saturday Evening Post*, 28 December 1901, pp. 7–8. The doubt exhibited by the foundry owner could be interpreted as representing typical business feelings toward useless college men.

28. Ibid.

29. Stephen Norwood's history of strikebreaking contains a chapter on college-student strikebreakers. He links their participation to the crisis of masculinity and notes that this activity received coverage in local newspapers and national periodicals. The *Post* story, "The Wedge" offers a very early (perhaps precedent setting) literary example. Stephen H. Norwood, *Strike-Breaking and Intimidation: Mercenaries and Masculinity in Twentieth-Century America* (Chapel Hill: University of North Carolina Press, 2002).

30. One of the earliest was Alvah Milton Kerr, "The Blacklisted Man," *Saturday Evening Post*, 11 November 1899, pp. 384–86.

31. Lloyd Osbourne, "The Great Bubble Syndicate," *Saturday Evening Post*, 26 March 1904, pp. 1–3 and 31–32. Two other examples are Eleanor Hoyt Brainerd, "Kidnapped by Bettina," *Saturday Evening Post*, 23 September 1905, pp. 1–3; and Will Payne, "Two Men and a Chance," *Saturday Evening Post*, 5 August 1911, pp. 6–8.

32. Katherine A. Whiting, "The Goddess from the Car," *Collier's Weekly*, 14 October 1905, pp. 19–21. An Edward Boltwood story in *Munsey's* integrated football and business success, while another *Munsey's* serial involving international adventure utilized two brothers, both of whom went to college and then into international business, with the lead character balancing his classical studies (his cultural side) by being good in athletics. Edward Boltwood, "The End of the Game," *Munsey's Magazine* 42 (February 1910): 753–56; and William Farquhar Payson, "Barry Gordon: A Story of Modern American Life," *Munsey's Magazine* 38 (March 1908): 749–63.

33. John Corbin, "The Cave Man," *Saturday Evening Post*, 26 January 1907, pp. 3–5 and 31–32. Another major serial in the *Post* that focused on business (and in this case international adventure), with a main character who boasted Yale sports greatness and working up through the shops, was Richard Harding Davis, "The White Mice," *Saturday Evening Post*, 13 March 1909, pp. 3–5 and 52–54. Still another story to feature a Yale baseball player who then goes on to international business adventures is Gouverneur Morris, "The Monitor and the Merrimac," *Saturday Evening Post*, 16 October 1909, pp. 5–7 and 64. Morris penned another relevant short story for *Cosmopolitan*, involving a Yale football player who "stood well in his class" and most certainly would have captained the team in his senior year if not forced to enter the business world after the death of his father. Gouverneur Morris, "The Penalty," *Cosmopolitan* 53 (August 1912): 293–305.

34. Corbin, "The Cave Man," 2 February 1907, pp. 15–17.

35. Ibid., 2 March 1907, pp. 9–11.

36. What started as a trickle of stories with college-educated businessmen became a steady stream by 1905 and after. The following list includes mainly those stories not yet mentioned. References to collegiate pasts for business-related characters in these stories may be termed generic. They do not mention football or the curriculum, etc.

The significant point is that they existed and became more numerous, indicating a growing acceptance of or familiarity with such a reference and all that it might possibly communicate: Daisy Rhodes, "My Wife's Son: How Donald and I Became Friends," *Saturday Evening Post*, 30 April 1898, pp. 5–6; Kerr, "The Blacklisted Man"; Osbourne, "The Great Bubble Syndicate"; Whiting, "The Goddess from the Car"; F. Hopkins Smith, "Muggles' Supreme Moment," *Saturday Evening Post*, 30 June 1906, pp. 5–6 and 30; Richard Harding Davis, "The White Mice"; Maximilian Foster, "Irene, the Single Cylinder Kicker," *Saturday Evening Post*, 8 July 1911, pp. 7–9 and 22; "Keeping Up Appearances," *Saturday Evening Post*, 11 November 1911, pp. 3–5; Will Irwin, "The Liar," *Saturday Evening Post*, 10 October 1914, pp. 14–16 and 46–48; Darragh and Rosemary Aldrich, "The Highest Room," *American Magazine* 82 (July 1916): 38–41 and 78.

37. Most of these stories were noted in chap. 2 and some were explored in chap. 4.

38. James H. Collins, "Bulwarks of Business Policy," *Saturday Evening Post*, 13 January 1912, pp. 18 and 40–41.

39. In Robert Herrick, "Common Honesty," *Saturday Evening Post*, 19 September 1903, pp. 2–5 and 28, the college-educated son goes into the business firm of his father. The reader is treated to a classic businessman's lament, as the father notes his regret of not having a college education's refinement. Both Gouverneur Morris, "The Spread Eagle," *Saturday Evening Post*, 4 September 1909, pp. 18–20 and 42, and Edgar Jepson, "The Shanghaied Son-in-Law," *Saturday Evening Post*, 10 December 1910, pp. 5–7, featured college-educated businessmen who attended Oxford, soaked in culture, and then settled down to business.

40. Corbin, "The Cave Man," 2 February 1907, pp. 15–17.

41. The only advertisements that mention college education or education generally in a *Post* College Man's issue from 1900, for instance, were prep schools, correspondence programs, or law schools such as Bard Hall Military School, Montclair Military Academy, and Chicago Kent College of Law, all appearing in *Saturday Evening Post*, 26 May 1900, p. 1110. The preponderance of ads researched for this book came from two sources: *Collier's Weekly* and the *Saturday Evening Post. Munsey's* and *Cosmopolitan*, of course, carried the same number of ads (sometimes even a greater number of pages), but the degree of variation between ads used in these periodicals is negligible.

42. In 1899/1900, a total of 977 institutions of higher education enrolled 237,592 students. That total number grew to 355,213 in 1909/10 in only 951 institutions and 597,880 in 1919/20. The percentage of male college students out of the male college-age population in 1889/90 was 3.8 and in 1899/1900 was 5.1. These were significant increases and not an unimportant market given the assumed income level of their families, but still the total college-going population totaled lass than 1 percent of the population. *Digest of Education Statistics*, 1977–78, pp. 85–94; and *Historical Statistics of the United States*, Series H, 751–65, cited in Leslie, "Toward a History of the American Upper Middle Class, 1870–1940."

43. On the advent of advertising and its part in transforming American culture, I have been particularly guided by Richard Ohmann. Ohmann's main point was that in working out a new "language of meaning" encoded in mass media ads, advertisers tried to instruct Americans in a new way of seeing the world: "In re-presenting objects, ads connect them to one another, to situations, to social processes, to us and our desires. They teach us the 'communicative function of goods,' and the place of goods in our way

of living and imagining." In doing this ads both reflected values and hoped to shape readers' ideals and, thus, their behavior. Richard Ohmann, *Selling Culture: Magazines, Markets, and Class at the Turn of the Century* (New York: Verso, 1996), 175, 212, and 215.

44. Ibid., 89–90.

45. Ibid., 204–6; and Roland Marchand, *Advertising the American Dream: Making Way for Modernity, 1920–1940* (Berkeley: University of California Press, 1985), xvii and 165. See also, Russell W. Belk and Richard W. Pollay, "Images of Ourselves: The Good Life in Twentieth Century Advertising," *Journal of Consumer Research* 11 (March 1985): 887–97.

46. My research bolsters the contention of Ellen Gruber Garvey that fiction and advertising in the turn-of-the-century mass magazines were enmeshed, each reflecting on the other. Ellen Gruber Garvey, *The Adman in the Parlor: Magazines and the Gendering of Consumer Culture, 1880s to 1910s* (New York and Oxford: Oxford University Press, 1996).

47. Ohmann, *Selling Culture*, 205–6.

48. Advertisements marketing class pins or badges include, Bastian Brothers, *Collier's*, 31 October 1903, p. 28; and Cecil H. Sherman and Company, *Saturday Evening Post*, 2 May 1903, p. 16. Potomac Press Publishers, *Saturday Evening Post*, 25 April 1903, p. 24, advertised "College Posters" for college rooms, fraternity houses, dens, and athletic quarters. The posters featured college athletes in action from Harvard, Yale, Penn, and Oberlin. *Frank Leslie's Popular Monthly*, *Saturday Evening Post*, 13 December 1902, back cover, promoted its magazine by offering "college girl" calendars for subscribing. Oliver Ditson Company, *Saturday Evening Post*, 3 February 1905, p. 15, was the first advertisement I saw for college songs.

49. In his look at fashion in advertising images in the 1920s, Richard Martin found that advertisers tried to educate the middle-class mass readers that they should fulfill an upper-middle-class lifestyle of formal dinner parties and comfortable living. Richard Martin, "Fashion in the Age of Advertising," *Journal of Popular Culture* 29 (Fall 1995): 235–54.

50. I did find one earlier instance of a ready-to-wear ad that used collegiate references. Hart, Schaffner and Marx marketed their "Varsity" model as early as 1901. Hart, Schaffner and Marx, *Collier's*, 29 June 1901, p. 2.

51. Daube, Cohn and Company, *Saturday Evening Post*, 26 March 1904, p. 32; and The Stein-Bloch Company, *Saturday Evening Post*, 9 November 1907, p. 2; The Stein-Bloch Company, *Saturday Evening Post*, 5 June 1909, p. 26.

52. Hart, Schaffner and Marx, *Saturday Evening Post*, 26 March 1904, p. 16.

53. Daube, Cohn and Company, *Saturday Evening Post*, 28 March 1908, p. 22; and Daube, Cohn and Company, *Saturday Evening Post*, 10 April 1909, p. 46. Both ads occupied an entire column and stretched at least half a page.

54. Chas. Kaufman and Brothers, *Saturday Evening Post*, 8 May 1909, p. 54; Chas. Kaufman and Brothers, *Saturday Evening Post*, 22 May 1909, p. 62. Each of these ads filled two columns and half the length of the page.

55. David Adler and Sons Clothing Company, *Saturday Evening Post*, 18 March 1905, back of front cover. Almost every ad contained some variation on the line "The Typical College Clothes." For instance, in 1907 when Adler faced competition apparently from other clothes-makers claiming to reflect the college man's tastes, Adler ran an ad with the line in all capital letters, "AMERICA'S ONLY TYPICAL COLLEGE CLOTHES." David Adler and Sons Clothing Company, *Saturday Evening Post*, 6 April 1907, p. 1.

56. David Adler and Sons Clothing Company, *Saturday Evening Post*, 8 April 1905, back of front cover.

57. David Adler and Sons Clothing Company, *Saturday Evening Post*, 2 December 1905, back of front cover.

58. David Adler and Sons Clothing Company, *Saturday Evening Post*, 17 April 1909, p. 33. The phrase "high art style" appeared in David Adler and Sons Clothing Company, *Saturday Evening Post*, 6 May 1905, back of front cover.

59. David Adler and Sons Clothing Company, *Saturday Evening Post*, 20 May 1905, back of front cover.

60. David Adler and Sons Clothing Company, *Saturday Evening Post*, 14 April 1906, p. 15; and David Adler and Sons Clothing Company, *Saturday Evening Post*, 17 October 1908, p. 33.

61. Examples with women include David Adler and Sons Clothing Company, *Saturday Evening Post*, 8 April 1905, back of front cover; David Adler and Sons Clothing Company, *Saturday Evening Post*, 28 October 1905, back of front cover; and David Adler and Sons Clothing Company, *Saturday Evening Post*, 3 April 1909, p. 41.

62. David Adler and Sons Clothing Company, *Saturday Evening Post*, 2 December 1905, back of front cover.

63. David Adler and Sons Clothing Company, *Saturday Evening Post*, 12 October 1909, p. 29.

64. Hart, Schaffner and Marx, *Saturday Evening Post*, 17 September 1910, p. 2. Other clothiers also offered suit models with collegiate names. Besides "Campus Togs" and "Harvard Clothes," there were Society Brand Clothes' "the Student," and Rosenberg Brothers' "Dartmouth." Collegian, the Varsity, Campus Togs, and the Dartmouth lasted a long time and, most notably, were not exclusively aimed at college men. Society Brand Clothes, *Saturday Evening Post*, 3 March 1912, p. 1; and Rosenberg Brothers Company, *Saturday Evening Post*, 26 September 1914, p. 44.

65. David M. Pfaelzer and Company, *Saturday Evening Post*, 26 September 1908, p. 52. Another ad asserted that "college men and young men in business" want style and individuality. Michaels, Stern and Company, *Collier's*, 13 May 1905, p. 3.

66. Society Brand Clothes, *Saturday Evening Post*, 5 February 1910, p. 1.

67. Schloss Brothers and Company, *Saturday Evening Post*, 17 September, 1910, p. 31.

68. The House of Kuppenheimer, *Saturday Evening Post*, 22 September 1906, pp. pp. 16–17.

69. Society Brand Clothes, *Saturday Evening Post*, 10 September 1910, p 1. Society Brand Clothes simply stated explicitly what other apparel ads featuring youthful illustrations implied—stay youthful and vigorous by wearing our clothes.

70. Two exceptions to this chronological delineation should be noted. A 1905 Hart, Schaffner and Marx ad illustration of three men pictured one of them in a hockey sweater. The ad still targeted the man in "college, business, or professions." Hart, Schaffner and Marx, *Saturday Evening Post*, 21 October 1905, p. 19. A full-page Adler's ad offered an illustration of one of the "highly artistic college posters" it would send free. The illustration was of a heavily muscled rower carrying his oar on his shoulder accompanied by a well-dressed student. David Adler and Sons Clothing Company, *Saturday Evening Post*, 8 April 1905, back of front cover.

71. Chas. Kaufman and Brothers, *Saturday Evening Post*, 22 May 1909, p. 62. Another ad, which illustrated a baseball game and referred to "the spirit of buoyant youth," was H. M. Lindenthal and Sons, *Saturday Evening Post*, 15 May 1909, p. 30.

72. Samuel W. Peck and Company, *Saturday Evening Post*, 12 March 1910, p. 40. Two other apparel companies who used similar scenes in their ads were House of Kuppenheimer, *Saturday Evening Post*, 15 April 1911, p. 71; and Schloss Brothers and Company, *Saturday Evening Post*, 15 March 1913, p. 65. The Kuppenheimer ad did not specifically mention college, but the Schloss Brothers ad noted the familiar "for college, school, or business."

73. Hart, Schaffner and Marx, *Saturday Evening Post*, 2 October 1909, p. 2. For instance, football action shots also appear in Alfred Benjamin and Company, *Saturday Evening Post*, 6 November 1909, back of front cover; and H. M. Lindenthal and Sons, *Saturday Evening Post*, 23 September 1911, p. 24.

74. Hart, Schaffner and Marx, *Saturday Evening Post*, 20 May 1911, p. 2.

75. Hart, Schaffner and Marx, in addition to the "Varsity" had the "Shapemaker," which supposedly helped make a good figure even for those who did not possess it. For an example, see, Hart, Schaffner and Marx, *Saturday Evening Post*, 20 May 1911, p. 2. Society Brand Clothes, too, were "cut to give the wearer the appearance of perfect physical development." They added that this would actually spur the person to achieve such a physical shape in reality. Alfred Decker Cohn and Company, *Saturday Evening Post*, 11 March 1911, p. 1.

76. Rosenwald and Weil, *Saturday Evening Post*, 8 May 1909, p. 55; and Rosenwald and Weil, *Saturday Evening Post*, 22 May 1909, p. 62.

77. Chas. Kaufman and Brothers, *Saturday Evening Post*, 30 October 1909, p. 28. They were still using terms like "virile" and "aggressive" in the next year and had moved their ad into a more prominent space, using the full page. Chas. Kaufman and Brothers, *Saturday Evening Post*, 1 October 1910, p. 1.

78. Samuel W. Peck and Company, *Saturday Evening Post*, 22 May 1909, p. 53; and Samuel W. Peck and Company, *Saturday Evening Post*, 26 March 1910, p. 72.

79. H. M. Lidenthal and Sons, *Saturday Evening Post*, 13 November 1909, p. 38. Hart, Schaffner and Marx pushed the "Varsity" until around 1915. For example, Hart, Schaffner and Marx, *American Magazine* 79 (May 1915): 74.

80. Alfred Benjamin and Company, *Saturday Evening Post*, 6 November 1909, back of front cover; Alfred Benjamin and Company, *Saturday Evening Post*, 24 September 1910, p. 1.

81. Hart, Schaffner and Marx, *Saturday Evening Post*, 31 October 1914, p. 38; and Hart, Schaffner and Marx, *Saturday Evening Post*, 1 October 1910, p. 2.

82. Hart, Schaffner and Marx, *Saturday Evening Post*, 12 September 1914, p. 2.

83. Chas. Kaufman and Brothers, *Saturday Evening Post*, 22 May 1909, p. 62.

84. "The University" and "The Oxford" may be found in Samuel W. Peck and Company, *Saturday Evening Post*, 30 September 1911, p. 50. The "Princeton" model was advertised in H. M. Lindenthal and Sons, *Saturday Evening Post*, 10 September 1910, p. 65. Another clothier had a style called "Dartmouth." Rosenberg Brothers and Company, *Saturday Evening Post*, 26 September 1914, p. 44.

85. H. M. Lindenthal, which had led the way with a more physical image for their clothes, continued to forward the ever present but often implicit complementary image of their clothes, as in a 1913 ad declaring their clothes were the "Clothes for Young Gentlemen." H. M. Lindenthal and Sons, *Saturday Evening Post*, 26 April 1913, p. 31.

86. Ederheimer, Stein and Company, *Saturday Evening Post*, 9 March 1912, p. 43.

87. Alfred Decker and Cohn, *Collier's Weekly*, 3 October 1908, p. 5; and Alfred Decker and Cohn, *Collier's Weekly*, 24 October 1908, p. 3.

88. Hart, Schaffner and Marx, *Saturday Evening Post*, 3 June 1911, p. 2.

89. Hart, Schaffner and Marx, *Saturday Evening Post*, 19 October 1912, p. 2.

90. Samuel W. Peck and Company, *Saturday Evening Post*, 12 March 1911, p. 40. Additional advertisements that pointedly intermingled their references to college men and businessmen include Adler Rochester Clothes, *Saturday Evening Post*, 2 October 1909, p. 53; House of Kuppenheimer, *Saturday Evening Post*, 18 March 1911, p 35; Hart, Schaffner and Marx, *Saturday Evening Post*, 28 September 1912, p 2; and Rosenberg Brothers Company, *Saturday Evening Post*, 26 September 1914, p. 44.

91. One excellent example is Chas. Kaufman and Brothers, *Saturday Evening Post*, 1 October 1910, p. 1. A Hart, Schaffner and Marx ad also employed the boy-leaving-home motif and conspicuously included a magazine as one of the items mother packed into the suitcase. Hart, Schaffner and Marx, *Saturday Evening Post*, 26 August 1905, p. 15.

92. Hart, Schaffner and Marx, *Saturday Evening Post*, 13 November 1909, p. 1.

93. Kuh, Nathan and Fischer Company, *Saturday Evening Post*, 18 April 1908, p. 22; and Kuh, Nathan and Fisher Company, *Saturday Evening Post*, 19 September 1908, p. 22.

94. Ibid.

95. Kuh, Nathan and Fischer Company, *Saturday Evening Post*, 19 September 1908, p. 22. Another ad also referred to their clothes as "strong." Kuh, Nathan and Fischer Company, *Saturday Evening Post*, 7 November 1908, p. 25.

96. L. E. Waterman and Company, *Saturday Evening Post*, 3 April 1909, p. 49; and A. Stein and Company, *Saturday Evening Post*, 18 May 1912, p. 60. Another Waterman ad pictured two campus illustrations—one of a grad with Gothic buildings silhouetted in the background, the other of a young man in a derby, carrying a suitcase, and arriving on campus. L. E. Waterman and Company, *Saturday Evening Post*, 21 September 1907, p. 28. For a dorm scene regarding shaving soap, see J. B. Williams Company, *Collier's Weekly*, 3 October 1903, p. 27.

97. E. Howard Watch Company, *Saturday Evening Post*, 3 April 1909, p. 49; and E. Howard Watch Company, *Collier's Weekly*, 3 October 1908, p. 31. A razor company played on the familiar cheering scene in one ad, one of the figures holding a Yale pennant (conveniently, the name of the company) and another figure wearing a turtleneck with a big *Y* on it. Yale Safety Razor Company, *Saturday Evening Post*, 29 February 1908, p. 27. Another large ad in prime space employing a rowing scene and fraternity reference was Wick Narrow Fabric Company, *Saturday Evening Post*, 7 September 1907, back of front cover.

98. Murad Cigarettes, *Collier's Weekly*, 25 November 1905, p. 2; Egyptian Deities Cigarettes, *American Magazine* 80 (November 1915): 86; American Tobacco Company, *Saturday Evening Post*, 25 July 1914, back of front cover; and American Tobacco Company, *American Magazine* 79 (March 1915): 82.

99. Onoto Pen Company, *Saturday Evening Post*, 11 September 1909, pp. 24–25.

Conclusion

1. Albert H. Atwood, "Do Opportunities Still Exist?" *Saturday Evening Post*, 3 July 1920, pp. 29, 90, 92, and 97. Western Electric (a division of AT&T) began recruiting on

college campuses around the turn of the century and also implemented special management training programs for these recruits. See George David Smith, *The Anatomy of a Business Strategy: Bell, Western Electric, and the Origins of the American Telephone Industry* (Baltimore: Johns Hopkins University Press, 1985).

2. Atwood, "Impatient Youth in the Business World," *Saturday Evening Post,* 10 April 1926, pp. 10–11, 205–6, 209–10, and 213.

3. A. H. Deute, "When the College Senior Becomes a Business Freshman," *Saturday Evening Post,* 15 September 1923, pp. 46 and 48.

4. David O. Levine, *The American College and the Culture of Aspiration, 1915–1940* (Ithaca, NY: Cornell University Press, 1986), 14.

5. See especially Levine, *American College and the Culture of Aspiration,* chaps. 3–5. For the importance of collegiate youth on American culture, see Paula Fass, *The Damned and the Beautiful: American Youth in the 1920s* (New York: Oxford University Press, 1977), chaps. 3–6.

6. Rita S. Halle, *Which College?* (New York: Macmillan, 1928), 3, quoted in Levine, *American College and the Culture of Aspiration,* 113.

7. See Levine, *American College and the Culture of Aspiration,* chaps. 3–5. Another good overall look at the curriculum controversy is found in Frederick Rudolph, *Curriculum: A History of the American Undergraduate Course of Study since 1636* (San Francisco: Jossey-Bass Publishers, 1977). Works covering the beginnings of business courses and separate schools of business on campuses are Steven Sass, *The Pragmatic Imagination: A History of the Wharton School, 1881–1991* (Philadelphia: University of Pennsylvania Press, 1982); Michael W. Sedlak and Harold F. Williamson, *The Evolution of Management Education: A History of the Northwestern University J. L. Kellogg Graduate School of Management* (Urbana: University of Illinois Press, 1983); and J. Cruikshank, *A Delicate Experiment: The Harvard Business School, 1908–1945* (Cambridge, MA: Harvard University Press, 1987).

8. These quotes come respectively from the *Duke Chronicle,* the *Daily Princetonian,* and the *Cornell Sun,* quoted in Fass, *Damned and the Beautiful,* 254–56.

9. Ibid., 233 and 126–27. Fass notes a comment from one college newspaper claiming that 65 percent of fashions in the 1920s were dictated by college students. She also observed that due to movies, magazines, and national advertising, "collegiate style" and college life were copied throughout the United States among American youth.

10. Judy Hilkey, *Character Is Capital: Success Manuals and Manhood in Gilded Age America* (Chapel Hill: University of North Carolina Press, 1997), 108–10.

11. Gail Bederman, *Manliness and Civilization: A Cultural History of Gender and Race in the United States, 1880–1917* (Chicago: University of Chicago Press, 1996).

12. For example, John L. Rury, "The Urban Catholic University in the Early Twentieth Century: A Social Profile of DePaul, 1898–1940," *History of Higher Education Annual* 17 (1997): 5–32.

13. On this notion of fashioning a "normal" way of being middle class, see Christopher P. Wilson, *White Collar Fictions: Class and Social Representation in American Literature, 1885–1925* (Athens: University of Georgia Press, 1992).

14. Levine, *American College and the Culture of Aspiration,* 148–61. See also Marcia G. Synott, *The Half-Opened Door: Discrimination and Admissions at Harvard, Yale, and Princeton* (Westport, CT: Greenwood Press, 1979).

Index

Margaret Fuller: Transatlantic Crossings in a Revolutionary Age
Edited by Charles Capper and Cristina Giorcelli

Creating the College Man: American Mass Magazines and Middle-Class Manhood, 1890–1915
Daniel A. Clark

Emerson's Liberalism
Neal Dolan

Observing America: The Commentary of British Visitors to the United States, 1890–1950
Robert P. Frankel

Picturing Indians: Photographic Encounters and Tourist Fantasies in H. H. Bennett's
    Wisconsin Dells
Steven D. Hoelscher

Cosmopolitanism and Solidarity: Studies in Ethnoracial, Religious, and Professional Affiliation
    in the United States
David A. Hollinger

Thoreau's Democratic Withdrawal: Alienation, Participation, and Modernity
Shannon L. Mariotti

Seaway to the Future: American Social Visions and the Construction of the Panama Canal
Alexander Missal

Imaginary Friends: Representing Quakers in American Culture, 1650–1950
James Emmett Ryan

The Trashing of Margaret Mead: Anatomy of an Anthropological Controversy
Paul Shankman

The Presidents We Imagine: Two Centuries of White House Fictions on the Page, on the Stage,
    Onscreen, and Online
Jeff Smith

Unsafe for Democracy: World War I and the U.S. Justice Department's Covert Campaign
    to Suppress Dissent
William H. Thomas Jr.